Yosemite *and* Sequoia

A CENTURY OF CALIFORNIA NATIONAL PARKS

EDITED BY

Richard J. Orsi, Alfred Runte, and Marlene Smith-Baranzini

UNIVERSITY OF CALIFORNIA PRESS

BERKELEY   LOS ANGELES   LONDON

CALIFORNIA HISTORICAL SOCIETY

SAN FRANCISCO

The introduction and first seven essays of this volume were originally published in *California History* 69, no. 2 (Summer 1990), reprinted here by arrangement with the California Historical Society. The design for *California History*, by The Arthur H. Clark Co., Spokane, has been adapted for this volume. *California History* is published with the cooperation and support of California State University, Hayward.

University of California Press
Berkeley and Los Angeles, California

University of California Press, Ltd.
London, England

Library of Congress Cataloging-in-Publication Data

Yosemite and Sequoia : a century of California national
  parks / edited by Richard J. Orsi, Alfred Runte, and
  Marlene Smith-Baranzini.
        p.   cm.
    "Introduction and first seven essays . . . originally
published in California History 69, no. 2 (Summer 1990)"—
T.p. verso.
    Includes bibliographical references and index.
    ISBN 0-520-08160-9 (alk. paper). — ISBN 0-520-08161-7
(pbk. : alk. paper)
    1. Yosemite National Park (Calif.)—History.   2. Sequoia
National Park (Calif.)—History.   3. Kings Canyon
National Park (Calif.)—History. 4. National parks and
reserves—California—History.   I. Orsi, Richard J.
II. Runte, Alfred, 1947–   .   III. Smith-Baranzini,
Marlene.
F868.Y6Y46   1993
979.4'47—dc20   92-42370

Printed in the United States of America
9 8 7 6 5 4 3 2 1

The paper used in this publication meets the minimum requirements of American National Standard for Information Sciences—Permanence of Paper for Printed Library Materials, ANSI Z39.48-1984. ∞

Contents

Preface

As is true with all subjects, the history of the California national parks demonstrates that we can never escape our history. Its legacy is ever present. Its study is at once fascinating, enjoyable, and useful in understanding and resolving the important issues that face us. There is universal interest in the great natural resources of California, especially the grandeur of Yosemite Valley, the giant sequoia, the greater Sierra Nevada of which they are a part, and the making of the state's national parks, which began back in Civil War times when Abraham Lincoln was president. The story of Yosemite and Sequoia national parks reflects the contradictory actions toward nature by all of us as Californians, Americans, and ordinary human beings, in our innocence, greed, and concern. It is a microcosm of what we as a people did to the land and its original inhabitants, as well as how we have tried, if belatedly, to save and properly preserve our extraordinary natural heritage.

This book began as the special Summer 1990 issue of *California History*, the quarterly journal of the California Historical Society, devoted to celebrating the centennial of the great California national parks. For "Yosemite and Sequoia: A Century of California National Parks," the Society was fortunate in being able to call upon the talents of renowned experts in the field. Serving as consulting editor of the special issue was Alfred Runte, one of the nation's foremost environmental historians. Runte and six other leading park historians contributed articles exploring broad periods and issues, as well as detailed case studies, of park history.

A signal event in the California Historical Society's publication history, the national parks issue was warmly received by readers and reviewers for its insights into important aspects of national park history, as well as its informative and attractive illustrations. In ironic testimony to its success, all copies of the magazine sold within a few months, and the issue was quickly out of print. Because the essays have enduring value beyond celebrating a centennial, the Society and the University of California Press are republishing the special issue in book form to make it available to a wider circle of readers. To make the story of California national parks more complete through the controversial events of the early 1990s, the book contains a newly written final chapter by Alfred Runte, "Planning Yosemite's Future: A Historical Retrospective."

The California Historical Society has published *California History* continuously since 1922, and it seeks to reach high standards of readable prose, sound content, and graphic excellence. This publication of California national parks essays in book form fulfills the society's purpose of making California's rich and varied history available to a wide audience.

For making this work possible, the Historical Society is particularly grateful to Lynne Withey, editorial director of the University of California Press, who suggested the partnership in the first place and who shepherded the project through to completion, and to Alfred Runte, historian and author, who graciously gave of his vast knowledge of the subject in the writing and editing of this book.

Michael McCone
Executive Director
California Historical Society

Richard J. Orsi
Editor, *California History*, and Professor of History
California State University, Hayward

Yosemite *and* Sequoia

"Monolith, the Face of Half Dome, Yosemite National Park, California, 1927." *Photograph by Ansel Adams.*
Courtesy of the Trustees of The Ansel Adams Publishing Rights Trust. All Rights Reserved.

Introduction

THE CALIFORNIA NATIONAL PARKS CENTENNIAL

by Alfred Runte

This special issue of *California History* recognizes California's seminal importance in the establishment and evolution of national parks. A century and a quarter ago, the national park idea was born in the High Sierra when so-called "gentlemen of fortune, of taste, and of refinement"[1] asked the state's junior United States senator, John Conness, to sponsor legislation setting aside Yosemite Valley and the Mariposa Grove of giant sequoias "for public use, resort, and recreation; . . . inalienable for all time."[2] Conness enthusiastically endorsed the proposal and shepherded it through a Congress grown weary by the tragedy of civil war. On June 30, 1864, President Abraham Lincoln signed the legislation, and the United States had its first park expressly devoted to the protection of natural scenery.[3]

Only because Congress designated California to be the actual guardian of the grant has the state's significance as the birthplace of national parks been challenged or discounted. The fact remains that the Yosemite Grant originated as a piece of *federal* legislation, and was awarded to California only so long as the state observed the express conditions contained in the act. Twice following its approval, in 1868 and 1871, California petitioned Congress for permission to recognize disputed land claims in Yosemite Valley. Josiah Dwight Whitney, writing on behalf of the Yosemite board of park commissioners, was among those who objected in 1868 on the grounds that Yosemite was "a National public park."[4] The historic case that emanated from the dispute, *Hutchings v. Low*, soon made it all the way to the U.S. Supreme Court. In December 1872 the court upheld the original legislation of June 30, 1864, and thereby reaffirmed California's legal obligation to hold Yosemite Valley and the big trees "inalienable for all time." The land claims in Yosemite Valley were "inoperative" unless "ratified by Congress." But no such ratification had been approved, "and it is not believed," the court concluded, "that Congress will ever sanction such a perversion of the trust solemnly accepted by the State."[5]

In fact, then, if not in name, Yosemite was indeed the first national park. Neither Congress nor the U.S. Supreme Court would allow California to renege on the absolute acceptance of the terms of

John Muir (left) and President Theodore Roosevelt leaving Yosemite Valley, May 15, 1903. It was at this famous meeting that Muir impressed Roosevelt with the importance of preserving wilderness in national parks and convinced the president that the valley, then under state management, should be returned to federal control for incorporation within Yosemite National Park, which had been created in 1890. *CHS Library, San Francisco.*

Yosemite's enabling legislation. Granted, Yellowstone, established as a public park in 1872, was the first area to eventually be *called* a national park. But its own precedent was Yosemite. By 1872 Congress was well aware of the disputed land claims in Yosemite Valley; the decision to hold Yellowstone in federal ownership was based in large measure on its sponsors' determination to avoid similar problems.[6]

With the exception of portions of Mackinac Island (established in 1875 as a national park, but later returned to the state of Michigan), the Yosemite Grant and Yellowstone Park represented the sum total of national parks for an entire generation. Then, in 1890, California gave rise to the national park *system* with the protection of Yosemite, Sequoia, and the General Grant Grove. In response to pressure from local residents and a nationwide group of preservationists led by John Muir, Sequoia was approved as "a public park" on September 25; the Yosemite high country and the General Grant Grove, initially designated as "reserved forest lands," were set aside on October 1. The act of October 1, 1890, further enlarged Sequoia. Shortly afterward, sensing that Congress also intended

Yosemite and General Grant to be managed as "public parks," Secretary of the Interior John W. Noble amended their titles accordingly. Henceforth, all three areas—Yosemite, Sequoia, and General Grant—would be known universally as national parks.[7]

Yosemite Valley and the Mariposa Grove, however, remained under state administration until 1906, when preservationists forced their return to federal management. General Grant National Park is now known simply as the General Grant Grove, which is a detached unit of Kings Canyon National Park. Indeed, this is not only the centennial year of Yosemite and Sequoia national parks but also the fiftieth anniversary of the establishment of Kings Canyon. For administrative purposes, Sequoia and Kings Canyon are generally recognized today as one and the same park. They were, nonetheless, originally established separately, and remain, in the minds of their loyal followers, distinct if adjoining units.[8]

Obviously, there is much to celebrate in 1990. Yet celebration must have a purpose. The perception and management of these three great parks is the subject of this special issue. By itself, Yosemite offers a remarkable example of the pressures for development that every national park in the United States has at times undergone. In Yosemite, debating environmental change is a process now a century and a quarter old. Yosemite, as the oldest park of its kind, has the longest history of modification. Tourists were familiar with Yosemite Valley well over a decade before the Grand Canyon and Yellowstone were even explored. The issues of park development were raised and debated first in Yosemite. Even today, no other national park more dramatically reflects America's alleged failure to reconcile the protection of the environment with the wants and demands of modern civilization. The histories of Sequoia and Kings Canyon national parks are also long and instructive. As Douglas Strong and Lary Dilsaver remind us, both parks have been especially important as proving grounds for new approaches in resources management.

The concentration of the remainder of this issue on Yosemite is in recognition of its overarching significance, including its far earlier promotion as one of the great icons of American culture. Kate Nearpass Ogden, Anne Hyde, and Peter Blodgett have combined a variety of important perspectives on the origins and distinctiveness of Yosemite's notoriety, exploring, among other topics, the role of Yosemite in landscape art and western tourism. Turning from the nineteenth to the twentieth century, Robert Pavlik describes how the growing

The high backcountry of Kings Canyon National Park along Bubbs Creek, as photographed in the early twentieth century. *CHS Library, San Francisco.*

Carleton E. Watkins, *Cathedral Rocks*. Watkins was the first major photographer to visit Yosemite. His mammoth prints made during the early 1860s were displayed in Washington, D.C., as part of the campaign in 1864 to preserve the valley as a national park. *Courtesy California State Library.*

popularity of Yosemite forced park officials to confront a host of management problems, most notably the need to harmonize new construction with the natural environment. That challenge, originally addressed during the 1920s and 1930s, still frustrates park designers, who nowadays often concede that the pressure to accommodate larger numbers of visitors detracts from the importance of other park values.

Perhaps if management had remained true to the principles of biological stewardship, as reflected in the wisdom of natural scientists such as Joseph Grinnell, the problem of overcrowding might have been headed off years ago. As director of the Museum of Vertebrate Zoology of the University of California at Berkeley, Grinnell argued that the purposes of Yosemite were strictly scientific, inspirational, and educational in nature. The privilege of learning in Yosemite, he argued, should be far more important than recreation for its own sake. But abandoning their initial emphasis on visitation would prove extremely difficult for the national parks. In the eyes of Congress, it was numbers that mattered. The surest measure of success for the National Park Service was to demonstrate that more and more Americans were enjoying the parks. People, not preservation, confirmed that

Yosemite, Sequoia, and Kings Canyon were worth the investment in congressional appropriations.

And so, even today, the issue remains joined. Indeed, every conflict in the history of the national parks, and therefore every suggestion of those conflicts yet to come, can be traced to some compromise of the ideal that the national parks first and foremost should exist for the preservation of their natural environments. As the authors in this issue remind us, the histories of Yosemite, Sequoia, and Kings Canyon national parks are filled with examples of attempts to impose layer upon layer of artificiality over the natural scene. It follows that the second century of California's centennial parks will be no less controversial than their first. The lessons of history, in that regard, are all the more relevant. California's wilderness parks are an unrivaled state, national, and international legacy. Each is too important to be just another place. In that perception, and no other, lie the only tried and true principles for guiding the future of these parks and their natural heritage.

California National Parks
Chronology

Yosemite Valley in the nineteenth century. Photograph by Carleton E. Watkins. *Courtesy California State Library.*

YOSEMITE NATIONAL PARK

1833 - Joseph Walker party crossed present Yosemite National Park and may have seen Yosemite Valley from the rim.

1851 - Mariposa Battalion under James Savage became the first non-Indians to enter the valley. The valley was then occupied by the Ahwahneeches, a tribal branch of the southern Sierra Miwok.

1855 - James Hutchings brought first party of sightseers to Yosemite Valley.

1856 - Lower Hotel, first permanent structure built, at base of Sentinel Rock.

1864 - Yosemite Valley and Mariposa Grove granted to California as a public trust.

1865 - Frederick Law Olmsted prepared the first detailed plan for the future needs and management of the Yosemite Grant.

1868 - John Muir made his first trip to Yosemite.

1874 - Coulterville and Big Oak Flat stagecoach roads completed to the valley.

1879 - Present building of Wawona Hotel constructed; Yosemite Chapel built.

1882 - Construction of Tioga Road began (completed in 1883).

1889 - Mirror Lake dam built to increase area of lake.

1890 - Yosemite National Park created on October 1. The Yosemite Valley Grant remained under California state management.

1891 - Captain A.E. Wood, first acting superintendent, arrived with federal troops (Fourth Cavalry) to administer national park from a base in Wawona.

Mid-1890s - Last grizzly bear shot in Yosemite (at Crescent Lake).

1899 - Curry Camping Company established at present-day Curry Village.

1905 - Area of national park reduced by Congress. Mt. Ritter, the Minarets, and Devil's Postpile eliminated on the southeast side, the south fork of the Merced River on the southwest side.

1906 - President Theodore Roosevelt signed the

John Muir, principal advocate of Yosemite National Park and the national park system, as photographed in 1912 by W. E. Dassonville. At this time, Muir's campaign against San Francisco's project to build a reservoir at Hetch Hetchy in Yosemite was nearing a climax. In 1913, however, Congress passed the reservoir bill, and the bitterly disappointed Muir died the next year. *Courtesy Bancroft Library.*

bill making Yosemite Valley and the Mariposa Grove part of the national park.

1913 - Raker Act authorized use of Hetch Hetchy as a reservoir for the city of San Francisco. Automobiles allowed to enter Yosemite Valley.

1914 - Civilian employees replaced military in administration of the park.

1916 - National Park Service Act passed, creating a new agency under the Department of the Interior.

1924 - New National Park Service administrative center and village site developed on north side of Yosemite Valley (Old Yosemite Village near present chapel site).

1925 - Yosemite Park & Curry Company formed by consolidation of Curry Camping Company & Yosemite National Park Company.

1926 - All-year Highway (140) opened.

1927 - Ahwahnee Hotel opened.

1930 - Rockefeller Purchase restored nearly 8,700 acres along the western boundary of park.

1932 - Wawona Basin added to national park.

1934 - Hetch Hetchy water flowed to San Francisco.

1935 - Ski lodge built at Badger Pass.

1937 - Carl Inn Tract added, rounding out the addition of endangered sugar pine forests along the park's western side. Legal entanglements held up acquisition until 1939.

1941 - Bear feeding program in Yosemite Valley eliminated.

1954 - Park annual visitation exceeds one million.

1956 - New Yosemite Lodge central buildings completed, and old lodge razed.

1967 - Park annual visitation exceeds two million.

1968 - Last Firefall from Glacier Point on January 25.

1970 - Free shuttle bus operation begun in Yosemite Valley on February 9. Mariposa Grove Road closed to private cars; tram cars available for transportation.

1971 - Prescribed burning of selected forest undergrowth began as a technique to decrease fire hazard and to encourage new tree growth. Mirror Lake dredged for the last time.

1972 - Wilderness permits required for backcountry use. Yosemite Village parking area converted to non-vehicular pedestrian mall.

1973 - Music Corporation of America (MCA) purchased Yosemite Park & Curry Company.

1977 - Trailhead quota system established to control backcountry use.

1980 - General Management Plan completed.

1984 - 677,600 acres (eighty-nine percent of park) designated wilderness under terms of the Wilderness Preservation Act of 1964.

1986 - First reintroduction of bighorn sheep on Yosemite's eastern boundary.

1987 - Park annual visitation exceeds three million.

1990 - Yosemite National Park celebrates its one hundredth anniversary.

SEQUOIA NATIONAL PARK

1858 - Hale Tharp, with an Indian guide, became the first white man to enter the Giant Forest.

1864 - The California State Geological Survey, led by William Brewer, explored the High Sierra and viewed the upper Kern River Canyon.

1873 - A silver strike at Mineral King opened this high mountain valley to settlement.

1875 - John Muir named the Giant Forest while exploring the giant sequoias south from the Mariposa Grove.

1881 - Senator John F. Miller of California introduced the first bill in Congress to establish a national park in the southern Sierra.

1885 - Members of Cooperative Land and Colonization Association (the Kaweah Colony) initiated an ill-fated attempt to claim lands in the Giant Forest.

1890 - A movement led by George W. Stewart, editor and publisher of the *Visalia Delta*, culminated on September 25, with creation of Sequoia National Park, the nation's second national park; on October 1, Congress passed separate legislation creating General Grant Grove and Yosemite

Giant Forest Lodge in 1918, showing some of the first automobiles to make it into Sequoia National Park. *Courtesy Sequoia National Park Archives.*

national parks and tripling the size of Sequoia National Park.

1891 - U.S. Cavalry troops began administering the park.

1893 - President Benjamin Harrison signed a proclamation creating the Sierra Forest Reserve, including the watersheds of the Kern and Kings rivers.

1903 - First wagon road reached Giant Forest.

1914 - Park management passed to civilian control under Walter Fry.

1916 - Congress created the National Park Service.

1920 - Colonel John R. White became superintendent.

1926 - Congress added Kern Canyon and the crest of the Sierra Nevada around Mount Whitney to the park, tripling its size. The Generals Highway opened to Giant Forest.

1933 - Completion of the John Muir Trail linked Sequoia to Yosemite National Park.

1933 - The Civilian Conservation Corps made
1942   major improvements in the national parks.

1953 - Visitation to Sequoia and Kings Canyon surpassed one million.

1956 - Mission 66 spurred development of na-
1966   tional park facilities.

1964 - Richard Hartesveldt conducted the first prescribed burn in Kings Canyon National Park; the Wilderness Act passed Congress.

1974 - The Park Service extended wilderness use limits to all the Sequoia and Kings Canyon backcountry.

1978 - Congress approved the addition of Mineral King Valley after a proposed development of a major resort by Walt Disney Productions resulted in a national controversy.

1980 - The Giant Forest development concept plan established removal of concession facilities from the grove as a primary goal.

1984 - Eighty-five percent of Sequoia and Kings Canyon national parks set aside in wilderness under the Wilderness Act of 1965; work commenced on a development zone in Clover Creek, to which Giant Forest concession facilities will theoretically move.

1987 - Annual visitation to Sequoia and Kings Canyon reached a record high of 2,220,561.

1990 - Centennial Celebration.

KINGS CANYON NATIONAL PARK

1873 - John Muir visited the Kings Canyon area and called for its protection.

1881 - Senator John Miller introduced an unsuccessful bill to create a national park in the Sequoia and Kings Canyon areas.

1902 - The U.S. Geological Survey published a water resource survey of the Kings River.

1920 - Creation of the Federal Power Commission spurred the city of Los Angeles and San Joaquin Valley interests to file plans for Kings River development.

1933 - The administration of General Grant National Park separated from that of Sequoia National Park.

1939 - Representative "Bud" Gearhart introduced a compromise bill to create Kings Canyon National Park without its two great canyons; the Forest Service completed road to Cedar Grove in Kings Canyon.

1940 - Kings Canyon National Park created on March 4, incorporating General Grant Grove.

1943 - The administration of Kings Canyon National Park combined with that of Sequoia National Park.

1965 - Cedar Grove and Tehipite Valley added to park.

1976 - The Park Service adopted a development plan for Kings Canyon calling for minimal development.

1990 - Kings Canyon National Park celebrates its fiftieth anniversary.

Kings River Canyon, as photographed from Bubbs Creek in the early twentieth century.
CHS Library, San Francisco.

The General Sherman Tree in Giant Forest is the largest living thing on earth.
Courtesy Sequoia National Park Archives.

Sequoia and Kings Canyon National Parks

ONE HUNDRED YEARS OF PRESERVATION AND RESOURCE MANAGEMENT

by Lary M. Dilsaver and Douglas H. Strong

In 1990, when Sequoia National Park marks its centennial, Kings Canyon National Park will celebrate its fiftieth birthday. These contiguous parks in the southern Sierra Nevada constitute one of the nation's finest wilderness regions. The history of their establishment represents a major success story in preservation efforts in the United States, and the account of their management adds a valuable chapter to the history of the National Park Service.[1]

Such success did not come easily. The creation of Sequoia resulted primarily from the determined efforts of a few San Joaquin Valley residents, and the expansion of the park and establishment of Kings Canyon came only after extended battles and compromises. The history of their management reveals the transiency of policies that depend on changing public awareness, lobby groups, and leadership.

Between 1772, when Europeans first sighted the Sierra Nevada, and the discovery of gold at Sutter's mill in 1848, few white people set foot in the Sierra Nevada.[2] Not until 1858 did cattleman Hale Tharp make the first known visit by a white person to the mountainous area east of the central San Joaquin Valley that became Sequoia National Park. Guided by local Indians, he traveled to Giant Forest, one of the finest concentrations of giant sequoias, where he later established a summer cattle camp. Although the Indians appealed to Tharp to protect their land, nothing could prevent the increasing influx of settlers into the Sierra foothills. Smallpox,

scarlet fever, and measles devastated the Indians. The survivors retreated into the high mountains and crossed the Sierra to the east. The Indians of Kings Canyon met the same fate.[3]

Soon sheepherders, prospectors, and lumbermen in pursuit of their trades entered the Kings-Kern-Kaweah watersheds in the Sierra east of Fresno and Visalia. Following the great California floods and drought of 1862-1864, sheepherders from the southern San Joaquin Valley drove their flocks north and east into the highest mountains in search of grazing land. Unfortunately, sheepherding practices at that time, combined with a complete lack of governmental control over the use of public land, resulted in widespread damage to the mountain watersheds. When sheep entered the mountains as the snow melted each spring, their sharp hoofs cut deeply into the moist soil, severely damaging the meadows. Sheepherders' fires, set in the fall to clear away brush and deadfall, ran unchecked over the mountain slopes.[4]

Fires and overgrazing alarmed some explorers of the Sierra. In 1873, Clarence King noted that the Kern Plateau, which had numerous meadows and lush grass when he had visited earlier, now appeared as a "gray sea of rolling granite ridges."[5] Two years later, John Muir vividly described the threat to Kings Canyon's fragile beauty. He urged that the forests be protected so the spring run-off would be sure to provide enough water for the San Joaquin Valley during the dry summer months. In Muir's opinion, "sheepmen's fires" did a great deal more damage than lumbermen's axes or mill fires.[6]

Prospectors also participated in the early exploration and utilization of the Kings-Kern-Kaweah watersheds. Their extensive prospecting came to little except for one strike at Mineral King. The discovery of silver in 1873 touched off a rush to this high mountain valley. With the completion of a road into the isolated mining camp by the end of the decade, Mineral King reached its peak of development. The boom soon ended, however. With the failure of the mines, the toll road passed into the hands of the county and became a public highway. A few summer tourists, attracted by the cool mountain air, built cabins and continued to visit the valley each year.[7]

In the meantime, discovery of the big trees elsewhere in the Sierra Nevada had attracted worldwide attention. In 1852, a hunter named A.T. Dowd, tracking a wounded bear, stumbled on the stand of giant sequoias now known as the Calaveras Grove of big trees. Together with Yosemite Valley, the enormous trees became a mecca for tourists. While the coastal redwood reached a greater height and the bristlecone pine of California's White Mountains was older, no other species of tree came even close to matching the giant sequoia in sheer bulk and grandeur.

In the 1860s lumbermen entered the forests of the Kings and Kaweah watersheds. At first lumber mills served only local communities, but the completion of the Southern Pacific Railroad line through the San Joaquin Valley in the mid-1870s opened more distant markets. Although pine and fir trees provided most of the lumber, many giant sequoias were cut to provide shakes, fence posts, and grape stakes. The worst was yet to come. Log flumes, introduced in 1889, opened previously inaccessible timberlands to loggers. Perhaps the finest stand of giant sequoias, in the Converse Basin, fell quickly.

Danger to the General Grant Grove first stimulated interest in protection of the giant sequoias of the Kings-Kaweah watersheds. As early as 1864 the Brewer expedition, in its report to the state of California, noted that big trees to the west of the grove were being cut for fence posts. Israel Gamlin established a squatter's claim to part of the grove in 1872 and completed a rough road to haul timber to the valley below. Three years later, within the very shadow of the General Grant tree, two men

Lumbermen Bill Mills (left) and S.D. Phips stand before the Mark Twain Tree in the area of modern Grant Grove in Kings Canyon National Park. They felled the tree in 1891 to provide exhibition sections for New York and London. *Photograph by C.C. Curtis. Courtesy Sequoia National Park Archives.*

The Kaweah Colony celebrates completion of their access road to the plateau of Giant Forest with a picnic in 1890. Soon thereafter their land ownership claims were suspended and Sequoia National Park created. *Photo by C.C. Curtis. Courtesy Sequoia National Park Archives.*

took nine days to fell an enormous tree and then set fire to its stump. Two 16-foot sections were cut into sections that could be shipped and reassembled in the East. But visitors at the exhibit the next year thought the whole thing was a hoax. How could a tree be that big? Beginning in 1878, editorials in the Visalia *Delta* criticized the destruction of the forests, including the cutting of giant sequoias for exhibit.[8]

In 1880 Theodore Wagner, the United States Surveyor General for California, wrote to the registrar of the United States Land Office in Visalia to request that four sections in the Grant Grove be suspended from entry, temporarily prohibiting anyone from claiming the land under existing land laws. He was responding to the concerns of Secretary of the Interior Carl Schurz, several scientists, and a growing number of local citizens who advocated protection of the big trees. In the following year, General John F. Miller of California introduced into Congress the first bill to establish a park.[9] The measure died in committee, however, perhaps because the proposed park was so large and would be opposed by timber and grazing interests.

In 1885 fifty members of the Cooperative Land and Colonization Association, with the intention of founding a utopian community, filed ownership claims on extensive tracts of land in Giant Forest under the Timber and Stone Act. They next sought capital for a railroad to connect with a road they planned to build from the foothills to the forestlands. When the railroad plan failed, they formed a joint stock company, the Kaweah Cooperative Commonwealth Company, and constructed an 18-mile road through rugged country to the edge of Giant Forest.[10] After setting up a portable sawmill, the colonists produced a small amount of lumber.

While a government land agent examined the Kaweah Company's land claims, local residents in Tulare County initiated a determined drive to protect the Sierra forests by having Congress permanently withdraw large tracts of land from the market. There were precedents for such action. Congress had granted Yosemite Valley to California in 1864 for "public use, resort and recreation." It was the first area in the country specifically set aside to be preserved for all future generations. As such, Yosemite marked the real beginning of the national park system, even though Yellowstone, created in 1872, was the first officially designated national park. Yosemite did not achieve this status

The two most important individuals in the history of Sequoia National Park stand before a big tree in Giant Forest. George Stewart (right), a Visalia newspaperman, led the fight to create the park in 1890. Colonel White served as superintendent for most of the period 1920 to 1947 and shaped both its development and preservation. *Photo by Lindley Eddy. Courtesy Sequoia National Park Archives.*

until 1890, and the valley actually remained under state management until 1906.

Farmers in the San Joaquin Valley wanted to protect the watershed on which they depended for irrigation, and they also wished to preserve the groves of giant sequoia remaining in public ownership as scenic and recreational areas. With these goals in mind, George W. Stewart, editor and publisher of the Visalia *Delta*, spearheaded the movement to protect the southern Sierra Nevada.[11]

Stewart became concerned when the state of California tried to acquire parts of the Grant Grove in 1889 as indemnity school land, and several private individuals also filed on part of the same grove. Although the grove had been withdrawn from the market in 1880, Congress had done nothing to guarantee its permanent protection. Stewart warned of the damage sheep and manmade fires could cause to the watershed and the valley below. Also, increasing numbers of vacationers needed protected areas for summer recreational use.

The *Delta's* editorials soon attracted local attention, and members of the Tulare County Grange called a meeting for October 9, 1889, in Visalia. Prominent residents from Fresno, Kern, and Tulare counties who attended agreed unanimously to petition Congress to establish a national park.

When Stewart and Tipton Lindsey, former receiver of the U.S. Land Office, drew a map of the proposed reservation, they expanded it to include the entire western slope of the Sierra from the present Yosemite National Park in the north to the southern end of the forest belt in Kern County. They wished to protect all major rivers flowing from the mountains into the San Joaquin and Tulare valleys.

A few months later, Stewart and his local supporters—including John Tuohy, Frank Walker, and Lindsey—became alarmed over rumors that the federal government was about to open the Garfield Grove—south of Giant Forest—to private land ownership under the Swamp and Overflow Act, Timber and Stone Act, and other statutes. Lumbermen coveted the timber, and sheepmen desired access to mountain meadows. Letters sent from the *Delta* office to interested groups and influential people from coast to coast warned of the danger to the world's largest trees, the giant sequoias. Lindsey notified Congressman William Vandever, initiating a full-scale campaign for a park.

By the end of July 1890, Vandever introduced a bill for a national park in the township that included the Garfield Grove.[12] The *Delta's* campaign attracted the support of *Garden and Forest, Forest and Stream,* and other publications. The California Academy of

Sciences, American Association for the Advancement of Sciences, and American Forestry Association also adopted resolutions favoring the park bill. Such support brought results; President Benjamin Harrison signed the bill on September 25, 1890. Sequoia National Park became the nation's second national park, created eighteen years after Yellowstone. The enabling act provided that two townships plus four sections be withdrawn from settlement, occupancy, or sale, and that they be set apart as a public park or pleasure ground for the enjoyment of the people.[13]

Wanting to see all the forests of the Sierra preserved, Stewart declared in the *Delta* that the first important step in a great work had been taken. Believing that the Kings and Kern canyons and other desirable areas could be added later, park advocates had not clamored for a large park because of the imminent danger to the Garfield Grove. They felt that any effort to secure a larger park, which would have included much privately held land, would be sure to fail without an educational campaign that they had no time to conduct.

On October first, less than one week after creation of the park, Congress passed a second bill that established Yosemite National Park, tripled the size of Sequoia, and set aside the Grant Grove as a small separate national park.[14] The measure came as a complete surprise to Stewart and others who had initiated the movement and worked so hard for the first bill. Daniel K. Zumwalt, a resident of Visalia and a land agent of the Southern Pacific Railroad who visited Vandever in Washington, has been credited with proposing both Grant National Park and the expansion of Sequoia, as well as for lobbying on behalf of establishment of Yosemite National Park. He had a personal interest both in protecting the watershed and preserving the giant sequoias. He knew of the 1889 petition and subsequent correspondence of the park advocates. More important, the Southern Pacific had long been concerned about protecting the water supply of the San Joaquin Valley, and it recognized that national parks would attract tourists and increase business.[15] Support by the powerful Southern Pacific helped win the day for Sequoia, Yosemite, and General Grant national parks.

The Kaweah colonists, however, were shocked and dismayed by the news of the October first legislation. To make matters worse, a special land

Courtesy of the Sequoia Natural History Association.

agent of the Department of the Interior reversed a previous report and ruled unfavorably on the colony's already-filed land claims in Giant Forest. Despite widespread support of the colonists by many residents of Tulare County, who respected the time and labor they had invested, Secretary of the Interior John Noble ruled against the colonists' land claims in April 1891. The government even denied compensation for the road they had built.[16]

The creation of the three national parks in California marked only the first step in protecting the Sierra watershed. Further prompt action was clearly needed. Within a decade, the population of Fresno and Tulare counties had more than doubled. The California State Board of Forestry frankly admitted that lack of funds prevented proper fire control. And as most of California was still the property of the national government, the state looked to Washington for legislative help.

Fortunately, in March 1891, Congress passed legislation that permitted the president to proclaim permanent forest reserves—today's national forests.[17] Protectors of the Sierra could now propose that land be set aside in forest reserves or national parks; it mattered little that no clear distinction between the two kinds of reserves existed at that time. In April, Stewart recommended that Sequoia and General Grant national parks be extended eastward to the summit of the Sierra Nevada. John Muir and Robert Underwood Johnson, editor of *Century Magazine*, both of whom had played a leading role in the establishment of Yosemite National Park, also continued to agitate for a large forest reserve in the southern Sierra.

In October, the commissioner of the General Land Office directed Special Agent B.F. Allen to investigate the forest reservation proposed in the Tulare County petition of 1889.[18] The petition had requested that the government reserve a tract of land embracing over 200 townships. On Allen's recommendation, the commissioner withdrew 230 townships from settlement under federal land laws, pending investigation of these lands. While an "Anti-Park Association," led by local sheepmen and lumbermen, protested that the forest reservation would hurt local prosperity, most residents of the San Joaquin Valley either approved the withdrawal of land or were neutral.

Early in 1892, Johnson suggested to Secretary Noble that President Benjamin Harrison reserve all of the Sierra Nevada above a certain altitude. If that were done, Johnson reasoned, later, at a moment of less urgency, Congress could convert some of it from forest reserve to parkland. He dreamed of an eventual large national park incorporating the southern Sierra.

Special Agent Allen redrew the boundaries he had been investigating to exclude arable land in the foothills, thus eliminating a good deal of potential opposition to the proposed reserve. When he completed his report in early 1893, he stressed the dependence of the economic future of the San Joaquin Valley on the protection of the watershed. Finally, on February 14, Harrison signed a proclamation establishing the Sierra Forest Reservation —a vast area of over four million acres stretching from Yosemite National Park on the north to a point well south of Sequoia National Park.[19]

While park advocates had presumed the adjacent Kings and Kern watersheds—part of the new forest reserve—might soon be added to Sequoia and General Grant national parks, pleas for park expansion fell on deaf ears. In 1905, the Department of Agriculture gained jurisdiction over all forest reserves and soon changed the name to national forests. Under Forest Service policy of multiple use and sustained yield, grazing and logging remained options on national forests of the Sierra Nevada. The Sierra Club and other park advocates continued to call for permanent preservation of outstanding scenic areas in national parks.

In 1911, California Senator Frank Flint introduced a bill to create a vast national park in the southern Sierra.[20] Earlier, William Colby of the Sierra Club had proposed a series of national monuments in the Kings River Canyon, Tehipite Valley, and other scenic areas, and Robert Marshall of the Geological Survey had initiated a plan for a large park incorporating both the Kern and Kings river watersheds. Advocates argued that an enlarged Sierra park would increase government appropriations, attract tourists, and stimulate the local economy.

But many local people opposed the enlargement. Stockmen, who paid only a small fee for grazing on national forest lands, would be excluded from a park. Hunters opposed the elimination of such a large hunting area. Prospectors claimed that much valuable ore would be excluded from use, and lumber interests decried the loss of valuable timber. Others argued that the natural features of the Sierra already had protection through their ruggedness and inaccessibility. Chief U.S. Forester Henry S. Graves insisted that all proposals for new national parks be deferred until a Bureau of National Parks was created.

The 1913 loss of the Hetch Hetchy Valley of Yosemite National Park to a dam site to provide water for San Francisco made park enlargement in the southern Sierra seem all the more important. Under heavy pressure, Congress established the National Park Service in 1916. Stephen Mather, its first director, led prominent guests into the Sierra to gain support for park expansion.

Opposition intensified, however. Cattlemen in the San Joaquin Valley still coveted summer grazing lands in the mountains; the Forest Service argued that any future park should exclude timber, mineral, and grazing lands of commercial value; the Los Angeles Bureau of Power and Light planned major dams at Cedar Grove in Kings Canyon and Tehipite Valley; its rival, the San Joaquin Light and Power Company, filed applications for its own power sites; and local irrigationists defended their need for the water and hydroelectric power of the Kings River.

The contest between rival interests ended in a standoff and left the door open for negotiations. The Federal Power Commission decided that Los Angeles had no immediate need for hydroelectric power from the Kings River and that the city's claims interfered with the park proposal. The Park Service and Forest Service, after lengthy discussions, compromised on drawing boundary lines. In the end, however, the irrigationists succeeded in excluding the whole Kings Canyon watershed from the proposed park expansion, claiming that they would need sites for future hydroelectric power projects. Mather and the Sierra Club, which had played a central role in the negotiations, decided to settle for what they could get—the Kern Canyon and the Sierra Nevada around Mount Whitney —and to work for a power-free Kings River park later. A Sequoia National Park enlargement bill received the president's signature on July 3, 1926.[21]

Discussions continued through the late 1920s on proposals to add the Kings Canyon region to the national park system. Once more, however, park advocates and irrigation and hydroelectric power interests could not agree on whether the area should be preserved for its wilderness and recreational values or for the construction of dams. Little happened until 1935, when Secretary of the Interior Harold Ickes proposed a bill to establish Kings Canyon National Park and announced that the new park would be treated as "primitive wilderness."[22] This meant access would be restricted to a state highway, then under construction, that was not to be extended farther than the canyon floor of the south fork of the Kings River. The Sierra Club, after receiving assurances that the Park Service would not overdevelop the region for recreational purposes, actively supported the park movement.

Ickes's park proposal, however, met with sharp criticism. Many valley commercial interests feared the Park Service would prohibit development, especially dams for hydroelectric power and irrigation. They favored continued administration by the Forest Service with its more utilitarian approach. Local Forest Service officials, opposed to the growing national park system, fought to defend its management principles and the land under its jurisdiction.

After a major battle in Congress, the contending parties reached a settlement. To win the support of the irrigationists, Ickes and local congressman Bertrand W. Gearhart supported separate legislation to develop the Pine Flat reservoir and related reclamation development projects to the west of the park. In addition, the dam sites of Cedar Grove on the south fork of the Kings River Canyon and Tehipite Valley on the middle fork were excluded from the proposed park, leaving the door open to future development. President Franklin D. Roosevelt signed the park bill on March 4, 1940, thus ending the lengthy struggle to establish Kings Canyon National Park.[23]

The park was perhaps the best compromise possible at the time. The Park Service gained a magnificent mountain wilderness of more than 450,000 acres. The small General Grant National Park, created in 1890 and administered jointly with Sequoia National Park until 1933, was converted into a part of the new Kings Canyon National Park. Since 1943, the neighboring parks of Sequoia and Kings Canyon have been administered jointly.

In the years that followed, the city of Los Angeles made new proposals for water and power development, not only in Tehipite Valley and at Cedar Grove, but within the park itself.[24] The Sierra Club objected, and the Federal Power Commission ruled once again against the applications. Although Cedar Grove and Tehipite Valley together embraced relatively few acres, they were important to the park. Cedar Grove represented the one area in Kings Canyon that could be reached by automobile and that could be developed for use by tourists; Tehipite Valley, dominated by a remarkable granite dome that rose high above the middle fork of the Kings River, provided a noted wilderness attraction.

The Forest Service had earlier agreed to Park Service management of Cedar Grove, but uncertainty about the ultimate fate of the south fork of the Kings River Canyon had blocked its development. When alternative dam sites, especially at Pine Flat, were identified downriver, the irrigationists finally withdrew their opposition to including the contested areas in the park. In 1965 Congress added Cedar Grove and Tehipite Valley to Kings Canyon National Park.[25]

Just as the decades-old battle over Kings Canyon ended, controversy broke out over Mineral King, just south of Sequoia National Park.[26] Excluded from the park in 1890, the former mining community had remained a quiet summer camping area ever since. The Forest Service administered the valley as part of Sequoia National Forest and, after 1926, as a game refuge. With the enlargement of the park that year, the valley became an enclave, surrounded on three sides by national park lands.

Responding to rapid increase in outdoor recreation following World War II, the Forest Service invited proposals from private developers for a ski resort at Mineral King. Due to the high estimated cost, especially of the construction of an improved road, no acceptable developer could be found until the 1960s. Early in 1966, the Forest Service granted Walt Disney Productions a preliminary planning permit for a year-round resort. The Disney proposal included a Swiss-style village, ski-lifts to serve 20,000 skiers daily, and parking for 3600 vehicles. The Sierra Club argued in opposition that, if it were developed, Mineral King would sustain irreversible damage and that its wilderness values made the valley worthy of national park status.[27]

When Secretary of the Interior Stewart Udall approved a proposal to construct an improved road across national park land into the valley, the Sierra Club responded, filing suit in 1969 in United States District Court for an injunction to block federal officials from issuing permits. Three years later, the United States Supreme Court upheld a ruling by the United States Court of Appeals that the club did not have the legal standing necessary to pursue the lawsuit. The court, however, left the door open for the club to amend its original complaint in the district court. Faced with further delays and possible defeat in the courts, disappointed by the California legislature's refusal to fund improvements of the road to Mineral King, and aware of growing public opposition to its plans, Disney looked elsewhere for a resort site. In 1978, Congress ended the controversy by adding Mineral King to Sequoia National Park.[28]

Looking back on the creation of Sequoia and Kings Canyon national parks, it is clear that various commercial interests—lumbermen, stockmen, hydroelectric developers, irrigationists, resort developers—managed to block broadly supported efforts to expand the national park system. It often appears that support for parks prevailed in Congress only when economic interests had been satisfied. On the other hand, the establishment of Kings Canyon as a wilderness park in 1940, and the more recent addition of Mineral King to Sequoia National Park, represent important steps toward protecting the ecological integrity of the national parks. Kings Canyon became one of the first parks specifically recognized for its wilderness qualities, and the protection of Mineral King, in the face of the determination of the Disney Corporation, marked a milestone in American preservation history.

The campaigns to establish and enlarge Sequoia and Kings Canyon national parks make up only one facet of their history. A parallel story concerns their management. Park managers and citizens asked how these national parks could best serve the public interest. Would they be best administered as natural preserves, or as recreation areas? These questions proved difficult to answer, and to this day no real agreement has been reached on the meaning and purpose of the national parks.

To begin with, Congress in 1890 provided no instructions or funding for Sequoia National Park.[29] At the request of Secretary of the Interior John Noble, the Secretary of War sent troops to protect the national parks of California from trespassers and vandals, a practice earlier introduced in Yellowstone. But the troops lacked authorization to patrol the Sierra Forest Reserve, and there were not enough soldiers for this purpose anyway.

Protection of just the parks proved difficult at first. When soldiers first arrived in June 1891 and camped outside the park at Mineral King, they found many parts of Sequoia inaccessible, even to patrols on horseback. Hunters killed game, particularly deer, as winter snows forced the animals down from the high mountains. Sheepherders persisted in driving their sheep across the poorly marked park boundaries and remained largely immune to punishment for repeated illegal entry. Wholesale devastation from overgrazing and fires resulted.

In 1898, Lieutenant Henry B. Clark, acting superintendent at Sequoia, pondered the purpose of a national park: "Is it a playground for the people, a resort for the tourist, a mecca for travelers, a summer house where the inhabitants of crowded cities can repair and fill their lungs with the pure air of mountain and forest?"[30] If so, he concluded, Sequoia was a failure, for its scenic wonders remained inaccessible. Clark and others urged construction of a road to the giant sequoias. In response in 1900, Congress finally authorized $10,000 for the protection and improvement of the park. These funds allowed for repair of the old Kaweah Colony road and its extension into Giant Forest. Completed in 1903, Colony Mill Road opened the door at last to the general public visiting Sequoia National Park. From this time on, the early trickle of tourists grew slowly, but inevitably, into a steady stream.

In spite of the valuable service provided by the military guard, the continued use of troops had its drawbacks. Soldiers, assigned temporarily, could neither know the parks well nor take the same interest in their protection that park rangers did. The almost annual rotation of acting army superintendents, each with his own interests and ideas, made continuity of management policy all but impossible. Whereas some superintendents called for protection of the wildlife, others urged removal of all predatory animals to protect "the deer and other smaller animals and game birds."[31]

Civilians were first employed in Sequoia and General Grant in 1898 during the Spanish-American War and then steadily after 1900. Park ranger Ernest

Britten provided the first winter protection for the parks from 1900 to 1905, and Walter Fry took on the responsibility until 1914. By that year, the military had withdrawn permanently, and Fry assumed full authority over the park's management. He inherited a park that had changed little since its establishment in 1890. It was still little known and almost wholly undeveloped. Lack of a consistent policy by the military superintendents and by the Department of the Interior continued to cause confusion.

The situation promised to change after August 25, 1916, with the establishment of the National Park Service. The new agency, with a small, committed staff of professionals, became a permanent advocate for the parks. It set forth a well-intentioned, but often contradictory, administrative guideline that caused no end of difficulty for future park managers: "to conserve the scenery and the natural and historic objects and the wild life . . . and to provide for the enjoyment of the same in such manner and by such means as will leave them unimpaired for the enjoyment of future

The U.S. Cavalry administered Sequoia and General Grant national parks from 1891 to 1913. *Courtesy Sequoia National Park Archives.*

Captain Charles Young (seated front-center) was the only active, commissioned black graduate of West Point when he served as park superintendent in 1903. During his park stint he supervised completion of the first road into Giant Forest. Here he poses with several of his men and the road crew. *Courtesy Sequoia National Park Archives.*

Early concession facilities concentrated at Giant Forest, where visitation increased markedly after the first auto arrived in 1910, as shown in this photograph. *Photo by Howard Hays. Courtesy Sequoia National Park Archives.*

generations."[32] How the parks could be preserved unimpaired and enjoyed by the public at the same time remained to be seen.

Two Californians, Stephen Mather and Horace Albright, took the lead in the formation and early operation of the Park Service, Mather as the first director and Albright as second-in-command. They were familiar with Sequoia and General Grant national parks and with their problems. For example, each summer hardy visitors on horseback or in stagecoaches struggled up the steep and narrow Colony Mill Road. After 1913 occasional automobiles, which chugged up the same dusty road, frightened the horses. At Giant Forest, visitors found ramshackle camps with inadequate water and sewage systems. In addition, private land claims in and around Giant Forest and the Grant Grove, acquired prior to 1890, threatened the parks with development and deterioration.

Mather first tackled the problem of private land inholdings. For more than two decades, military superintendents had tried to buy 3877 privately-owned acres, scattered in many different plots. Captain Charles Young had even managed to obtain an option on most of these lands for about $19 per acre. Yet time and again a frugal Congress had rejected requests for appropriations.[33] To help overcome this obstacle, Mather offered to match congressional funding with private donations. Between 1916 and 1927, he cajoled money from the National Geographic Society and wealthy industrialists and contributed more than $50,000 from his own pocket. With the eventual approval of Congress, the Park Service bought most important inholdings, with the notable exception of a 160-acre plot near the Grant Grove. This area, developed in 1919 for summer cabins, remains today as Wilsonia Village.[34]

The campaign to acquire privately-owned lands had been best left in Mather's hands. The development of tourist and resource management policies, however, needed strong local leadership. Mather found such a person in Colonel John Roberts White. Oxford educated and recently returned from the Great War, White had met Albright while canvassing Washington for a job. In only eight months he advanced from temporary ranger to assistant superintendent at Grand Canyon National Park. In June 1920, he assumed the superintendency of Sequoia and General Grant. He would play a leading role at the two parks for most of the next quarter-century.[35]

Like Mather and Albright, White believed the best way to preserve the parks was to make them popular with the public. This meant new roads and visitor centers, more trails, and advertising to explain park wonders. Construction of a new road began in 1922 to replace the inadequate Colony Mill Road. The new route, via the middle fork of the Kaweah River, provided much easier access for automobiles. Plans soon included a thirty-mile link between Sequoia and General Grant. The "Generals Highway" would allow visitors to drive into one park and out the other in the same day. Indeed, with great fanfare, it opened to Giant Forest in 1926, and nine years later connected both parks. Construction of axial roads to Crescent Meadow, Lodgepole, and Wolverton, plus a state highway to Cedar Grove, virtually completed the present road network of Sequoia and Kings Canyon.[36]

As road construction proceeded, Mather looked for ways to improve the concession services at Giant Forest and Grant Grove. He believed a single concessioner would provide the best service and be the most accountable. Fortunately, some small local operators in the parks declined to renew their options, and after one trial monopoly failed, Mather convinced an old business friend, Howard Hays, to take over the Sequoia and General Grant operations.

With Mather's promise to support development, Hays and his brother-in-law George Mauger began operations in 1926, just as the new road opened to Giant Forest. After moving the dining and retail facilities to the new road, Hays began replacing old, dilapidated cabins with new ones. Between 1926 and 1930 the concessioner built more than two hundred cabins and tent-tops at Camp Kaweah, Pinewood Auto Camp, and Giant Forest Lodge. Hays and Mauger also rebuilt cabins in Grant Grove, but said their primary interest would remain Giant Forest, where the chief tourist attractions and the greatest opportunities for profit were to be found.[37]

The 1926 addition of the Mount Whitney country to the park also demanded attention. White regarded access to backcountry wilderness as essential to educating visitors in the ways of nature. A trail-building program received vigorous support from the Sierra Club, whose members sought expanded opportunities to explore and enjoy the new alpine parkland.[38]

The Park Service, which inherited a network of former Indian, livestock, and military trails, soon undertook construction of two highly publicized special trails. The John Muir Trail, from Yosemite to Mount Whitney, began as a state project in 1915. Completed in 1933, the trail linked Sequoia to its more famous northern neighbor. White took a greater interest in the second project, known as the

The Auto Log has been a major Giant Forest attraction since the earliest cars arrived. *Courtesy Sequoia National Park Archives.*

High Sierra Trail. This carefully designed trail connected Giant Forest with Mount Whitney and provided easy access to the backcountry for hikers and people on horseback. By 1934, Sequoia's trail system, like its road system, was virtually complete.[39]

With the expansion of the parks' infrastructure during the 1920s, visitation to Sequoia and General Grant increased markedly. Mather and Park Service personnel sought further ways to encourage the visiting public to participate in park advocacy. Radio addresses, newspaper articles, and public speeches by White and others helped. The most effective means, however, began with inauguration of an "interpretation" program in Yosemite in 1920. Two years later Walter Fry introduced the program at Sequoia with a series of now-familiar guided walks, campfire programs, and museum displays. This service proved so successful and dovetailed so nicely with White's ideas of visitor education that by 1931 he had manipulated his budget and the National Park Service's Washington office, and had successfully created a department of naturalists. The impact of the program can be gauged only by its overwhelming popularity.[40]

Interpreting the natural world became a Park Service trademark in the 1920s, but park management left much to be desired. In keeping with the prevailing misconceptions about wild animals, wildlife was handled on a good animal/bad animal basis, much as it had been under the military super-

intendents. Good animals included deer—often made tame by visitor feeding—while bad animals included any that preyed upon good animals. Thus mountain lions, coyotes, and bobcats were systematically trapped or poisoned. Fire supression became truly effective with the addition of new fire roads, specially trained crews, and regular funding. Although well-intended, vigorous fire fighting also resulted in the dangerous accumulation of inflammable materials. World War I had brought a return of cattle grazing to Sequoia, a wartime expediency that Mather and his new agency diplomatically allowed. It took until 1930 to remove the livestock —an early lesson to the Park Service that a policy once established, no matter how destructive, was hard to reverse.[41]

During the first decade and a half of Park Service administration, visitation to the two parks increased more than eightfold, as tourists enjoyed the new road, filled the new cabins, hiked the new trails, and attended the new campfire programs. Although most visitors thought the parks were well run and fully protected, White and many of his staff during the late 1920s began to suffer doubts about the efficacy of park management policies. The construction and publicity had succeeded in drawing unwieldy crowds. On July 4, 1930, more than 2000 cars carrying some 4300 people had entered the park. White grimly recorded the scene at Giant Forest, where a jostling, honking, mechanical jam spilled out of the parking lots and alongside roads. Campsites overflowed onto access roads, and trash littered built-up areas. Visitors ran shouting through the groves, scaled fences protecting the best-known sequoias, and engaged in every form of amusement from softball to square dancing. Lost in the disarray was the inspiration of the massive sequoias. In the face of such intensive recreational use, the original idea of a park as a preserved area faded. White realized that development for tourists had gone too far and that a park experience should encompass more than fun and frolic.[42]

Even before road and housing construction were complete, Colonel White began to suggest new goals for park planning—goals of "atmosphere preservation" and visitor education. In order to avoid the mistakes of the past, White, who felt a personal responsibility for the two parks in his charge, declared himself an obstructionist—ready to block or remove any policy or development that threatened the parks' natural atmosphere. Additional impetus for this policy came from profes-

sional landscape architects, who advised White on almost every decision.[43]

From the mid-20s through the mid-40s, the last two decades of his superintendency, White tried to recreate the parks in the image of his vision of natural preservation. Because of an unusual combination of circumstances, he achieved remarkable success. His seniority and experience, coupled with eloquence and diplomacy, gave him an air of command rare in the Park Service. The Great Depression placed a powerful tool in his hands; White took charge of as many as 1100 men of the Civilian Conservation Corps, choosing projects within the parks and allocating labor. Had he been given this opportunity earlier in his career he might have built roads and buildings, opening thousands of acres to recreational development. Now he used the CCC to maintain and replace existing facilities, to landscape large areas of the visitor complexes, and to develop special attractions like Crystal Cave, Tunnel Log, and the stone staircase up Moro Rock.[44] The CCC also increased White's influence indirectly. In administering this huge program nationwide, the Park Service developed a system of regional

Prior to the 1930s, scientific wildlife management did not exist in Sequoia National Park. Predators were systematically eliminated because they harmed deer and other animals popular with visitors. Shown here in the late 1920s (left to right) are mountain lion hunters Clarence Fry, Jay Bruce, and George Brooks, with Park Superintendent John White. *Courtesy Sequoia National Park Archives.*

The Civilian Conservation Corps operated in Sequoia National Park from 1933 to 1941, primarily building roads and trails and landscaping. *Courtesy Sequoia National Park Archives.*

offices and functional divisions that still exist. During the early days of this expanded bureaucracy, the Park Service director and his Washington office became more distant from local park decisions, thus creating a temporary power vacuum into which Colonel White stepped.[45]

The opening round in the battle to control park development occurred in 1927. Barely a year after concessioner Howard Hays came to Sequoia, White suggested he abandon plans to develop the area of Giant Forest and instead develop the less environmentally sensitive pine-forested valley at Lodgepole. Hays reacted with alarm. Citing visitor preference for "sleeping beneath the Big Trees," he went over White's head to appeal directly to Mather, who supported his position. Thus, the first round in what became Sequoia's greatest management battle went to Hays and his company.[46]

Athough White acquiesced for a time, his consuming interest in restoring Giant Forest to its natural state led him to confront the concessioner again in 1931. Hays requested permission to add a few cabins to a housing complex known as Giant Forest Lodge. Recalling the distressing images of the previous Fourth of July, White rejected the

application and again proposed that the company evacuate the grove. Hays again went over White's head with similar success. This time, however, Horace Albright, the new National Park Service director, recognized the need for some restrictions on construction. He established a so-called "pillow limit" for the lodge area.[47] Park planners later identified this decision as the first limit of its kind in any national park. Pillow limits on other Giant Forest complexes soon followed.

White successfully blocked other new developments. He defeated a proposal for another road from Ash Mountain to Giant Forest via the middle fork of the Kaweah River. According to White, a proposal for a widely promoted high-altitude highway to run the length of the Sierra Nevada died when he refused appropriations to build the portion in Sequoia.[48] He also blocked installation of electric power lines in Giant Forest and rejected a variety of proposals, ranging from golf courses and dance halls to hayrides and cable cars. Again and again, citing potential damage to the "atmosphere" of the parks, White assumed the high moral ground and portrayed prodevelopment forces as tawdry and greedy.

Despite pillow limits, the problem of crowding in Giant Forest continued to concern park planners. White and his assistants explored different strategies for restoring the grove's inspirational atmosphere. They limited the amount of time campers could stay at the four government campgrounds. They encouraged winter use, hoping it would distribute visitors seasonally. Instead, it added to the swelling numbers. When they encouraged the concessioner to add improvements to Kings Canyon and Grant Grove, the offer was spurned as unprofitable. Park planners moved some government administration and maintenance buildings from Giant Forest to Lodgepole Valley, but they were too few to make a difference. They even pondered redesigning the road system to decrease auto traffic. Nothing worked or promised any real hope except full removal of concession facilities from the grove.[49]

As the new decade of the forties dawned, White maneuvered to gain even tighter control over park planning and the concessions. The onset of World War II halted nearly all development and resource management programs in the national parks. Nationwide, visitation dropped by 80 percent, the parks' budget suffered a drastic cut, and the ranks of Park Service and concession employees declined sharply.[50] Given the respite, planning for future development accelerated. In Sequoia, concessioners Hays and Mauger hoped to replace some of the older Giant Forest cabins after the war and to expand the visitor complex. Superintendent White hoped for a return to CCC-type labor, for repair of roads and trails neglected during the war. He also hoped a combination of luck and pressure would enable him to remove concession facilities from Giant Forest. In order to strengthen his position, White called on his traditional allies, landscape architects. To a person, they recommended removal of concessions.

Unfortunately, White's control over local development decisions weakened after the war when the Washington office reassumed the reins. The imminent termination of the concessioner's contract in 1946 intensified direct negotiations between Hays and the national office. Feeling powerless, White railed against the concessioner, the policy of lengthy contracts for monopoly concessions, and what he regarded as usurpation of his duties. When Hays received a temporary extension of his contract, the colonel bitterly predicted that the concessioner would forestall his contract termination by obtaining indefinite contract extensions until a more amenable Park Service administration took over.[51]

White's acrimony henceforth proved a stumbling block in the concession contract negotiations and in 1947 resulted in his forced retirement. The era of John Roberts White, of local control, and of atmosphere preservation had ended. One of the most powerful superintendents in the system, White was replaced by a more pliant and development-minded man, Eivind Scoyen. A few years later, Park Service Director Newton Drury and Regional Director Owen Tomlinson also retired, to be replaced by people less committed to restoring Giant Forest to its natural state. Finally, in 1952, Hays and Director Conrad Wirth signed a new contract that ignored the question of Giant Forest. White's prediction proved remarkably accurate. The loss of this battle for Giant Forest marked the diminished influence of landscape architects and the philosophy of atmosphere preservation.

During World War II and its aftermath, Congress had provided minimal financial support for the national parks. While visitation to Sequoia and Kings Canyon increased nearly 125 percent between 1940 and 1955, for example, funding increased at less than half that rate. Partly in an effort to garner public support, the Park Service advocated a major development program, Mission 66. At the two southern Sierran parks, the project included three new visitor centers, extensive new employee housing, and expansion of park infrastructure.[52] Some in the Park Service feared Mission 66 would damage the parks and wondered what would save the "preservation" side of the Park Service's charter.

Science provided a possible answer through the application of ecological principles to park management.[53] Pioneering wildlife biologists Aldo Leopold and Joseph Grinnell helped shape future policy through their writings and by placing their students in the Park Service.[54] In the southern Sierra, forest pathologist Emilio Meinecke contributed with a 1926 study of human impact on Giant Forest.[55] In the 1930s scientific resource management gained a foothold in Sequoia and Kings Canyon, as well as nationally. George M. Wright, an independently wealthy scientist, funded a program of wildlife surveys in the national parks that revealed the inadequacy of earlier preservation efforts. Wright became the first national chief of the Park Service's Wildlife Division, but his untimely death in 1936 left it rudderless. The onset of World War II then eliminated his division and the incipient Park Service program of ecological management.[56]

Nevertheless, some impetus from this ecological concern continued. At Sequoia and Kings Canyon, research scientist Lowell Sumner experimented with a deer reduction program, discontinued the Bear Hill show (a bizarre tourist attraction with bleachers surrounding a bear-infested garbage dump), institutionalized predator protection, and encouraged studies of backcountry meadows.[57] Meinecke issued another report on Giant Forest in 1944 in which he reinforced his earlier warnings about threats to the big trees.[58] This was followed in 1955 by a report of a special commission investigating damage to the sequoias in Yosemite National Park.[59] Meanwhile, a burst of activity from 1947 to 1951 produced several extensive reviews of back-

During the 1960s, as the environmental movement caught hold, the philosophy of ecosystem management came to the fore. In 1963 a committee of scientists commissioned by Secretary of the Interior Stewart Udall released a path-breaking report named after its chairman, A. Starker Leopold.[62] Relying in part on data from Sequoia National Park, the report spelled out ecosystem preservation as the best means to protect the national parks for future generations. It insisted that all management policies allow or mimic natural processes. This meant removal of some development, the complete

Giant Forest Village in August 1953 demonstrated the problem of overcrowding in a sensitive environment. With the exception of the gas station, the facilities and crowding are still present in 1990. *Photo by Wayne Alcorn. Courtesy Sequoia National Park Archives.*

country resources in Sequoia and Kings Canyon. These were followed by a specifically commissioned scientific appraisal of backcountry meadows by Carl Sharsmith.[60]

Then, in 1959, ecologist Richard Hartesveldt released the first of several studies on giant sequoias, challenging policies that had allowed construction and suppressed fires among the big trees.[61] In questioning fire suppression, Hartesveldt struck at one of the oldest and most dearly held directives of the earlier preservation policy. He argued that older trees were endangered by abnormal accumulation of fuel around the base of their trunks, and pointed out that sequoia seeds rarely germinated in areas choked with vegetation. Periodic fires, he concluded, would clear the debris, solving both problems.

reorientation of resource management, and a vigorous program of scientific research. Udall ordered the Leopold Report implemented as the major policy guide for all national parks.

Faced with a groundswell of public environmentalism and the hard evidence of scientists, Congress in the 1960s passed important legislation that altered Park Service policies and planning. In 1964 the Wilderness Act provided a means for protecting roadless and undeveloped areas, much as the founding act of Kings Canyon National Park had done nearly a quarter century earlier.[63] In 1969, Congress passed the National Environmental Protection Act, requiring federal agencies to prepare statements on the environmental effect of all major federal projects and to propose alternatives to mitigate damage. Preservation groups, whose

Bear feeding was a major attraction in Giant Forest from the early National Park Service years until 1940. Its cancellation due to its "unnaturalness" turned garbage-hungry bears loose in the campgrounds to the dismay of rangers and visitors. *Courtesy Sequoia National Park Archives.*

membership was growing rapidly because of the environmental movement, became the loudest and most persistent participants in public planning.[64]

At Sequoia and Kings Canyon, the impact of these changes first affected the backcountry. The 1961 publication of a *Backcountry Management Plan* followed reports on meadow ecology, a massive litter cleanup, and tighter controls over hikers and large parties of tourists on horseback or using pack animals. The plan became a blueprint for all other backcountry parks in the system. In it the Park Service called for some meadows to be closed to livestock use, and for the establishment of meadow and trail monitoring, litter cleanup programs, and better organization of research projects. As the 1960s progressed, park planners closed more meadows to visitors using livestock and, in some cases, even to backpackers.

While the environmental movement led the Park Service to confront its problems of livestock use, litter, and meadow damage, it also encouraged increasing numbers of backpackers to enter the backcountry. Annual visitation to the Sequoia and Kings Canyon backcountry jumped from 8000 in 1962 to more than 44,000 in 1971.[65] Armed with its ecological agenda and faced with the risk that people might love the delicate wilderness to death, the Park Service took a novel and important step. In

1972, in cooperation with the Forest Service, rangers began issuing wilderness permits that limited the number of people allowed into the most popular areas of the backcountry. For the first time the Park Service limited the number of people visiting a park area. That it did so on the basis of ecologically-based principles was even more remarkable.[66]

The combination of public concern for preservation and ecological planning also affected development plans elsewhere in the southern Sierra parks. Shortly after the creation of Kings Canyon National Park in 1940, San Joaquin Valley businessmen had proposed a major recreation complex outside the park at Cedar Grove. Concessioners Hays and Mauger, lacking interest in that area and fearing construction of a reclamation dam, refused to build visitor facilities in the canyon. With the addition of Cedar Grove to the park in 1965, the threat of reclamation ended. In the ensuing planning process for the area, the Park Service scaled down its own development plans in the face of opposition by park users, the Sierra Club, and others.[67]

Upon acquisition of Mineral King, the Park Service encountered similar public opposition to development. Although the Disney plan of the 1960s had called for a major resort, most people who participated in a public hearing rejected development.[68] In the resulting *Mineral King Comprehensive Management*

Despite cessation of cattle and sheep grazing, massive erosion continued in the backcountry from overgrazing by horses and mules. Studies such as the one underway in this 1949 photo show the damage along popular trails. *Photo by Lowell Sumner. Courtesy Sequoia National Park Archives.*

Plan (1980), the only change in the status quo was a decision to eliminate existing leases and cabins upon the deaths of their owners.[69]

Meanwhile, the Leopold Report of 1963 had a profound impact. Park scientists at Sequoia and Kings Canyon attempted to correct past mistakes with programs to eliminate exotic plant and wildlife species that had been introduced in the past, to reestablish native species such as golden trout and bighorn sheep, and to separate bears from campers.[70] The most startling change came in fire management. In 1964 Hartesveldt began experimenting with controlled fires in the sequoia groves. The successful regeneration of giant sequoias that resulted from these experiments encouraged the Park Service to establish a permanent policy of prescribed burning and monitoring natural fires. By 1969, the program was fully underway and has since gained widespread public acceptance.[71]

Of all management issues, development at Giant Forest remained the most difficult. In response to a report by a blue-ribbon Park Service panel, the government moved campgrounds, picnic areas, and most of its structures out of the area by 1972.[72] However, the concessioner's more than 350 buildings remained scattered throughout the forest. In

1980 the Park Service released its *Giant Forest Development Concept Plan*, which called for the relocation of concession facilities to Clover Creek just north of Lodgepole.[73] Despite Park Service and public support for removal and the weakness of Howard Hay's old argument that the public demanded to "sleep beneath the Big Trees," the new concessioner, Guest Services, resisted moving its buildings.

In the 1970s and 1980s, the Park Service continued to struggle with its original mandate: to provide for recreation, while protecting the parks unimpaired for future generations. At Mineral King, cabin leaseholders searched for ways to maintain their presence in the valley. In the backcountry, livestock use associations successfully defeated a plan that would have drastically reduced their access. Fishermen forced the Park Service to continue stocking some lakes and streams in spite of the unnaturalness of the procedure.[74] The controversy ignited by the explosive Yellowstone fires of 1988 temporarily forced a return to fire suppression in all the parks. Although the ban was lifted in Sequoia and Kings Canyon in December 1989, the fire management question and the whole philosophy of ecosystem management continues to be rigorously scrutinized.[75] And at the Giant Forest, the removal of concessions remains uncertain. As the concession company negotiates its next contract for 1992, no one can say what twist of circumstances may again be a reminder that parks are human creations, set aside by human design and controlled by human ideas and interests.

As the first century of Sequoia and Kings Canyon national parks draws to a close, ecological preservation seems well established as the operating management philosophy. Yet it is just a philosophy, a set of current beliefs and practices. The future of Sequoia and Kings Canyon rests in the hands of those who will manage their preservation and use in the century to come.

Lary M. Dilsaver is an associate professor of historical geography at the University of South Alabama and a volunteer researcher for the National Park Service. With William Tweed he recently completed Challenge of the Big Trees, *a centennial history of Sequoia and Kings Canyon national parks.*

Douglas H. Strong is a professor of history at San Diego State University and has written extensively on American environmental history and the history of the national parks, including Tahoe: An Environmental History *(1984);* Trees—or Timber: The Story of Sequoia and Kings Canyon National Parks *(revised edition, 1986); and* Dreamers and Defenders: American Conservationists *(1988).*

The Keyhole prescribed burn was conducted on June 22, 1987, in Giant Forest. Sequoia and Kings Canyon scientists pioneered research and development of Park Service fire management. *Photo by Elizabeth Knight.*

This photograph of a tourist party on Glacier Rock, ca. 1890, was marketed by the C.I. Hood Company of Lowell, Massachusetts, as an energetic sales pitch for Hood's Pills, which could combat "bilious turns, headache, constipation, or any liver troubles." The site itself, with a party of travelers poised on the rock overhanging eternity, was a conventional image in nineteenth-century Yosemite photography. Through their commercialism, such images captured and advertised the spectacular natural formations of Yosemite. *Courtesy Huntington Library.*

Visiting "The Realm of Wonder"

YOSEMITE AND THE BUSINESS OF TOURISM, 1855-1916

by Peter J. Blodgett

Only five years after white men first descended into it on March 27, 1851, the Yosemite Valley began to attract curious and intrepid sightseers with reports of its scenic magnificence. Among them came artists, writers, and photographers. Their works, distributed initially across the state, then the nation and eventually the world, inspired many other people to visit the great valley and absorb its glories firsthand. Thus, through the six decades between the American Civil War and World War I, the numbers of visitors grew ever larger, and, as a consequence, stimulated the development of a substantial tourist industry in the valley that sought to profit from tourist dollars. Close study of that industry, therefore, contributes to better understanding of the evolution of commercial use of scenic wonders. Such study also illuminates tourism's impact on the fate of the Yosemite region through its encouragement of both natural preservation and commercial development.

Yosemite's first white "tourists," the volunteers of the Mariposa Battalion, a militia tracking Indians, for the most part proved quite impervious to the valley's marvels. Their pursuit of the local Indians in 1851 occupied most of their attention. The rapid eviction of most of the native population, however, opened the valley for peaceful excursions. In the early 1850s, newspaper reports drawing on the accounts of militiamen or prospectors who had explored the valley incited other Californians such as James Mason Hutchings, an English emigrant, to venture into the region. In turn, *their* descriptions of the valley's beauty, appearing in local newspapers or in Hutchings's *California Magazine*, drew still more travelers to the valley. Hutchings himself, as organizer in 1855 of the first sightseeing party to visit the valley, had taken care to capture a visual record of Yosemite by inviting the artist Thomas A. Ayres to accompany the party. Ayres's drawings, widely reproduced as lithographs, enhanced the valley's publicity during the 1850s.[1]

Shortly after Hutchings's pioneer visit to the valley, therefore, news of Yosemite's matchless scenery spread widely in California. Hutchings's account of his travels in the Mariposa *Gazette* was followed by other articles, freely reprinted by many newspapers in the state. Through these stories, word of the valley's existence also filtered east as early as 1856, when *The Country Gentlemen* of Albany, New York, reprinted an article from the *California Christian Advocate* that depicted the "Yo-ham-i-ty" Valley. Illustrated by lithographs based upon the work of Thomas Ayres, this piece presented the spectacle of Yosemite to an eastern audience for the first time. Further stories about Yosemite in the next few years increased public awareness of the valley and tempted a few more

hardy visitors every summer, including the celebrated New York editor Horace Greeley in 1859.
Publication of Thomas Starr King's series of Yosemite letters in *The Boston Evening Transcript* during the winter of 1860-61 and exhibition of the
first photographs taken in the valley by Charles L.
Weed and Carleton Watkins brought interest in the
Yosemite to new heights, despite the nation's pre-
occupation with the course of the Civil War.[2]

Measured by the number of visitors who trekked
to the valley each year, Yosemite tourism remained
inconsequential through its first decade. Only 653
people between 1855 and 1864 had overcome the
many obstacles that surrounded the valley. The
valley's psychological impact upon these visitors,
however, was enormous. In recounting their experiences, travelers routinely reported the "awe and
veneration" that overcame them at first sight of the
valley, describing in reverent tones what one tourist in 1856 called the "gorgeous array of the vast
and wonderful combined in this superb display of
the beautiful and the sublime." To many "literary
tourists" such as Greeley and Bayard Taylor who
had begun exploring California's natural wonders
in the 1850s, such special glories as the Yosemite
deserved special protection against exploitation.
Thus, despite the modest total of eyewitnesses, a
movement to ensure the preservation of the valley's beauty was making rapid headway among
some of the leading citizens of the state by the
early 1860s. Deeply worried about the impact of
uncontrolled development on the valley, they dis-
creetly agitated for its ownership and management
by the state. As Israel W. Raymond, California
representative for the Central American Steamship
Transit Company of New York, wrote to California's
Senator John Conness in February 1864, "I think it
important to obtain the proprietorship soon, to
prevent occupation and especially to preserve the
trees in the valley from destruction . . . ." As historian Kevin Starr later observed, the state's residents and its visitors could find in the valley a
symbol of "all that California promised: beauty,
grandeur, expansiveness, a sense of power and a
sense of . . . an assured and magnificent future."[3]

In response to such concerns, Senator Conness
successfully carried legislation through Congress
that ceded control of both the valley and the Mariposa Grove of sequoias to the state of California in
June 1864. Congress laid the grant squarely in the
hands of the state, under the management of the
governor and an appointed board of eight commissioners, who were enjoined to hold it for "public
use, resort, and recreation . . . inalienable for all
time." Although Senator Conness argued in debate
that the land to be preserved had no value for such
pursuits as cultivation, the legislation recognized
an inherent value in providing the general popu-
lace with places of relaxation and scenic beauty. As
one student of Yosemite's history has pointed out,
the grant "became the first official recognition that
man should not always subjugate nature, but also
enjoy it recreationally and aesthetically, and that
the government's role was to preserve areas for
that purpose."[4]

Creation of the grant with its mandate for dedication of the valley to public purposes in perpetuity came at a crucial moment in Yosemite's history.
Increasing traffic to the valley had already begun
to attract the attention of various commercial interests. Three brothers, Houston, Andrew, and Milton
Mann of Mariposa, had built a toll road to the
valley in 1856, only one year after Hutchings's first
visit there. Along their route, on the south fork of
the Merced River, Galen Clark, another Yosemite
pioneer, founded his first hotel in 1857. In 1859,
the Lower Hotel, owned by Stephen Cunningham,
opened in the valley itself to offer visitors crude
but effective shelter.[5] Although the Mann Trail,
Clark's Station, and the Lower Hotel would all
soon pass into other hands, and their names disap-
pear, each venture represented an outcropping of
the entrepreneurial energy that characterized California during the Gold Rush.

Even before the state formally assumed management of the valley, some local businessmen, such
as the Mann brothers, considered how they could
profit from the growing numbers of visitors. For
these early entrepreneurs, the Yosemite represented
what one historian has dubbed "the new bonanza."
If prospectors could find no gold ores in the valley,
businessmen could still "mine" gold from the valley by supplying the needs of the travelers.

Given the unspoiled state of most of the valley
and the surrounding region in the 1850s and 1860s,
the needs of the early tourists were particularly
great. With the exception of a few primitive hostelries such as the Lower Hotel and Clark's Station

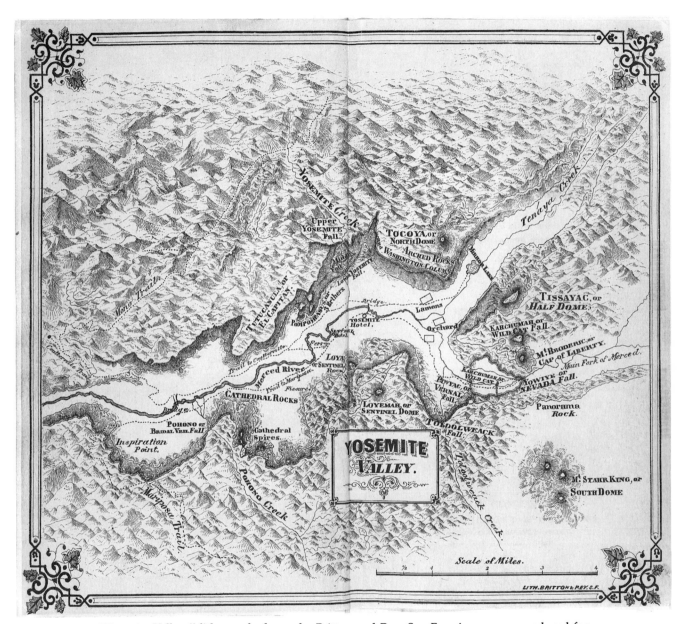

"Yosemite Valley," lithographed map by Britton and Rey, San Francisco, was reproduced for the first Yosemite Valley guidebook, *Yosemite*, by John S. Hittell, 1868. The map reflects the continuing influence of Indian names in the early tourist era, as well as the earliest development of valley trails, hotels, and ferry. *Courtesy Huntington Library.*

and a few improved paths such as the Mann brothers trail, the valley's visitor facilities remained, for the most part, unimproved. Consequently, both travel to the valley and a stay in it for any length of time demanded hardiness, persistence, and a taste for adventure.

Simply approaching the valley proved a significant adventure in itself. Before 1872, no wagon roads reached the valley floor; travelers took to horseback many miles from the valley and rode in on dusty, rocky mountain tracks that pitched up and down steep inclines. Those tourists who braved the primitive trails found the trip to the valley dirty, exhausting, and nerve-wracking even in the best of circumstances. One visitor, writing in the summer of 1861, characterized the trip as "a hard one for the hardiest and terrible for ladies." They suffered "the wounds and bruises of 100 miles of the roughest and steepest mountain traveling on horseback," as well as the punishing effects of exposure that left them with "sunburnt faces wrinkled and drawn down with excessive fatigue."[6]

The cause of road improvement, therefore, achieved considerable importance in the early history of Yosemite's tourist industry. Some of the communities in the Yosemite region, such as Mariposa, eager to divert tourist dollars into the local economies, pressed hard for better roads. In several instances where the Yosemite Board of Commissioners seemed slow to act, local commercial interests launched their own projects. The commissioners sanctioned other toll roads to the valley rim or even down into the valley floor.[7]

Despite the formidable difficulties that road building in mountain country entailed, construction crews were approaching the valley from several directions in 1869 and 1870. The Mariposa and Big Tree Grove Turnpike Company, the Chinese Camp and Yo Semite Turnpike Company, and the Coulterville and Yosemite Turnpike Company all endeavored to link the valley by wagon roads to surrounding towns. Their progress significantly reduced the length of the saddle trip into the valley. During the same period, as the Central Pacific Railroad finished its short line east from Stockton into Calaveras County and then south into the San Joaquin Valley, other stage roads connected rail stops at Milton, Berenda, Raymond, and Merced to the valley turnpikes. Still larger numbers of

tourists then could reach the valley in less time and with less discomfort than ever before. In the early 1870s a new transportation network grew up that could carry tourists from San Francisco to Oakland by ferry, from Oakland to Stockton, Milton, and eventually Merced by train, by stage to Gentry's or Clark's Station, and finally by horse or mule to the valley. In 1874, the Coulterville and Yosemite Turnpike Company finally pushed over the edge of the valley and laid out a wagon road down to the valley floor. Despite improved roads, as one 1871 guidebook urged, visitors to Yosemite should be "strong and fresh" when they made their plans for the excursion and take special care to equip themselves with "plenty of something soft and thick to come between [them] and the horse, during the necessary miles in the saddle."[8]

The greater number of visitors borne to the valley on these improved roads and new rail connections, in turn, created a growing market for other business ventures. More tourists demanded more services and facilities of all kinds in the valley itself. Many new commercial enterprises thus appeared in the valley during the 1860s and 1870s. Although neither Cunningham's Lower Hotel nor its neighbor the Upper Hotel were disturbed by competitors for some years after opening, the hospitality business in Yosemite directly felt the impact of Yosemite's expanding popularity. The rough cast of accommodations at the Upper and Lower hotels lessened, though it persisted in many aspects for as long as the valley was beyond reliable rail or wagon freight service. In particular, James M. Hutchings's return to the valley in 1864 as proprietor of the Upper Hotel brought much physical improvement to what became known as the "Hutchings House." Adding porches and partitions to increase privacy and soften the harsh edges of the main hotel, he also erected outbuildings, including the renowned "Big Tree Room" surrounding a 175-foot cedar tree and serving as both kitchen and sitting room.[9]

Completion of the first transcontinental railroad in 1869 established a direct, if somewhat rickety, connection between California's scenic attractions and the rapidly expanding pool of upper-class easterners interested in visiting natural wonders. In the particular case of the Yosemite Valley, the anticipation of greater tourism inspired much new

Hotel operators in Yosemite Valley employed various strategies to attract patrons. Leidig's Hotel trade card (left), closely modeled a familiar Carleton Watkins photograph of Sentinel Rock. The Cosmopolitan, not to be outdone, became renowned for its cleanliness and amenities such as billiard tables and its extremely well-stocked bar. *Courtesy Huntington Library.*

development in 1870 and 1871. Just as the Lower Hotel, the Hutchings House, and Clark's Station underwent considerable upgrading, so other aspiring capitalists founded La Casa Nevada between Vernal and Nevada falls, Leidig's Hotel near the Lower Hotel, Mountain View House on the trail between Clark's Station and the valley, and the Cosmopolitan Bath-house and Saloon near the Hutchings House. Each establishment tried to fashion its own identity, usually based on the character of its service.

None was more effective than the Cosmopolitan. Its success in providing the amenities living up to its name astonished visitors. The saloon advertised a "ladies' parlor," a "gents' reading room" furnished with the latest newspapers, a barber shop, hot and cold baths, billiards tables, games of quoits and shuffleboard, and a very well-stocked bar. With the promise that "No pains or expense will deter the Proprietor from rendering it A Desirable and Favorite Place of Resort!", the Cosmopolitan became an attraction in its own right for those tourists who had imagined that they would have to abandon clean towels, full-length mirrors, and carpeting for the duration of their visit.[10]

The transfer of Yosemite Valley from the public domain to state management in 1864 thus fostered a setting ripe with commercial possibilities. Dedicated in perpetuity to the purposes of public pleasure and recreation, the grant represented a guaranteed market for businesses engaged in serving the tourist. At the same time, however, the terms of the grant imposed significant restrictions on all uses of the valley. If the valley were to be protected for the use and enjoyment of future generations, unrestrained development in it could not be permitted. Upon the state of California, through the agency of the State Board of Commissioners, fell the ultimate responsibility for preserving the valley, while making it as accessible as possible to the general public.

During their tenure as managers of the Yosemite reservation, the commissioners sought to reconcile the interests of public and private enterprise and to create a harmonious balance between them. The board encouraged private road building with grants and authorized toll roads when the legislature provided insufficient funds for construction.

The commission improved trails and roads and erected bridges in the valley to assist sightseers. And they waged a long, bitter struggle through the courts against several private landholders, including James Lamon and James Hutchings, who claimed land in the valley by virtue of settlement predating the 1864 act of cession.[11] In all these instances, the commissioners were wrestling with aspects of the single overriding dilemma that confronted them throughout their existence: how could they foster development in the valley for the benefit of visitors without irreparably damaging the valley's unspoiled character?

The continuing increase in the number of visitors, however, always lent weight to the arguments of those who favored further development. Especially in the last quarter of the nineteenth century, Yosemite drew hundreds and then thousands of visitors each year, including hundreds of foreign sightseers. In one three-year stretch between 1883 and 1885, an average of 2361 American tourists came each year to the valley, in comparison to the total of 653 who had made the journey between 1855 and 1864 and the 2073 who had visited between 1865 and 1868. During the same period, a grand total of 1166 foreign nationals arrived in the valley, averaging 388 per year. The wide variety of nationalities among the foreign tourists demonstrated Yosemite's world-wide drawing power. Although the peripatetic residents of Victorian Britain predominated, most other European nations were also represented in each year's influx from abroad. One party traveling from San Francisco to Yosemite in 1884 reflected this diversity in microcosm: two Americans, four Britons, three Irishmen, a doctor serving in the Indian army, a German, a Spaniard, and a Dutch sea captain.[12]

Surging tourist numbers, especially in the 1880s, put new pressure on both the state commissioners and the private concessioners to accommodate all the newcomers. Drawing on more generous state appropriations, the commissioners launched an extensive program of renovations between 1885 and 1889. Decaying roads and trails were rebuilt, worn bridges were replaced, pipelines to carry fresh water were laid, new trails and footpaths were cleared, and repairs were made to the basin of Mirror Lake to relieve the accumulation of debris. The commissioners even erected a grand new hotel, the Stoneman House, in 1888, and then dismantled Leidig's and Black's hotels. Those aging and "unsightly" establishments, the commissioners decided, were no longer fit to serve the public.[13]

Private operators serving tourist travel to the valley took the same course of action, striving to emulate and then surpass earlier improvements at the Hutchings House and the Cosmopolitan Saloon. New stage routes linking stations along the Central Pacific line through the San Joaquin Valley to Yosemite competed aggressively with each other for business. Firms such as the Great Sierra Stage Company and the Yosemite Stage and Turnpike Company built up large operations encompassing not only horses, stages, and drivers but also smiths, stables, barns, and way stations located at strategic points along the trails. All of them boasted of their success in reducing the length and discomfort of the stage journey through the excellence of their drivers and their equipment.

Despite the expense of hauling in everything from bar stools to bath towels, other concessioners expanded their facilities. Under the management of the Washburn brothers, for example, the old Clark's Station on the south fork of the Merced evolved by the 1880s into the large Wawona Hotel operation, connected to the valley by the Yosemite Stage and Turnpike Company. Wawona included not only lodgings and barns but vegetable gardens, pasture, slaughterhouses, a dairy, an icehouse, granaries, and repair shops for the stage equipment. James M.. Hutchings's successors, George Coulter and A.J. Murphy, continued Hutchings's construction work, adding a two-story hotel to the various cottages built by Hutchings. Their successor, John K. Barnard, completed the main building, later named the Sentinel Hotel, and pursued further improvements to Hutchings's original structures.[14] Private business interests thus accelerated the development of the valley and of the surrounding region in order to benefit from the growth of tourism.

The commissioners and the private operators had to respond to more than the sheer press of numbers, however, as they confronted the implications of expanding tourist travel to Yosemite. While many early visitors had been satisfied with a saddle blanket for shelter and biscuits and beans for a bill of fare, many of their successors sought

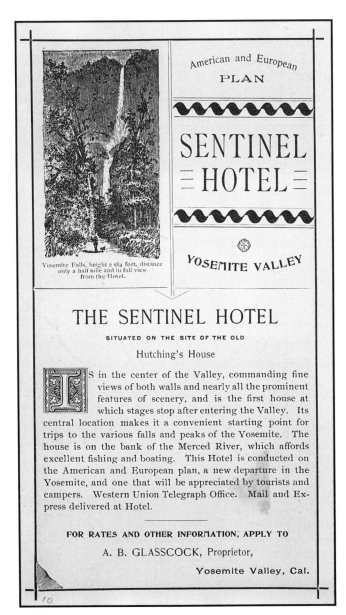

The Sentinel Hotel situated on the site of the old Hutchings House ca. 1895. A trade card for one of the most familiar of Yosemite's hostelries, going back even before J. M. Hutchings, this advertisement, with its references to American and European plan accommodations, mail deliveries, and Western Union telegraph connections, demonstrates the growing interest of tourists in a more civilized vacation. *Courtesy Huntington Library.*

more comfort and refinement in their travel circumstances. Even many aspiring outdoorsmen preferred to "rough it" more gently in the structured setting of a developed campground. Despite a mounting popular enthusiasm for outdoor recreation, most tourists indulged a taste for nature only through short expeditions beyond a relatively civilized base of Pullman sleeping cars and resort hotels.

Fewer tourists seemed willing, therefore, to accept the advice of one 1873 guide book that they should expect "some inconveniences" on a Yosemite trip: "You cannot carry the Grand Hotel with you into the mountains." Construction of the well-appointed but ill-fated Stoneman House and the expansion of the Wawona Hotel represented not only an effort to house more tourists but to offer them as luxurious an experience as possible during their stay. Even Yosemite's first formal campground, operated by Aaron Harris between 1878 and 1887, provided such amenities as corrals and fodder for livestock, preselected campsites, and supplies of fresh meat and produce for the campers.[15] Such establishments as Harris's campground and the Wawona complex with their many facilities and amenities for the tourist, allowed visitors to partake of the outdoor life without being bothered by all its discomforts.

Renovation, reconstruction, and improvements notwithstanding, however, Yosemite in the 1870s and 1880s remained a resort in a "rustic" setting. Although the human inhabitants had begun to domesticate the valley to many civilized purposes, their efforts were still confined largely to portions of the valley floor. Travel through the region remained difficult and that difficulty, in turn, deprived the concessioners of access to reliable freight service. Without such service, they had considerable trouble importing the supplies and equipment needed to enhance their operations. One lodger at Barnard's Hotel during the summer of 1878 reported that "all arrangements here are of the simplest—quite comfortable but nothing fine . . . . It must be confessed that the rooms are rough-and-ready; and the partitions apparently consist of sheets of brown paper, so that every word spoken in one room is heard in all the others!" The trip itself was still an agony to be endured, not a pleasure to be anticipated. Most tourists remembered

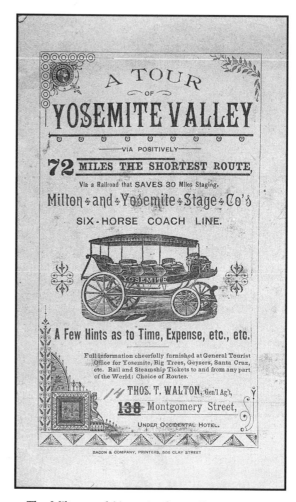

The Milton and Yosemite Stage Company was one of many private concessionaires established during the 1870s and 1880s to profit from the upsurge of tourists into the valley. *Courtesy Huntington Library.*

their journey as an unremitting physical assault on their persons, relieved only by a series of welcome but too-brief layovers. As one traveler in 1878 rememberd it, "We were thankful to rest our weary battered bones, ere starting again to complete our twelve hours of violent shaking and jolting over loose stones and roads not yet repaired after their winter's wear." Another, in 1884, described the frightening combination of a dangerous road and stagecoach at full gallop: "On we dashed—our rattling driver, with a wild look in his eye, a wide-brimmed hat and a pointed beard, reckless of the discomforts of his male passengers and evidently enjoying the nervous excitement of the females . . . . The road was absolutely awful; and at times the four wheels were off the ground and in the air together . . ."[16]

Whatever difficulties confronted them, Yosemite's visitors continued to succumb to its magic allure on first sight. As pilgrims to a religious shrine in another age might have been moved to ecstasy by the majesty of the divine presence, so were many tourists inspired to acclaim the "unique glory" of the valley in similar terms. Writing of one moonlit evening on the banks of the Merced River below the Yosemite Falls, one visitor in 1884 reported that "I felt absolutely thrilled with delight at the beauty, grandeur, and solemn silence that surrounded us. The stillness was almost awful, broken only by the distant continuous whisper of the great waterfall, or the shrill cry, now and then, of some bird." Writing of her journey into the valley during a summer storm in the following year, another tourist captured the emotional force of the scenery heightened by the convulsion of the elements: "When our feeling of awe seemed most intense and we thought nothing would make the scene grander, there came a startling clap of thunder & flash of lightening [sic] and a heavy shower of rain came rattling down upon us, and the storm made grandeur sublimity." An astounding natural glory so dominated the valley that even one sardonic British critic, deriding the impact of the tourists on the landscape, conceded that their worst efforts could not undermine the essence of the valley's wonder.

They have made roads and bridle-paths to it, built hotels and drinking saloons in it, brought the

cosmopolite cockney to it, excursioned to it, pick-nicked in it, scraped names upon its rocks, levied tolls by its waterfalls, sung "Hail! Columbia" beneath the shadows of its precipices, swallowed "smashes" and "slings" under its pine trees; outraged, desecrated and profaned it but it still stands an unmatched monument hewn by ice and fire from the earth itself.[17]

Not all observers of the valley's development, however, were so sanguine about the ability of its natural environment to withstand the inroads made by the tourist business and the busy tourists. Worried that the desecration of the valley lay close at hand, various critics in the late 1880s pointed to the State Board of Commissioners, Yosemite's official managers, as the source of the valley's worst problems. Decades of controversy culminated in 1906 in the recession of the Yosemite grant by California to the federal government and the dissolution of the board. During its lifetime, the board of commissioners' efforts to manage the valley had involved it in many acrimonious disputes, beginning with its efforts to oust Hutchings and Lamon in the 1860s. In its dual role as guardian of the valley and regulator of all business enterprises within the grant, the board possessed sufficient power to guarantee the success or failure of any business subject to its authority. The abuse of that power, whether fancied or actual, consequently became the subject of complaints against the board, sometimes carried as far as the state legislature. Opposition to the board's alleged support of "monopoly power" proved especially telling, as in 1874, when the legislature, at the urging of the Yosemite Turnpike Road Company, broke the board's exclusive grant to the Coulterville and Yosemite Turnpike Company of the right to enter the valley from the north. The legacy of bitterness created between the board and some of the private operators may even have contributed to dissolution of the original board under provisions of the new state constitution of 1879, which limited the terms of state officeholders.[18]

In time, new opposition to the reconstituted board of commissioners arose, for only the personnel of the board had changed after dissolution in 1880. The board's power had not been lessened, and some of its actions still provoked charges of favoritism, venality, and ineptitude. At last, in 1888, concessioner Charles Robinson's conflict with the board erupted into a nasty dispute that embroiled the state legislature. Robinson, an artist who had operated a small studio in the valley, became so outraged at his dispossession by the commissioners that he filed formal charges against them. He accused them of diverting public resources to the control of their allies, of abusing the landscape of the valley for commercial uses such as agriculture and stock raising, and of using their regulatory powers to build up uncontrolled monopolies for their friends. Apparently with the support of William Randolph Hearst's San Francisco *Examiner* in 1888 and 1889, Robinson obtained hearings on his long list of grievances before each house of the legislature. Although the reports of the investigative committees essentially upheld the commissioners on many points, various reforms in management of the valley were suggested, including a significant restructuring of the board. Moreover, the controversy over Robinson's charges arose just at a time when pressure for federal protection of Yosemite's wonders was peaking.[19]

John Muir, long-time devotee of the valley's beauty, had become as deeply disenchanted with the valley's management by 1889 as had his acquaintance Charles Robinson. After a visit to the valley that summer with Robert Underwood Johnson, the conservation-minded associate editor of *The Century Magazine*, Muir accepted Johnson's urgings to campaign for a new natural reserve encircling the valley. Their aim was to preserve Yosemite's Sierra watershed from destruction through unrestrained exploitation by lumbermen and stock growers. With great literary force, Muir and Johnson hammered away at the need to protect the greater Yosemite region from what Johnson denounced as California's "amateur management" of the valley, which led to

> the spectacle of the most phenomenal of the national pleasure grounds ignorantly hewed and hacked, sordidly plowed and fenced, and otherwise treated on principles of forestry which would disgrace a picnic ground.

Johnson's editorials in *The Century* demanded more able and professional oversight of the valley, thus further impeaching the caliber of the current state board's management.[20]

In their campaign for federal protection, Muir and Johnson advanced their aims successfully by the judicious use of publicity directed toward receptive and influential audiences. Johnson's magazine, a pre-eminent force in cultivating literary realism among American authors and good government in American politics, gave Muir an entrée into the homes of thousands of middle- and upper-class families. Many of them, in turn, shared Muir's apprehension about the fate of unprotected wild lands and sympathized with the burgeoning movement to safeguard natural resources, including scenic beauty, from destruction. Some probably had read Muir's earlier writings or seen the Yosemite photographs of Carleton Watkins; a few had probably visited the valley in person. Other eastern publications lent their weight to the cause, mobilizing more support for the legislation pending in Congress. This support, along with that of California's Southern Pacific Railroad, translated into a successful legislative campaign in the fall of 1890, spearheaded by Muir's eloquent pieces in *The Century*.[21]

Although the establishment of Yosemite National Park surrounding the valley inspired joy in many quarters, criticism of the state board's management of the valley did not abate. The mounting pressure on the valley's open land and water resources by the growing tourist population only intensified the agitation fomented by Muir and his allies to prod California into receding the valley to the federal government. Muir rallied old comrades such as Robert Johnson and drew in powerful new friends such as E.H. Harriman and other Southern Pacific Railroad leaders and President Theodore Roosevelt. The recession movement also gained support from many reform-minded middle- and upper-class Americans who by the early 1900s had begun to coalesce into the broad movement identified as "progressivism." Among them, Muir could count many members of his own Sierra Club, founded in 1892, who applauded both political reform and preservation of unspoiled nature. After 15 years of debate and discussion, the recession was accomplished in 1906, incorporating the valley into the national park, under the authority of the Department of the Interior and the protection of the United States Army.[22]

Almost as soon as the transcontinental railroad was completed in 1869, travelers were encouraged to visit Yosemite on their trips to California. Even eastern railroads and steamship lines advertised the valley. The Southern Pacific Railroad used Yosemite on brochures and timetables to advertise its special relationship with California. *Courtesy Huntington Library.*

Both before and after recession of the valley to the federal government, the Army had engaged in considerable surveying and construction of roads and trails throughout the national park to improve its accessibility not only for travelers but for cavalry patrols as well, protecting the back country from trespassing poachers and stock growers. Although the cavalry troops assigned to the park detail only patrolled in the summer months and were ill-equipped by either training or statute to serve as civil guards, their continuous patrolling generated much information about previously-unexplored sections of the region. Following the valley's recession, the Department of the Interior also contracted for engineering work within the valley, establishing new trails and bridges and renovating or replacing dilapidated structures. As in the case of the state board, the federal managers of the park now struggled to keep up with deterioration that followed each tourist season.[23]

The park's administration had to give such work a top priority, for new developments in transportation to the valley made possible the middle-class invasion in great numbers. As one historian of tourism has observed, "Each decade saw more families with leisure time and money to spend in it; the West as well as the East was becoming urbanized, and even its modest towns spawned their vacation spots." This new growth in tourism encouraged a "mass market" whose importance came to outweigh "the patronage of the elite."[24]

The continuing approach of railroads toward the valley made this massive influx possible by shrinking distances significantly, especially after the completion of the Yosemite Valley Rairoad. Built between 1905 and 1907, that road ran 78 miles from Merced through the Merced River canyon to El Portal just outside the park. Although the railroad never received permission to extend its route into the valley, its rail link from Merced to the terminus at El Portal left tourists with only a four-hour stage ride from El Portal to the valley instead of one lasting two days. Within a few years, the railroad had secured contracts with the Southern Pacific to carry Pullman sleepers originating in Los Angeles and San Francisco through to El Portal, leaving their passengers undisturbed and relieved of the necessity to change cars. The Yosemite Valley Railroad provided other luxuries such as a diner

car and an open-observation car; in 1913, the company's new motorized transportation from El Portal reduced the last leg of the tourist trip to an hour and a half. By 1916, the railroad was carrying over 14,000 passengers per year.[25]

Adoption in 1913 of gasoline-powered transport in place of horse-drawn wagons to convey tourists from El Portal into the park also marked the beginning of the automobile's enduring relationship with Yosemite National Park. The same year, Interior Secretary Franklin K. Lane lifted the 1907 ban imposed by the Army that exiled early motorists from the park. While the age of mass ownership and use of the automobile was still some years in the future, the auto exerted considerable influence on many phases of park affairs from its first appearance. It put new demands on the park's road network, required new regulations to manage the movement of traffic around the park, and created a necessity for all kinds of new services and facilities, from garages and gasoline stations to parking lots. A few years after the end of World War I, automobiles would make possible an enormous increase in the number of annual visitors.[26]

Continued road improvements and the mechanization of travel to the valley thus brought the possibility of visiting the park within reach of an ever larger number of Americans. The growing number of visitors who took advantage of this opportunity promised concessioners in the national park a wider market for their services, especially as more and more middle-class Americans acquired the disposable income and leisure time required for pleasure travel. Many visitors took advantage of an American variation on an English innovation pioneered by Thomas Cook, the personally-conducted railroad tour. When the Boston firm of Raymond and Whitcomb launched their first tour to the Pacific Coast in 1881, it offered travelers what a later observer has described as "self-conscious gentility and reassurance of safety from discomfort." Conducting as many as fifty or sixty tourists about the great circuit of western attractions, including Yosemite, the tour operators introduced Americans of secure but not exalted means to the genteel life of the grand resorts, providing the paradoxical experience of "exclusiveness on a large scale." Despite the rapid pace of their tours, these travelers reveled in the companionship of their parties,

Not everyone who traveled to Yosemite complained of its primitive facilities. Captain William Banning, of the prominent Los Angeles transportation family, hosted a coaching vacation for friends and relatives in the Yosemite-Big Tree region, ca. 1902. With them went a Belgian cook and a supply wagon carrying food, kitchen equipment, and camping accoutrements. *Courtesy Huntington Library*.

as well as the scenic wonders around them. "Everyone seems at home and the car is full of pleasant conversation," observed one tourist bound to Yosemite from Boston in 1882, while ten years later another client of Raymond and Whitcomb wrote enthusiastically that "the sociability of this company is a joy and a delight."[27]

Those amiable parties of tourists, hustled through their Yosemite visit by tour operators, thus enlarged the concessioners' business, especially for the Sentinel Hotel. As the only hotel in the valley after the destruction of the Stoneman House in 1888, the Sentinel monopolized business, while others outside the valley, such as the Wawona or, after 1907, Yosemite Valley Railroad's Del Portal, absorbed the demand for comfortable accommodations on the way to the park. The Del Portal, with its "wide halls" and its "large, airy rooms" warmed with steam heat and illuminated with electric light, allowed each guest to indulge in "all the luxury of hotel living," representative of "a most careful provision for comfort and enjoyment." Such comfortable establishments guaranteed, in the words of one pamphlet, that "the visitor to Yosemite does not have to 'rough it,' or undergo any discomfort or hardship."[28]

Tourists who *did* seek at least a modicum of "roughing it," however, found little accommodation to their interest. After fire wiped out Harris's campground in 1887, organized arrangements or facilities for camping were uncommon. The possibilities of profiting from that pastime, though, attracted a new entrepreneur to the valley at the end of the nineteenth century. David A. Curry, a schoolteacher who had come from Indiana to settle in northern California, and a man with a yen for a more secure occupation involving life out-of-doors, established a primitive family-run campground on the south side of the valley in the summer season of 1899. Offering nothing more in the beginning than "a tent, a good table, and a clean napkin at every meal," Camp Curry set out to furnish "service aimed at making every guest feel at home." Although the Currys' location in the valley meant importing everything from eggs and butter to mirrors and blankets, they slowly made a go of their enterprise, assisted by favorable word-of-mouth publicity that spread first among educators throughout California. Stanford students staffed the camp during the summers, while teachers and administrators came to enjoy an inexpensive and congenial stay in Yosemite.[29]

Like the valley's hotels, however, Camp Curry continued to offer more services in hopes of attracting more customers. While the camp retained its familiar wood and canvas tent cabins, it added a permanent building in 1901 to house a kitchen and dining room. In the next year came sewer lines, restrooms, a bath house, and even space for tennis courts and a croquet lawn. Curry, a natural showman, revived the firefall down Glacier Point as an evening entertainment and presented an array of campfire programs for his guests on the natural and human history of the region. Curry's success in capitalizing on an important new dimension of the tourist market is measured by the rapid growth in Camp Curry's share of the valley's tourism. Whereas Camp Curry attracted only 290 guests during its inaugural season compared to 2600 at the Sentinel Hotel, its attendance rose to 800 in 1902 and 1300 in 1904. By 1912, Camp Curry, with 3516 guests, outstripped not only its competitors, Camp Ahwanee (1162) and Camp Lost Arrow (954) but also the Sentinel Hotel (2615). Only three years later in 1915, during the season of the Pacific expositions in San Francisco and San Diego, Camp Curry drew 11,715 guests, while only 8323 stayed at the Sentinel Hotel, 2611 at Camp Lost Arrow, and 1426 at Camp Ahwanee.[30]

Camp Curry's success, as well as the popularity of other campgrounds in the valley, demonstrated the increasing appeal of outdoor recreation among American tourists, particularly of middle-class circumstances. Its great variety of facilities and David Curry's constant improvement of them, however, also demonstrated that most tourists in the 1890s and the early 1900s did not aspire to lose themselves in the wilderness. Camp Curry's development mirrored the on-going development throughout the valley, intended to offer tourists more comforts and "civilized" conveniences. By 1908, for example, Yosemite Village comprised a very busy community of 46 structures including offices and shops, barns and stables, and homes for concessioners and representatives of the federal government. Electrification had been made possible by construction in 1901 of the Happy Isles power plant, while daily mail service during the summer and a spreading network of telephones eroded the valley's quiet insularity. El Portal, the small community that sprouted around the Yosemite Valley Railroad's terminus and its Hotel Del Portal, grew up in the same manner, force-fed by the money earned from legions of tourists who shuttled through each summer.[31]

Whether they spent only two days at the Sentinel Hotel with a Raymond and Whitcomb excursion party or two months in a tent cabin at Camp Curry, the valley's visitors in general appreciated the services available to them and their patronage encouraged further development. When the valley returned to the federal government in 1906, Yosemite's concessioners included not only lodgings and transportation, curio dealers, grocery stores, and photographic studios, but also a butcher shop, bakery, laundry, bowling alley, billiards room, and barber shop. Those who visited Yosemite early in this century thus had to give up far fewer comforts of their daily existence than any of their predecessors. They could obtain fresh bread, clean clothing, close shaves, and even a regular newspaper, *The Yosemite Tourist*, published by D.J. Foley, who also operated a print shop and a photographic studio. As one commentator wrote in 1911, "One lacks for no comfort" in visiting Yosemite, "a spot of infinite loveliness set as a resting place amid the stress and turmoil of the mighty world."[32]

The many concessioners that settled in the park by the beginning of World War I had created a man-made environment replicating many features of urban life. In number and variety, they presented a complicated challenge to the public officials who had managed the valley since its cession by the federal government in 1864. As travel to the valley grew and as tourists expected more and better facilities decade by decade, first the California State Board of Commissioners and later the United States Army and the Department of the Interior struggled to balance commercial development against preservation of the natural environment. After World War I, Yosemite's new guardian, the National Park Service, would find it a problem whose solution would be frustratingly elusive.

Peter Blodgett is working toward completion of the doctorate in history at Yale University. He has authored several articles and chapters in anthologies on such subjects as California bibliography and national park history. Currently, he is assistant curator for western historical manuscripts at the Huntington Library.

Figure 1: Albert Bierstadt, *Valley of the Yosemite*, 1868. *Courtesy Yale University Art Gallery, photograph by Joseph Szaszfai.*

Sublime Vistas and Scenic Backdrops

NINETEENTH-CENTURY PAINTERS AND PHOTOGRAPHERS AT YOSEMITE

by Kate Nearpass Ogden

During the second half of the nineteenth century, Yosemite Valley rapidly became the Niagara Falls of the West Coast. As one of the most popular scenic attractions in the country, it was thus frequently rendered in paintings and photographs. Scores of artists visited Yosemite between its discovery in 1851 and the creation of the national park in 1890, and they continued to paint and photograph the valley in later years. The landscapes created in the first forty years of Yosemite's history played an important communications role on several notable occasions: when the valley was first publicized in the 1850s, when its status as a state-managed park was promoted in 1864, and when the land surrounding the valley was set aside as a national park in 1890.

Artists went to the valley because it offered some of the grandest, most sublime scenery in the country. Yosemite and other newly discovered sites in the West gave them fresh subject matter and an opportunity to make a splash with something new. A prime example is the New York artist Albert Bierstadt, whose fame was based on his numerous large paintings of the Rocky Mountains, Yosemite Valley, and other western landscapes (fig. 1).

Yosemite appealed to artists for ideological reasons as well. As an American "Eden" or an immense "natural cathedral," the valley carried a spiritual significance that was recognized by many visitors of the period. Accounts of the 1860s and 1870s are full of religious rhetoric, in which the Yosemite trip was referred to as a "pilgrimage" and tourists posed as transcendentalist worshipers of God-through-nature.[1] Yosemite also served the cause of nationalism, since it was bigger and better than any area like it in Europe. Artists painting the valley felt they were promoting knowledge of and pride in their country, as well as helping to develop American landscape art. For California artists and their patrons, Yosemite further served as a focus of state pride.[2]

Geological investigation was one of several important influences on the art and artists of Yosemite. A number of Yosemite painters and photographers were brought west by the expeditionary parties exploring America's territories and national boundaries, although most visited the valley on their own time. Some artists worked directly with the geologists studying Yosemite Valley itself.[3] On a general level, geology was of interest to *all* the artists who painted and photographed the geological monuments and curiosities that serve as focal points in the Yosemite landscape.

Although religion, nationalism, and geology were important, tourism was probably the most pervasive influence on Yosemite image-making.[4]

49

Figure 2: Thomas A. Ayres, *Valley of the Yosemite, California,* 1855, drawing in charcoal, white chalk, and pencil. *Courtesy Yosemite Museum, Yosemite National Park, Photograph by Ted Orland.*

Tourists served as both subject matter and market for artists in the valley. Photographers and painters alike profited from the tourist trade, and their images were influenced by it in turn.

Artist Explorers

The early years of Yosemite history, in which the valley was first explored and publicized, might be considered the expeditionary phase of Yosemite image-making, and the earliest artists were "artist-explorers" in the tradition of George Catlin, Carl Bodmer, and A.J. Miller. The first draftsman to visit Yosemite was Thomas A. Ayres, who arrived in 1855, four years after the valley's discovery by the Mariposa Battalion (fig. 2). Ayres was brought to the valley by the budding entrepreneur James Mason Hutchings, who would soon become a publisher and self-appointed publicity agent for Yosemite and would later run a hotel in the valley. Realizing that visual proofs of this amazing landscape would be of widespread interest (and perhaps profitable as well), Hutchings decided to reproduce Ayres's drawings in the first issue of his new journal, *Hutchings' California Magazine.*[5]

According to a Yosemite visitor in 1859, "Ayres' sketches are truthful, but do not approach to giving an idea of this wonderful Valley."[6] It was thus logical for Hutchings to think next of using photographs in his magazine, since photography was credited with even greater verisimilitude than drawing or painting. In 1859, Hutchings traveled to the valley again with Charles L. Weed, Yosemite's first photographer, and subsequently reproduced Weed's images in several issues of his magazine.

The trials of nineteenth-century landscape photographers, who carried their heavy equipment, chemicals, and fragile glass plates into the wilderness, certainly qualify Weed for designation as an "explorer-artist." Also, Weed's trip was made a decade or so earlier than the four great scientific surveys led by King, Powell, Hayden, and Wheeler. The use of photography as a tool of western exploration was thus still in its adolescence when introduced in Yosemite in 1859.

One of the painters who visited Yosemite around this time, James Madison Alden, was a survey draftsman by profession, although he apparently visited Yosemite on his own. Alden, who had previously worked for the Pacific Coast Survey, made a number of watercolors depicting Yosemite in 1859 while employed by the Northwestern Boundary Survey.[7] Other painters who visited Yosemite in the early years were new residents of San Francisco and Sacramento. One of these was Frederick Butman, the first California painter to concentrate exclusively on landscape. Butman is said to have painted the first oils of Yosemite in 1857, and a few of his Yosemite landscapes still exist. Another early arrival was the Frenchman Antoine Claveau, whose now-lost Yosemite panorama (probably a series of paintings) was, like Butman's work, exhibited in San Francisco in 1857.[8]

Other early Yosemite artists include James Lamson, whose extant diary documents his journey from Maine to California; George Tirrell, whose 25,300 square foot California painting (now lost) was believed in 1860 to be the longest panorama ever painted; and William S. Jewett of New York, better known than the others and hailed as California's first successful portraitist. Among the earliest European-born artists to paint Yosemite were Eugene Camerer from Germany and the Englishman George Burgess, a forty-niner who later helped establish the San Francisco Art Association in 1871.[9] A few Yosemite drawings and paintings by most of these artists still exist, although Camerer's images of the valley are best remembered through the lithographs based on them.

The trail of the early artists of Yosemite winds through a variety of sources, including newspapers, travel books, diaries, letters, and art work. Two extant drawings, for example, indicate that George Tirrell visited Yosemite in September 1858, and one of Hutchings's articles mentions Tirrell's presence there the following year as well.[10] James Lamson's diary tells us that he and Eugene Camerer also visited Yosemite in 1859; a watercolor by Lamson and a comment by Hutchings provide additional evidence of their visit that year.[11] An article in the *Overland Monthly*, 1884, written by another early Yosemite explorer gives a plausible reason for the current obscurity of Antoine Claveau's paintings. After explaining that Milton and Houston Mann had commissioned the artist to paint a Yosemite panorama, the writer, James H. Lawrence, added that Claveau "was a fraud, and humbugged them —dawdling away his time for the best part of a year, and giving them, instead of a panorama, a series of wretched daubs."[12] Although much has been discovered about these early Yosemite painters, many gaps in the record still remain.

Drawings, paintings, and photographs provided visual proof of the valley's wonders at a time when many California stories were regarded as tall tales. News of the valley's amazing landscape had somehow failed to spread after Yosemite was seen in 1833 by Joseph R. Walker's party and in 1849 by the miners William Penn Abrams and U.N. Reamer.[13] After the Mariposa Battalion entered Yosemite in 1851, however, visitors published newspaper accounts of the valley; others sketched and painted what they saw. Hutchings's use of drawings and photographs in his magazine did a great deal to anchor Yosemite firmly in the public imagination. Lithographs published in the 1850s after Ayres's and Camerer's drawings also helped to call attention to the valley.

The first images of Yosemite to be seen in the East were Ayres's drawings, which were exhibited at the Art Union in New York in 1857.[14] Next came Weed's 1859 photographs, which were acquired in 1860 by the New York stereo publisher Edward Anthony & Company (later E. & H.T. Anthony); these were distributed by Anthony as far as England.[15] Photographs taken by Carleton Watkins in 1861 were exhibited at Goupil's Gallery, New York, in December of 1862.[16] Ayres's, Weed's, and Watkins's images served as publicity to an ever-widening audience and confirmed the claims made about Yosemite in the eastern press by Horace Greeley, the Reverend Thomas Starr King, and others.

Yosemite images were considered so compulsory among publishing companies that *Ballou's* magazine of Boston reproduced an invented, fictitious view of the region on two separate occasions. The first appeared in the May 21, 1859 issue, during the initial explosion of interest in Yosemite. The second followed in the June 1870 issue, during the California craze ignited by the opening of the transcontinental railroad. Fictitious Yosemite landscapes were also published as lithographs by Currier and Ives in the mid-1860s, one of them drawn by the artist Frances F. Palmer. The distribution of these invented landscapes indicates the pervasiveness of public interest in Yosemite and the West.

Artists of the 1860s

Benjamin Parke Avery, a writer and editor for the San Francisco *Bulletin* and the *Overland Monthly* and an early commentator on the California art scene, considered 1862 a watershed date in the history of California art. "With the year 1862," he wrote, "began a period of more activity and promise for Art on the Pacific . . ."[17] The same is true of Yosemite; during the 1860s, artists began to visit the valley in ever greater numbers. They came from New York and Boston as well as San Francisco, then the fastest-growing art center on the West

Coast. A few artists came from foreign countries, particularly Great Britain.

One of the most important and best known artistic expeditions of the early 1860s was made by New York artist Albert Bierstadt and his painter companions, Virgil Williams and Enoch Wood Perry. Their August 1863 visit is important for several reasons: its relatively early date, the prominence of the artists involved, the number of pictorial documents still extant, and the presence of Fitz Hugh Ludlow, an able writer who documented the trip. Ludlow's account of their excursion first appeared as a series of articles in *The Atlantic Monthly*. Profiting by the California craze of 1869, Ludlow later republished his account in book form as *The Heart of the Continent* (1870).

Bierstadt's 1863 Yosemite visit did much to inspire local artists in their commitment to painting as a career, their interest in landscape, and their concentration on Yosemite Valley as a subject. Five years after Bierstadt's visit, Benjamin P. Avery wrote that the New York painter had greatly stimulated resident artists. According to Avery, the effects of Bierstadt's visit were generally positive, "though they were first visible in a violent outbreak of Yosemite views, good, bad and indifferent." Avery noted that the valley was already a mecca for California artists, but he recognized, even then, the "danger of having a little too much of even such a good thing as Yosemite."[18]

Establishing Yosemite Valley as a Wilderness Preserve

Bierstadt's Yosemite paintings played a subtle, but important, role in the designation of Yosemite Valley as a park. Returning to New York in December 1863, he began painting Yosemite scenes based on his oil sketches. The first to be shown to the public was a small oil sketch exhibited and auctioned at the Metropolitan Fair in April 1864, a benefit held by the New York Sanitary Commission to raise money for wounded Civil War veterans. At that time, *Night at Valley View* (Yosemite Museum) and *Cho-looke: The Yosemite Fall* (Timken Gallery, San Diego) were also available for viewing in the artist's studio, where they were seen by the artist's ever-widening circle of admirers.[19] Yosemite had been a familiar name for several years, but Bierstadt's paintings provided eastern viewers with their first technicolor visions of its sublime landscape.

Figure 3: Carleton Watkins, *Vernal Fall,* 1861, mammoth albumen photograph. *Courtesy Yosemite Museum, Yosemite National Park, photograph by Robert Woolard.*

Carleton Watkins's photographs (fig. 3) were used even more directly to convince Congress to set aside the valley as a park. Israel Ward Raymond, a prominent San Francisco businessman, is credited with suggesting that the Yosemite park proposal would be stronger if photographs were included. It was certainly Raymond who mailed them to Senator John Conness in Washington, D.C., on behalf of the park promoters.[20] Legend has it that Watkins's photographs were also forwarded to the White House, where President Lincoln studied them prior to signing the 1864 bill setting aside Yosemite Valley for preservation in California's custody.

Bierstadt's, Weed's, and Watkins's images continued to serve as advertisements for Yosemite and California long after the valley was designated a park. Like Thomas Cole's paintings of the Catskill Mountains of New York, which had promoted awareness of that region earlier in the century, these Yosemite images piqued the curiosity of easterners. The same was true of Thomas Hill's paintings later in the decade. Hill painted two of his largest Yosemite canvases while working in Boston between 1867 and 1872. The first so impressed the local art world that the prominent Boston publisher Louis Prang commissioned a smaller version of it, which he reproduced as a chromolithograph. *Ballou's Monthly Magazine* thus had good reason to claim in June 1870 that Hill and Bierstadt were the artists who had introduced their town to Yosemite.

Many artists who visited Yosemite in the 1860s were originally from the East Coast. Some were only traveling through (like Bierstadt and Perry), while others had or would settle permanently in California. Virgil Williams, for example, moved to San Francisco eight years after his Yosemite excursion with Bierstadt and became one of the state's leading art teachers. At least one Yosemite visitor of the late 1860s, watercolorist John Henry Hill, was brought west by his scientific affiliation as a staff artist with Clarence King's survey of the fortieth parallel. Hill arrived in California in 1868 and probably visited Yosemite on his own that year as well.[21]

A significant few who visited during the 1860s were from Great Britain. One of these was the photographer Eadweard Muybridge, who took his first Yosemite photographs in 1867. Others included the painters Thomas Hill and William Keith (figs. 9 and 10). Hill, born in England, came to the United States at the age of fourteen and moved to California as an adult in 1861. Hill's earliest existing Yosemite paintings are dated 1863 and 1864, suggesting that his first visit occurred around that time.[22] The Scottish-born William Keith painted Yosemite in 1866—probably for the first time—and exhibited his paintings in San Francisco that fall.[23]

The predominant painterly style of the 1860s has sometimes been called "romantic realism." It is generally characterized by picturesque compositions, tightly detailed handling of subject, emphasis on "local" colors (blue sky, green foliage, gray rocks), relatively bright color schemes, and foreground figures that provide a focal point and a sense of scale. The mood is often one of midday sunlight and everyday realism, although exceptions include Bierstadt's glowing sunsets and Fortunato Arriola's moonlit landscapes. Many of these early Yosemite canvases were painted in a minutely detailed manner that reminds us of contemporaneous scientific interests and, at the same time, evokes the spiritual beliefs of the period. Nature was considered "part and parcel" of God, and the divine presence was evoked most clearly by nature in its most sublime manifestations. Such places obviously included Yosemite Valley.

The sources of romantic realism were the so-called Hudson River School of New York and its European predecessors, including picturesque French and British styles. The academy of Düsseldorf, Germany, which taught a tightly detailed realism, most often combined with sentimental subjects, was also an influence. Bierstadt's *Valley of the Yosemite* (fig. 1) evokes the spiritual qualities as well as the quasi-scientific realism of the period. Equally detailed, if less dramatic, are the landscapes painted by Bierstadt's companions of 1863, including Perry's *Sentinel Rock, Yosemite*. The early paintings of Thomas Hill and William Keith also fit this mold.

The Golden Age of Yosemite Photography

The great competition among Yosemite photographers of this period is well known, having been discussed at length by Weston Naef and others.[24] It began in 1861 with Carleton Watkins, who arrived in Yosemite with mammoth plate glass negatives (so named for their remarkable size, approximately 18"x22") apparently determined to outdo Weed's earlier 11"x15" photographs. Weed responded by returning with mammoth plate negatives in 1863

Figure 4: Charles L. Weed, *Mirror Lake*, 1863-4, mammoth albumen photograph. *Courtesy Yosemite Museum, Yosemite National Park, photograph by Ted Orland.*

or 1864 (figs. 3 and 4). After his initial visit in 1861, Watkins returned to Yosemite in 1865 and 1866; other visits during the 1860s are less easily verified.[25] Eadweard Muybridge photographed Yosemite for the first time in 1867 and returned with mammoth plates in 1872. Muybridge apparently had every intention of outshining his predecessors in turn, for he openly invited the public to compare his work with that of the competition.

The 1860s and early 1870s thus encompassed a golden era of Yosemite photography, during which photographs of exceptional quality were taken by the valley's first photographers. The elegance of Watkins's compositions and his sensitivity to light and texture resulted in photographs that evoke a landscape of Edenic beauty (fig. 3). Muybridge's Yosemite landscapes, like Weed's and Watkins's, improved a great deal during his second visit, both in technical and compositional respects. Some of Muybridge's images are as picturesque as Watkins's; others are more dramatic, and capture the valley at its most sublime.

Another photographer from the early years is the intriguing W. Harris, whose first name remains a mystery. In 1867, the same year Muybridge took his first Yosemite photographs, Harris supplied photographs for *The Yosemite Book*, an elegant publication by the California state geologist, Josiah D.

Whitney. Harris photographed distant sites in the High Sierra for Whitney, locations Watkins had not reached the previous year. Four of Harris's original prints were included at the end of *The Yosemite Book*, following twenty-four by Watkins.[26]

Olmsted and the Artists

An important but poorly documented trip to Yosemite was made by Thomas Hill, Virgil Williams, and Carleton Watkins in August 1865. Hill and Williams, who had become acquainted in Boston, may have traveled to the valley together on a sketching tour. It seems less likely that Watkins traveled with them, but their eventual meeting is confirmed by a photograph he took of them at their Yosemite campsite (fig. 5). While working in the valley, all three were solicited by the landscape architect Frederick Law Olmsted for their views on scenic enhancements to the park, as well as on conditions affecting it adversely.

Olmsted, who had come to California in 1863 to manage the troubled Mariposa Mining Company was probably one of the proponents of the bill setting aside Yosemite Valley as a public park. After the bill passed in 1864, Olmsted was appointed to the board of commissioners, and on August 9, 1865, he presented a preliminary park management plan to his fellow commissioners. In it he proposed that the board solicit assistance from "landscape artists" and "students of natural science," whom he considered the best advisors on aesthetic and ecological matters, respectively.[27] Olmsted wrote the same day to Hill, Williams, and Watkins, asking their advice on scenic issues.[28] As landscape artists who had worked in the valley before, all three were logical choices; in addition, they were already on the spot.

Olmsted's decision to consult "aesthetic specialists" is significant, as it indicates the importance he placed on scenic values in park management. Nothing is known of the artists' response, however, and Olmsted himself returned to New York that fall. After his departure, the park commission apparently lost its impetus to involve artists in policy-making decisions, although the idea resurfaced occasionally in later years.

The Transcontinental Railway Era

The number of artists visiting Yosemite increased dramatically after 1869, an obvious watershed year when the transcontinental railroad was com-

pleted and overland travel improved markedly. For the first time, established eastern painters could make the trip with relative comfort and ease. Among the best known artist-visitors of this period were Albert Bierstadt (on his second California trip), Thomas Moran, Samuel Colman, Benjamin Champney, George and James D. Smillie, and William Bradford. Others, some of them California residents by then, included Charles D. Robinson, Ransom Gillet Holdredge, Gilbert Munger, Herman Herzog, John Ross Key, Raymond Dabb Yelland, Frank Shapleigh, George Holbrook Baker, Henry Cheever Pratt, William Marple, Ferdinand Richardt, H.O. Young, Lemuel Wiles, Hiram Bloomer, and Peter Toft.

Thomas Hill and William Keith also continued to paint Yosemite during the 1870s. Hill was becoming nationally known by then, and Keith was well on his way to prominence in California. Later arrivals included George Inness, Louis Eilshemius, William Stanley Haseltine, Charles H. Harmon, Nicholas Row, Andrew Melrose, James Everett Stuart, and W.W. Armstrong.[29]

Figure 5: Carleton Watkins, *Virgil Williams and Thomas Hill in Camp, Yosemite,* 1865, half of albumen stereoview. *Courtesy Yosemite Museum, Yosemite National Park, photograph by Robert Woolard.*

After 1869, more and more foreign artists also began to visit Yosemite. Among them were two British watercolorists: Washington F. Friend, about whom relatively little is known, and Lady Constance Frederica Gordon-Cumming, whose 1878 display of paintings on the veranda of her hotel was probably the first exhibition held in the valley by a non-resident artist.[30] Several foreign artists who painted Yosemite decided to make California their permanent home. These included the British-born painters Edwin Deakin and Juan Buckingham Wandesforde, the Mexican Fortunato Arriola, the Germans William Hahn and Frederick F. Schafer, and Henry Cleenewerck, who was born in Belgium to French parents.

Transportation to Yosemite improved further when coach roads were completed to the valley in 1874 and 1875. Better roads meant easier transportation for photographers, as well as painters, and their numbers likewise began to increase. Those who came to Yosemite in the 1870s included John J. Reilly, Martin M. Hazeltine, Charles L. Pond, Thomas C. Roche, George Fiske, Gustavus Fagersteen, S.C. Walker, and Albert Bierstadt's brother Charles. (Hazeltine, who had photographed Yosemite in 1867, continued to take stereoviews up and down the West Coast well into the 1890s.)[31]

Albert Bierstadt, whose earlier paintings of the valley were famous by then in the East as well as in California, returned to San Francisco from July 1871 until October 1873. Always looking for ways to expand his repertoire, he returned to the valley in February 1872 to sketch its appearance in winter. He also visited Yosemite on at least two other occasions during his 1871-1873 trip, once in May 1872, when he worked with the photographer Eadweard Muybridge (fig. 6), and again for six weeks in June and July 1873.

Thomas Moran, another nationally known painter, visited Yosemite for the first time in August 1872 with his artist wife Mary Nimmo Moran. While at Yosemite, Moran executed a number of pencil drawings and watercolors of the valley. One of the most famous is *South Dome, Yosemite* (fig. 7), an image that was engraved as the frontispiece of John Muir's elegant gift book, *Picturesque California* (1888). The vantage point from which the artist sketched was named Moran Point in his honor, the second Yosemite locale named for an artist. (The first was Mount Watkins, named for the photographer in 1865.)

Moran created only a few oil paintings of Yosemite after his 1872 trip, perhaps because Bierstadt had already established the valley as his own artistic turf. Moran's interest in Yosemite and California reawakened years later, however, after a visit he made to the valley in May 1904. Most of his seven extant Yosemite oils were painted after this later trip. At least one additional painting was inspired by his last trip to the valley in 1922.[32]

Figure 6: Eadweard Muybridge, *Albert Bierstadt at Work in Yosemite Valley,* 1872, half of albumen stereo photograph. *Courtesy Eldon and Susan Grupp, photograph by Ted Orland.*

Numerous artists painted and photographed the valley after 1869, more than can be discussed here, but many of them deserve further research. Little is known about the Yosemite visits of Samuel Colman and William Bradford, although both are relatively well known painters and a few Yosemite scenes by each still exist. Colman, who is known for western as well as Hudson River landscapes, traveled to California in 1870 and visited Yosemite either that year or the next.[33] He probably returned to the valley during later excursions as well. Several Yosemite watercolors resulted from these trips, including a painting of Yosemite's Illilouette Canyon that was engraved for the *The Ladies' Repository* in June 1871. William Bradford, the "iceberg painter," was in California by 1875. He traveled to Yosemite in 1878 and probably made other excursions there during the late 1870s and early 1880s.[34] Several of Bradford's paintings of the valley in winter appear curiously unfinished, as if he had despaired of realizing his vision of Yosemite.

Gilbert Munger, James D. Smillie, and Herman Herzog may be less well known than Colman and Bradford, but they were more prolific in their pictorial treatment of Yosemite. All three artists visited the valley during the early or middle 1870s, and each painted a number of excellent Yosemite landscapes. Gilbert Munger, who worked in the West with Clarence King's fortieth parallel survey, spent "two seasons" at Yosemite, possibly the summers of 1872 and 1873 (fig. 8).[35] James D. Smillie came to California in 1871 with his younger brother George, also an artist, and the two spent most of July and August in Yosemite. Smillie's purpose in making the trip was to obtain material for William Cullen Bryant's gift book *Picturesque America*. Smillie's diaries provide the most detailed account of a Yosemite trip by any of the artists who went there.[36] The German-born painter Herman Herzog traveled to California and Yosemite in 1874.[37] Herzog continued to concoct Yosemite landscapes long after his return to the East Coast; his *Sentinel Rock, Yosemite* won a medal at the Philadelphia Centennial Exhibition of 1876.

Monumental Paintings for California's "Big Men"

The California market supported a great deal of artistic growth during the 1870s. Impressive fortunes were made by barons of commerce like William C. Ralston, Leland Stanford, Charles Crocker, and Collis Huntington. Some of these profits found their way into the pockets of California

Figure 7: Thomas Moran, *South Dome, Yosemite*, 1873, watercolor and pencil on gray paper. *Courtesy Cooper-Hewitt Museum, Smithsonian Institution/Art Resource, New York.*

artists, whose paintings were purchased to decorate the homes of the wealthy. Thomas Hill, for example, sold his first two 6x10-foot Yosemite panoramas to railroad magnate Charles Crocker of San Francisco and Judge E.B. Crocker of Sacramento. A third was purchased by E.J. "Lucky" Baldwin, a wealthy rancher from southern California, and a fourth by former governor Leland Stanford. Other large Yosemite paintings by Hill were acquired during the 1870s by San Francisco banker William C. Ralston for his home, as well as for his Palace Hotel; several were also purchased by James Lick for the Lick House hotel.[38]

Hill's monumental Yosemite canvases represent an important link between commerce and art. Most were purchased by the financial giants of the time for their homes (or for their hotels). In depicting the "crowning glory" of the California landscape on a monumental scale, these canvases symbolized their owners' positions and power. There is an element of local or state pride at work here as well; paintings of California subjects would have appealed to men whose fortunes were founded on California industry and transportation. The fact that so many were purchased within a few years' time further suggests a degree of competition among the owners.

There is another correlation between the monumentality of Hill's Yosemite paintings (or the mammoth photographs taken by Watkins and Muybridge) and the size and grandeur of the landscape they depict. It has often been noted that the vastness of the American West inspired paintings of epic proportions; Bierstadt's *Rocky Mountains* (1863) was influential in this respect, and Thomas Moran followed suit with his Yellowstone and Grand Canyon paintings.

The largest painting of Yosemite ever attempted was the circular panorama conceived by Charles D. Robinson in 1883 and begun in 1892. Robinson's panorama was an impressive 50x380 *feet* in size, and its creation required the help of several assistants (Von Perbandt, Bloomer, Peixotto, Valencia, and Pages). Robinson took his panorama to the Paris Exposition of 1900, but did not succeed in having it exhibited. In order to finance his trip

Figure 8: Gilbert Munger, *Royal Arches and Half Dome, Yosemite*, n.d., oil on canvas. *Courtesy Montgomery Gallery, San Francisco.*

Figure 9: Thomas Hill, *View from Glacier Point, Yosemite* ca. 1875 oil on canvas. *Courtesy Oscar and Trudy Lemer, photograph by Kate Nearpass Ogden.*

home, he was forced to cut it into smaller pieces, which he sold. The location of the pieces is unknown today, but the panorama can still be seen in the illustrations accompanying an article Robinson himself published in the *Overland Monthly*.[39] In the absence of Robinson's panorama, the largest surviving Yosemite painting is Bierstadt's 9x15-foot canvas *The Domes of the Yosemite* on display at the St. Johnsbury Athenaeum in Vermont.

Thomas Hill, William Keith, and Later Trends

Thomas Hill and William Keith are representative of changes in Yosemite art, and American art in general, that occurred in the last quarter of the nineteenth century. By the 1870s, more and more California artists were traveling to Europe for artistic training.[40] Rather than continuing the Hudson River- and Dusseldorf-inspired realism of the 1860s, they looked instead to the artists of Munich and Paris for stylistic guidance. From these artists they learned to work in a looser, less detailed manner. The painters of Munich and Barbizon (near Paris) painted with a dark, predominantly brown palette which was also adopted to varying degrees by California artists, most notably by William Keith.

Hill and Keith began evolving their signature styles as they continued to paint Yosemite during the 1870s. Hill studied in Paris in 1866 with the German painter Paul Friedrich Meyerheim, and painted in the French countryside with the Barbizon painters. Hill's *View from Glacier Point, Yosemite*

(fig. 9) exemplifies the loose, impressionistic brushwork that was a hallmark of his mature style. In later years this loose handling would allow him to produce painting after painting in a facile, formulaic manner. Keith's *Sentinel Rock, Yosemite* (fig. 10) likewise indicates the direction of the artist's mature style, although it is less intimate in scope than many of his late paintings. Keith probably saw the work of the Barbizon painters during his trip abroad in 1869-71, and he later studied in Munich for three years in the early 1880s. *Sentinel Rock* brings to mind the dark brown tones and loose, painterly handling of both schools.

During his trip to San Francisco in the spring of 1891, the important American painter George Inness further reinforced William Keith's Barbizon tendencies. The two artists painted together in Keith's studio and traveled to Yosemite for a week. According to Keith's biographer Brother Cornelius, Inness, unlike Keith, declared Yosemite impossible to paint and attempted very few landscapes of the valley.[41] Only two are extant; one is unlocated and the other so closely resembles George Fiske's photograph of Yosemite from Inspiration Point that it seems Inness based his painting on the photograph.

The only photographs that seem readily comparable to these late-nineteenth century Barbizon-style paintings are those by Anne Brigman and Alvin Langdon Coburn. In the first two decades of the twentieth century, Brigman and Coburn both took moody, soft-focus, "pictorialist" photographs at Yosemite. Coburn's images are pure landscape, while Brigman's depict female nudes in an outdoor setting thought to be Yosemite.[42] Their images might be considered the photographic equivalent of Keith's dark, intimate landscapes or Hill's impressionistic ones.

Changing Views of the Valley: Development and Tourism

Ever since Charles Weed photographed the Upper Hotel (later Hutchings' Hotel) in 1859, Yosemite photographers have documented the buildings, bridges, roads, and other changes made in the valley. Painters, who could more easily edit manmade structures out of their compositions, generally concentrated on the landscape itself. There are a few notable exceptions, however, and these are historically interesting: Raymond Dabb Yelland's painting of the Miwok Indians' wooden huts, William Hahn's landscape including the Indians' acorn cache constructions, Herman Herzog's image of the Cosmopolitan Saloon, and Hiram Bloomer's painting of an early Anglo-American building at El Portal.[43]

Commercial development and tourism have been among the most pervasive influences on Yosemite Valley and its artists. Tourists themselves first began to appear in Yosemite landscapes as early as 1859, when the articles in *Hutchings' California Magazine* were illustrated with engravings of tourist activities. Tourists appeared in landscape paintings the same year. One of the first such paintings was a now-lost Yosemite scene by Frederick Butman that included travelers boarding a ferry on the Merced River. Butman's tourists received a decidedly negative response from the *Alta California's* art critic, who complained that human figures in modern clothing detracted from the beauty and religious connotations of the landscape. "Modern cut garments," he wrote, "seem ridiculous in contrast with such wonderful works of the Almighty . . . It is some such feeling as might be excited on seeing Praxiteles' or Canova's beautiful creations enveloped in crinoline."[44]

Indians, on the other hand, were usually acceptable in paintings, since they carried connotations of the "noble savage" and maintained the wilderness quality of the landscape. The use of the Indian foreground detail was an artistic rather than eth-nographic decision for many years. Indians in the foreground added a touch of color, a human focal point, and a sense of scale. The first photographers to depict the Yosemite Indians probably did so for financial rather than ethnographic reasons. Stereoviews of such subjects, like the one seen in figure 6, were highly marketable among eastern armchair travelers and in the local tourist market.[45]

Two of the earliest extant landscape paintings with tourists were painted by William S. Jewett, California's first successful portrait painter. Jewett's *Yosemite Falls* (1859) contains two men, apparently travelers, wearing the linen "duster" or "dust-coat" so important for travel in the west. His *Bridalveil Falls* (1861) includes a group of tourists clambering about on the rocks below Bridalveil.[46] The female tourists in *Bridalveil* serve as a reminder that women had accompanied exploring parties to Yosemite since 1856, only a year after the first "tourist trip" made by Hutchings and Thomas Ayres.

Yosemite tourist painting had really arrived by 1874, when William Hahn finished his series of three canvases: *The Trip to Glacier Point, Yosemite Valley from Glacier Point,* and *The Return Trip from Glacier Point.* The first and third, which depict riders on a steep, wooded trail, are barely recognizable as Yosemite landscapes.[47] The largest of the three, *Yosemite Valley from Glacier Point* (back cover), depicts the same group of visitors surveying the view after reaching their destination atop the mountain. Hahn's *Glacier Point* painting is important because it says as much about tourism as about the landscape itself; figures and scenery are given equal weight. It also documents the horse trail to Glacier Point that was opened to the public in 1872. There is a certain contradiction to the foreground still life of discarded trash and empty bottles in Hahn's painting. Tourists in the nineteenth century were obviously no more conscientious about picking up trash than their twentieth-century descendants.

In the 1870s, the emphasis in Yosemite photography began to shift away from unpopulated landscapes to images of tourists posing in front of scenic attractions (fig. 11). Although these tourist portraits are a far cry from the sublime landscapes taken by Watkins and Muybridge, many of them are fascinating in their own right. This change from virgin wilderness to scenic backdrop is significant for several reasons. First, it parallels the corresponding change in the valley itself, from an Edenic wilderness, populated only by native Indians, to a

Figure 10: William Keith, *Sentinel Rock, Yosemite*, ca. 1880, oil on canvas, private collection. *Photograph by Nan and Roy Farrington Jones.*

peculiarly American resource of scenic beauty, a national tourist site accessible to everyone. The change also illustrates quite literally the growth of tourism in the valley. From a total of forty-some visitors in 1855, tourists in the late 1880s averaged over four thousand a year. Third, it shows that Yosemite was already becoming somewhat hackneyed as a subject for art. What was important to the tourists of 1880 was proof of their own visits, rather than (or in addition to) documentation of the valley's glories. Tourist portraits provided evidence that visitors had "done" Yosemite, to use the contemporary idiom.[48]

In 1870, John J. Reilly was the first photographer to open a studio in Yosemite Valley. Reilly's studio, a special tent with a sign announcing it as "J.J. Reilly's Stereoscopic View Manufactory," was situated so tourists could pose with either Yosemite Falls or the Royal Arches as a backdrop. Reilly photographed some of Yosemite's best known visitors during his first summer in the valley, including P.T. Barnum, the geologist Joseph LeConte, and Therese Yelverton, Viscountess of Avonmore.[49] Reilly operated his studio from 1870 until about

1877 with various partners and assistants, including Martin M. Hazeltine, Dan Folsom, E.D. Ormsby, S.C. Walker, and Gustavus Fagersteen, who took over the studio when Reilly left. Fagersteen and his competitors continued to take "Photographs with the Yosemite in the Background," as one of them advertised in a sign over his studio door.[50] Yosemite Falls was a logical choice as backdrop; not only was it the most famous of the valley's waterfalls and its "namesake," but it was located conveniently close to several hotels and what passed for a village.

Other photographers of this period included Charles L. Pond, Charles Bierstadt, Martin Mason Hazeltine, and Thomas C. Roche, all of whom came to the valley in the late 1860s or early 1870s to supplement their commercial photographic stock with Yosemite views. Stereo photographs were especially popular, and were collected for entertainment and educational purposes across the country. Pond and Bierstadt, who had establishments at Niagara, published their own stereoviews. Roche was working for the publisher E. & H.T. Anthony of New York when he visited the valley in 1870 and 1871. Hazeltine's Yosemite work was published by John P. Soule of Boston and by the Kilburn Brothers of Littleton, New Hampshire.[51]

The famous western photographers William Henry Jackson and John K. Hillers also deserve mention. Like Pond and Roche, Jackson made a special trip to Yosemite to supplement his commercial stock with views of the valley. Jackson's visit occurred in 1888 or 1889, while he was operating his own photographic studio in Denver. Jackson's Denver firm was later absorbed by the Detroit Photographic Company, which sent Jackson or another photographer to Yosemite again in the early twentieth century to update their stock once more. [52] John K. Hillers, who had accompanied John Wesley Powell's expeditionary surveys in the West and Southwest in the 1870s, photographed Yosemite a few years after Jackson. Working on assignment for the U.S. Geological Survey, Hillers traveled to Yosemite in 1892 and took a series of photographs intended for display at the 1893 Columbian Exposition in Chicago.[53] Jackson's and Hillers's Yosemite views are large, picturesque, and in the grand style established by Watkins and Muybridge (fig. 12).

Photos and Paintings as Souvenirs

Tourists were not merely the subject of Yosemite artists; they were also a prime market. Photographs, in particular, were a logical mass-market item, since they were easily produced in large quantities, and souvenir photography constituted a booming business in San Francisco and the valley. Weed's 1859 photographs, for example, were exhibited and sold in the San Francisco gallery of his employer, Robert Vance. His 1864 series was handled by the opticians Lawrence and Houseworth (later Thomas Houseworth & Co.), who had sponsored his trip that year. Houseworth likewise intended to sponsor Eadweard Muybridge's 1872 trip to Yosemite, but the photographer's negotiations with Bradley & Rulofson resulted in their publishing and promoting his work instead.[54] Carleton Watkins sold

Figure 11: Gustavus Fagersteen, *Tourist Portrait*, ca. 1880, albumen cabinet card photograph. *Courtesy Yosemite Museum, Yosemite National Park, photograph by Ted Orland.*

his own photographs at his San Francisco studio, which he named "Watkins' Yosemite Gallery" around 1871. The publisher Isaiah W. Taber was another force in San Francisco's photography market. Taber acquired and began publishing many of Watkins's negatives around 1875-6, in the wake of the 1874 national economic recession; this forced Watkins to re-shoot his Yosemite photographs as well as many other subjects.[55]

Competition in the valley itself was less fierce. In 1879, a young visitor named Sarah Locke noted in her diary that there were two photographic galleries in the valley that spring.[56] One was probably that of Gustavus Fagersteen, who took over Reilly's studio in 1877; the other may have been George Fiske's establishment. Ten years later, Fiske and Fagersteen were still the primary competitors in Yosemite's studio trade (fig. 13). As Hutchings commented in his 1886 book, *In the Heart of the Sierras*, both photographers sold work at their studios, and Fiske's work was also for sale at the Big Tree Room in Barnard's Hotel. Isaiah Taber's stock, which included many of Watkins's early photographs, was sold at John J. Cook's Hotel, giving Fiske and Fagersteen additional competition.[57]

In addition to taking tourist portraits, photographers like George Fiske and Gustavus Fagersteen continued to produce landscape images as well. Rather than searching for new approaches, however, they photographed Yosemite's familiar monuments from what had by then become standard points of view. Such photographs show what we might consider today a "post-card aesthetic"; they invariably depict the most characteristic side or feature of a monument, and they include as many picturesque conventions as possible. Tourism thus increasingly affected the style, as well as the content, of Yosemite photographs.

A more exclusive use of photographs as souvenirs occurred when the photographer Adam Clark Vroman visited Yosemite in 1900 or 1901 with H.E. Hoopes and several of Hoopes's friends. Best known for his photographic documentation of the American Indian, Vroman took pictures of his traveling companions, as well as the standard Yosemite tourist attractions, and compiled the prints afterward in a souvenir album for Hoopes.[58] Pictorially, Vroman's images are comparable to the souvenir prints made by other photographers late in the century. In market terms, however, the album is unique, and was created for a very limited clientele —for Hoopes himself, and perhaps other members of the party.

Ordinary tourists were not the only ones buying photographs of Yosemite. The scientists William H. Brewer and Josiah D. Whitney bought Yosemite prints from Watkins, and Whitney also used Watkins's images in several of his publications about the valley.[59] Albert Bierstadt, William Keith, William S. Jewett, and Hiram Bloomer were among the painters who subscribed to Eadweard Muybridge's 1867 photographic series. Bierstadt and several other California painters also placed orders for Muybridge's 1872 series.[60] Thomas Hill and James D. Smillie are known to have acquired Yosemite photographs for use in composing their paintings. The latter visited the San Francisco studios of both Watkins and Muybridge during his 1871 visit to California and purchased additional prints after arriving in the valley. Smillie even proposed a trade to Watkins: paintings in exchange for photographs.[61]

For tourists with enough money, paintings could also be purchased as mementos of the trip. Oddly enough, the photographer J.J. Reilly seems to have been the first to recognize that paintings might be marketable in the valley as souvenirs. The studio/gallery he established in 1870 was stocked with his own Yosemite paintings and photographs, although none of the former seem to have survived.[62] When Thomas Hill established a studio in the valley in 1883, and in 1886 set up shop in nearby Wawona, he too sold Yosemite paintings to travelers. Although Hill continued to paint and exhibit elsewhere after he settled in Wawona, as time went on he spent more and more time in the valley. By the mid-1890s, the tourist trade may well have been his primary source of income.[63]

By the early 1880s, Charles D. Robinson also had a studio on the valley floor, where his paintings competed with Hill's in the local market.[64] Both artists took orders from visitors, who specified the Yosemite subject(s) of their choice. Hill's business notebook from the mid-1880s gives us an idea of the orders he received. Page after page lists the names and addresses of clients, followed by the artist's standard subject types: "Yosemite Fall," "Morning, Yosemite Valley," "Bridalveil Meadow," and so forth.[65] Most of Hill's clients during this period were from New York and San Francisco, although others came from Great Britain, Germany, New Zealand, Australia, and India. Hill's prices ranged from $50 to $400 per painting, with one "general view" priced at $2,500. Considering the effects of quantity upon quality, it is no wonder his later paintings became more facile and formulaic.

Figure 12: John K. Hillers, *Yosemite Falls in Dry Season*, 1892, albumen photograph.
Courtesy Yosemite Museum, Yosemite National Park, photograph by Robert Woolard.

By his own account, Robinson sold about eighty-four canvases to British clients during the course of his career, although not all were Yosemite landscapes. In a manuscript of 1927, Robinson wrote that "Sir Morell Mackenzie had four [paintings] of mine . . . Lord Henry Paulet had a large 'Yosemite at Sunset' of mine and Lord Capell had one also . . . I remember that I did some canvases for C. Orr Ewing, I think, living on the southern borders of Scotland next to Yorkshire in England, but I have forgotten."[66]

Other artists working in the valley on a more temporary basis also sold paintings occasionally as souvenirs, most frequently to visitors from Great Britain. In 1872 or 1873, for example, Gilbert Munger was reputedly paid $10,000 to paint local scenery for Lord Skelmersdale and two other English gentlemen.[67] William Bradford, visiting Yosemite in 1880, was similarly commissioned by the Earl of Grosvenor, who ordered paintings of two standard subjects, Bridalveil Meadows and Sentinel Rock.[68]

Chromolithography, then a relatively recent development in color printmaking, made reproductions of paintings affordable to a wide audience. By the late 1860s, tourists who could not afford originals by Bierstadt and Hill could instead buy "chromos" based on their work. Bierstadt's 9x15-foot painting, *The Domes of the Yosemite* (1867), was reproduced as a suitably large chromo, approximately 22x33 inches in size. Prang's chromo of Thomas Hill's *Yosemite Valley* (1868), probably the most popular item of its kind, was copied by more amateur painters than any other Yosemite image. In the early 1870s, Yosemite chromos were copyrighted by a number of artists who evidently hoped their prints would be as lucrative as those by Hill and Bierstadt. Among them were Benjamin Champney, John Ross Key, Robert Wilkie, and an otherwise unknown painter, Charles Clark, whose Yosemite chromo is very similar to Hill's.[69] The Key and Wilkie chromos were small in size, but formed part of Prang's series of California subjects, an indication of the ever-growing demand for inexpensive souvenir images.

Valley Residents

An important change that occurred in Yosemite art around 1880 was the decision of a few artists to make the valley and its environs their permanent residence. Some of the artists most closely associated with Yosemite, like George Fiske and Thomas Hill, are those who lived there. Fiske became the first photographer to live in the valley year-round the winter of 1879-80.[70] In the 1880s, Thomas Hill began dividing his time between the valley, where he painted during the summer, and nearby Wawona, where he spent the winter.

Several later artists also lived at Yosemite. Christian Jorgensen, who specialized in watercolor scenes of the valley, first came to Yosemite on a camping trip in 1898, and decided to make it his permanent summer home.[71] Harry Cassie Best,

Figure 13: George Fiske's photograph store, Yosemite Valley, in the 1890s. *Courtesy Huntington Library.*

who visited Yosemite in 1901 with the artist Thaddeus Welch, also decided to stay, and opened his first studio/gallery there in 1902.[72] Years later, Harry Best's daughter Virginia married and settled in the valley. She and her husband, the photographer Ansel Adams, continued to operate her father's studio and gallery. The name of their establishment was later changed from Best's Studio to the Ansel Adams Gallery, as it is known today.

The publicity value of art is obvious. Drawings, paintings, photographs, and prints of Yosemite initially served to bring the valley to public attention and contributed to the establishment in 1864 of a park under state management in the valley. By the middle of the 1860s, photographs of the valley had begun to serve a new function as advertisements to tourists. Weed's, Watkins's, and Muybridge's photographs were shown in the windows of San Francisco establishments like those of R.H. Vance and Thomas Houseworth, where they served as enticements. Once inside, tourists found maps, guidebooks, and other information on travel routes and hotels.

Establishing the National Park

Yosemite landscape images later played an important role in the crusade to establish a national park in the region. In 1889 and 1890, a number of articles appeared in the press complaining about state management of the valley and supporting a new national park for the surrounding area. Among the most persuasive articles were those by John Muir in the August and September 1890 issues of *Century Magazine*. Muir's articles were heavily illustrated with engravings based on drawings, photographs, and paintings. Most were drawn by J.A. Frazer after photographs taken by George Fiske, although a few were by other artists, including Thomas Moran and Charles D. Robinson.

The rhetorical bias of the illustrations was positive for the most part and concentrated on presenting the valley's features to best advantage. A few photographs, however, illustrated the ravages recently inflicted on the valley by local residents. Probably taken by Fiske specifically for Muir's articles, these images depicted a section of valley floor that had been plowed over for hay, hundreds of tree stumps left by the creation of "state pasturage," and the results of uncontrolled trimming of trees.

Letters published in the *Century Magazine* of January 1890 by Judge Lucius P. Deming of Connecti-

cut, George G. Mackenzie of Wawona, and Robert Underwood Johnson, editor of the magazine, also focused attention on recent problems in the state park and the surrounding area. Although not illustrated, their letters were significant because they revived the idea of soliciting professional advice on aesthetic aspects of park management. In the realm of "positive" publicity, the gift book *Picturesque California*, edited by John Muir and published serially in the middle 1880s, helped revive consciousness of Yosemite's importance to California. All of these efforts were successful, at least ultimately. In October 1890, some 1500 square miles surrounding Yosemite Valley were placed under federal protection, and in 1906 the valley itself was added to Yosemite National Park.

The publicity value of paintings and photographs hardly ended there. The work of the next generation of Yosemite photographers—Arthur Pillsbury, Daniel Foley, and Julius Boysen—was often used in promotional literature and other publications about the park in the early twentieth century. Ralph Anderson, park photographer from 1932 to 1953, and Ansel Adams, the most famous Yosemite photographer of all, provided countless illustrations for later publications on Yosemite.[73] The twentieth century has witnessed an explosion of scenic photographs of the type used in Sierra Club publications. Such photographs became even more numerous and varied after the advent of improved color processes.

Yosemite in the twentieth century has never been the painters' mecca it was in its first fifty years, although it continues to attract artists interested in sublime landscape. The most celebrated painters of this century who have painted Yosemite landscapes are William Zorach and Georgia O'Keeffe, who visited the valley in 1920 and 1938, respectively, and Wayne Thiebaud, who has worked there more recently. The emphasis in their paintings is on formal elements like shape, color, and texture, rather than landscape details. In contrast to their work are the more traditional watercolors of Gunnar Widforss, whose name has been linked with that of Yosemite and other national parks since the 1920s. As modern painters have turned for inspiration more often to the inner landscape of emotions and ideas, and less often to observation of the natural world, Yosemite (and sublime scenery in general) have grown less compelling as subjects for high art.

Important contributions to our vision of Yosemite, however, have been made by a number of recent photographers working in black and white. The best known of these are Ansel Adams, who first photographed the valley in 1916 and lived there periodically between 1928 and 1961, and Edward Weston, who visited Yosemite in 1937 and 1938 on a Guggenheim fellowship. Paul Caponigro, Jerry Uelsmann, and Michael A. Smith have all photographed Yosemite in the last two decades. The work of these five photographers ranges widely in subject and style, from Adams's grand panoramas, Weston's textured studies of trees, and Caponigro's intimate landscape spaces, to Uelsmann's surrealistic double exposures and Smith's subtle formal arrangements. With the exception of Uelsmann, however, all of them share an interest in the evocative power of pure landscape (see frontispiece to "Introduction" of this issue).

Other intriguing developments have occurred in the work of contemporary photographers like Roger Minick, Bruce Davidson, Richard Misrach, Ted Orland, and David Mussina. The work of this last group tends to focus on the ironic, sometimes humorous confrontation between nature and today's tourists, with Yosemite's geological curiosities and sublime panoramas appearing as backdrops for more mundane human concerns. Landscapes by these contemporary photographers seem diametrically opposed to the pristine wilderness captured by Ansel Adams and his nineteenth century predecessors, although they have much in common with Fiske's and Fagersteen's tourist portraits. As perceptions of the valley have changed, from Yosemite as "God's great temple" to Yosemite as a national playground, photographers have reflected this change in their work. Given the cyclical nature of art, it is hardly surprising that the nineteenth-century development from sublime wilderness to scenic backdrop has already been recapitulated in our own century. It should be interesting to watch what happens in the next hundred years.

Kate Nearpass Ogden is a doctoral candidate in art history at Columbia University in New York, where she currently holds a Luce Fellowship in American Art. Her dissertation, entitled "Yosemite Valley as Image and Symbol: Paintings and Photographs from 1855 to 1880," is a study of Yosemite landscapes in their historical and cultural context.

Yosemite Valley as photographed by the renowned Carleton E. Watkins. Watkins's large photographs of Yosemite's grandeur lured many early tourists to the valley and helped convince Congress in 1864 to make Yosemite the nation's first wilderness park and to entrust it to the custody of the state of California. *Courtesy California State Library.*

From Stagecoach to Packard Twin Six

YOSEMITE AND THE CHANGING FACE OF TOURISM, 1880-1930

by Anne F. Hyde

As part of a national park system, Yosemite National Park shares management, ideals, architecture, concessionaires, and campground reservation systems with parks all over the United States. In spite of these similarities, Yosemite has a history that makes it distinct from the other parks created in the American West in the same era, particularly in the ways in which the park was developed for tourist use. In the first place, Yosemite began its history as a park under the management of California, which had received the valley and surrounding cliffs in trust from the federal government in 1864. The earliest of the western parks, Yosemite was the first to become popular with tourists.[1] Because of its spectacular beauty and its location in California, a tourist mecca, Yosemite received more visitors and publicity than other scenic areas in the West. Particularly, the completion of the transcontinental railroad in 1869 that connected California with the eastern part of the nation and opened the gate to floods of tourists made Yosemite relatively accessible to the traveling public. Yellowstone, Grand Canyon, and Glacier, in comparison, received few visitors in their early years because of their remote locations.

The relative ease of reaching Yosemite and its well-publicized scenery, however, were not its most important features for nineteenth-century tourists. As the only major park *not* to be reached directly by a railroad in its early years, Yosemite was unique in terms of its development for the traveling public.

Many visitor facilities in Yellowstone, the Grand Canyon, and Glacier were initially built by railroads to improve public relations and to increase ridership on their lines. Although the government owned the land in these parks, the railroads held much power over access, facilities, and publicity.[2] This was not true in the case of Yosemite. In the absence of any railroad-owned facilities, the state of California and then the United States government controlled the development and use of Yosemite by turning over its operation to a wide variety of managers and concessionaires until the beginning of the National Park Service era in 1916.

Such a system had advantages and disadvantages and had a clear impact on Yosemite's development for public use. For the nineteenth-century tourist, the fact that no single, wealthy corporate entity dominated access to the park contributed to a number of difficulties. Haphazard management, insufficiently capitalized and supervised concessions, and competing interests made travel in Yosemite at best an uneven experience and at worst a nightmare. The relative lack of railroad-controlled facilities in the park, however, gave Yosemite and its managers more flexibility to deal with the enormous changes brought about by automobiles, new kinds of tourists, and the creation of the National Park Service in the early twentieth century.

In the late nineteenth century, Yosemite's scenery had strong appeal for wealthy tourists and many of them flocked to the new park as part

Hutchings' Hotel with a view of Sentinel Rock, Yosemite Valley, 1872. *Courtesy Huntington Library.*

of their western tours. In the summer of 1870, the first year that transcontinental trains brought significant numbers of tourists to California, John Muir noted that "all sorts of human stuff is being poured into our valley this year."[3] A tourist who visited Yosemite that summer explained that the trip had become "*de rigueur.*" She warned potential visitors that "woe betide the wandering easterner if he seeks the Pacific without bringing a trip to Yo Semite back with him!" By 1877, another tourist wrote that "the visit to the Yosemite Valley is, of course, inevitable."[4]

Visiting Yosemite had become "inevitable" because of the reputation of its scenery. A popular railroad guidebook promised that Yosemite "presents a scene of beauty and magnificence unsurpassed, except *possibly* in childhood's fairy dreams." Most visitors did react with enormous enthusiasm to the glacially sculpted rock walls and formations, waterfalls, and mountain landscapes present in the valley. One satisfied tourist wrote that "among all the natural wonders of this world, the great Yosemite Valley ranks first without dispute." He concluded that "the Yosemite must be seen, and

once seen it can never be forgotten." Another observer described a typical reaction to the first view of the valley: "We looked, drew breath, and gave vent with such powers as God had given us to the wonder, delight, admiration, and awe which all persons, I believe, experience in first beholding this marvel of nature."[5]

Even though nearly all visitors who wrote about the experience were thrilled by the beauty of Yosemite, many of them wondered if the trip had been worth it. Because of the chaotic management of the park, a trip to Yosemite offered few comforts, and according to many travelers, it presented many hardships. The accommodations along the way to Yosemite and in the valley itself varied enormously, but at best they were uncomfortable, and at worst they were unbearable, especially given the high standards of wealthy tourists. To add to these discomforts, the only way to get to Yosemite involved a stage coach trip to the edge of the valley, and for the first twenty-three years of tourist travel, a ride on mules or horses down into the valley itself.[6]

To make matters worse, the difficult trip and the

poor accommodations cost a significant sum. In 1873, a writer in *Scribner's* magazine warned her readers that "the Yo-Semite excursion is an extremely costly one." She estimated that the traveler should expect to spend about $150 and at least ten days on the trip, and "to reckon it as less would be to mislead." This represented a considerable outlay of money and time for even the wealthiest and most leisured tourist. Eleven years later, little had changed. An 1884 visitor noted "a person going from San Francisco into the valley needs about a hundred and fifty dollars . . . the least one should think of doing the valley with and staying a week or ten days." She cautioned prospective travelers that without careful attention the trip could cost much more because many unscrupulous businesses threatened to "strand the visitor in the valley unless he pays a significant sum."[7]

For this substantial cost, the Yosemite tourist found few luxuries. Lodgings located on the roads into the park and in the valley itself hardly merited the appellation "hotel," according to many travelers. One visitor described the dubious accommodations in Merced as "a large commodious wooden building" whose proprietor "is so afraid of offending people that a set of riotous tourists are permitted to come in and take possession of the house, to sing and tear round all night, while their hunting dogs are kept in the bedrooms howling a mournful vesper for the benefit of persons who are to ride by stage sixty-eight miles the next day." The food served at such hostelries did little to improve visitors' impressions of them. "Our supper consisted of badly cooked potatoes, heavy rolls of fat bacon," remembered one woman, adding crabbily, "as I could not get accustomed to eat this kind of food, I did not fare too sumptuously."[8]

Travelers expecting more glamorous accommodations in the park were inevitably disappointed. Businessmen hopeful of making a profit from tourist interest in the valley built a series of shoddy hotels, including the Lower Hotel, the Upper Hotel, later known as Hutchings' House, the Sentinel Hotel, Black's Hotel, and the Cosmopolitan. These structures varied in location, size, outward grandeur, and name, but resembled each other in poor service and inadequate facilities.[9]

Tourists complained bitterly about the discomforts they faced. A minister visiting Yosemite in 1868 noted that "there are in it two hotels, as they

Black's Hotel, also known as "Lower Hotel," Yosemite Valley, 1880s, as photographed by Carleton E. Watkins. *Courtesy Huntington Library.*

call themselves." He went on to describe his room, which "consisted of a quarter of a shed, screened off by split planks which . . . enabled us to hear everything that went on in the other rooms." He complained further that his room "had no window, but we could see the stars through the roof." The situation had not improved nearly two decades later when a tourist explained that "the hotels in Yosemite are of the bandbox order—cloth and paper." Pointing out the disadvantages of such construction, she commented, "My first morning's dreams were disturbed by the wail of some venerable spinster who had lost her washrag."[10]

Travelers were forced to endure such dismal accommodations because hotel operation in the valley was sometimes an unprofitable endeavor. Most material for the construction and operation of a hotel had to be carried in on stagecoach and on horseback, and the tourist season in the valley only lasted the few months of the year that offered pleasant weather and passable roads. Such conditions increased overhead and reduced profits, forcing many concessionaires out of business, or at least to scrimp on services and to charge high rates. Even when the state stepped in and appropriated $40,000 for a new hotel in the 1880s, the results were less than desirable. The new four-story Stoneman House proved to be a disaster from the beginning. Described by visitors as "strangely commonplace and repellent" and "of cheap construction and unsafe," the Stoneman was plagued by poor management and design until it burned to the ground in 1896.[11] In comparison to the limited lodgings offered to Yosemite visitors even after the turn of the century, Yellowstone, dominated by the Northern Pacific Railroad, the Grand Canyon, associated with the Sante Fe, and Glacier, influenced by the Great Northern, all offered their visitors more comfortable, and sometimes even luxurious, accommodations.[12]

Although only some visitors complained about the lodging facilities in Yosemite, the outcry over the condition of the roads into the valley was universal. Until the late 1870s, tourists who wanted to see the valley took stagecoaches for most of the journey and then mounted horses for the final descent into the valley itself. Most visitors in this era were wealthy easterners and Europeans unaccustomed to mountain trails, and in John Muir's words, they clung to their horses like "overgrown toads." Even though a popular guide-book claimed that "no lady who is not physically or mentally incapable of walking a mile, or sitting on a very gentle and sure-footed horse, need have the slightest apprehension," many tourists found the trip to be an ordeal. An 1870 traveler described the condition of her party upon arrival in the valley after the grueling ride as "inert masses of what were once tolerably strong-minded and particularly strong-bodied women."[13]

The stagecoach portion of the trip received equal condemnation. The fact that special "Yo Semite suits" for women could be purchased in San Francisco shops indicated the trip's hardships. Even though special clothing might protect them from the elements, tourists complained about uncomfortable coaches, rough roads, and choking dust. One disenchanted visitor recalled that "the weary, worn, and sore human freight are thrown violently from side to side until their necks are well-nigh dislocated." Another person found the dust to be the most bothersome aspect of the journey because "you are coated with dust, your eyes are smarting, your tongue is clogged, your hair is caked, your limbs are sore, your flesh is inflamed, you want to go home."[14]

As a result of such discomforts, visitors often wondered if even the spectacular sights of Yosemite were worth the effort required to see them. As one English traveler put it in 1871, "Two-hundred and fifty miles of staging upon the Rocky Sierras, beneath an August sun and half the time enveloped in red dust, are enough to make one seriously ask, Does it pay to visit Yosemite?" Even years later tourists answered that question in the negative, declaring that "the journey in and out by public stage is so hateful that one feels to have paid too dearly for the wonderful and soul-awing scenery that greeted us at the end." An official of the Pennsylvania Central Railroad claimed that the trip to Yosemite "was the most inhuman experience in the world," and further that "if my business interests lay upon this coast, I would build a railroad to this truly marvelous valley."[15]

Poor management caused many of the difficulties faced by tourists who chose to visit Yosemite during the first fifty years of its existence as a park. Even after the federal government created the large Yosemite National Park surrounding the valley in 1890, the valley remained in the hands of the state of California and a myriad of concessionaires. A report of the Secretary of the Interior in 1892 noted the inferior administration of the park under state management. The report claimed that tourists paid exorbitant charges for poor accommodations and that transportation costs were "beyond all reason." As a result, the report concluded that Yosemite was "inaccessible except to persons of ample time and means."[16]

Largely, the problem was one of too many concessionaires, creating a situation in which some of them had difficulty turning a profit even while providing inadequate service at high rates. Conditions of operating a business in the park—the short season, the high cost of deterioration during the winter, the expense of hauling supplies long distances, and the capriciousness of government leases—did not encourage good businessmen to risk capital in a Yosemite concession. Thus, many of the operations were rather fly-by-night and lasted only a season or two while offering poor service to

Yosemite's visitors. Tourists complained bitterly about "the little clap-traps organized to get money out of the traveling public" and "of being rushed in and out of the valley as if the object was to pick their pockets and let them go."[17]

However, despite the complaints of tourists about high costs, poor accommodations and travel conditions, and the laments of the federal government about shoddy administration, little changed in the valley until well into the twentieth century. Neither the state of California nor the concessionaires who operated facilities in the valley could, or would, provide the kind of improvements visitors seemed to want.

The Southern Pacific Railroad had recognized the profitable possibilities of the park, but its efforts to gain access to park operations beyond a stage service that carried passengers from

Hotel at Mammoth Hot Springs, Yellowstone National Park, ca. 1890, as photographed by F. Jay Haines. In contrast to the modest accommodations available at Yosemite through the early 1900s, grand hotels were built by railroads in some of the western national parks. Reflecting its greater accessibility and superior facilities, many times more tourists visited Yellowstone, as compared to Yosemite, until well into the automobile era of the twentieth century. *Courtesy Huntington Library.*

its Central Valley railroad lines into the park had been unsuccessful, largely because of the Sierra's imposing topography. Unlike the other important national parks, which allowed the railroads much influence over operations within the parks near their lines, Yosemite had to rely instead on a conglomeration of individual concessionaires loosely supervised by the state agency governing the valley. Without the active sponsorship of a major railroad, Yosemite remained remote and it continued to suffer from laggard management and poorly conceived development. The Yosemite Valley Railroad, an independently-owned spur from the main Southern Pacific line, did reach El Portal, twelve miles from the valley, in 1907, but by this time railroads were about to become outmoded by the new automobile tourism that characterized the twentieth century.

The difficulties created by Yosemite's disorganized pattern of development and its lack of a railroad patron, however, did open up some new opportunities with the changes in park management and tourist travel in the early twentieth century. The automobile, camping, and the new middle-class traveler created significant shifts in travel patterns and in what Americans demanded from their national parks. In addition, the creation of the National Park Service in 1916 and Stephen Mather's implementation of its new and powerful role in the operation of the parks ushered in changes that other parks and their railroad patrons fought vigorously. Yosemite, however, because of its unique early development, was in a better position to accept these changes.

Few observers predicted the tremendous impact the automobile would have on tourist travel in the United States or the rapidity with which it would occur. In fact, "motoring" in the first decade of the twentieth century was limited largely to eccentrics. Car travel was slow, inconvenient, dangerous, and expensive. Before 1910, automobile makers produced only custom-made cars that cost thousands of dollars. This, in addition to the high cost of operation and the unreliable quality of roads in the United States, made traveling by car a sport hazarded by only a few wealthy enthusiasts.[18] When the first cars appeared in the national parks at the turn of the century, park officials, including those who governed Yosemite, banned them, considering automobiles noisy and disruptive menaces.[19]

Such actions proved to be premature, as Americans started buying automobiles in startling numbers. In 1910, less than half a million people owned cars in the United States, but by 1920, the number had increased to nearly eight million, and this was only the beginning. By 1927, there was one car for every 5.3 persons in the United States. Even though ownership of these cars was limited to the middle and upper classes of American society, this represented a revolution in transportation.[20]

It also revolutionized tourism, taking tourists out of trains and placing them in control of individual vehicles. Driving a car gave American travelers a sense of freedom and personal choice that riding in a train could not provide. The automobile liberated the traveler from the restrictions of railroad schedules and tracks. The artist James Montgomery Flagg expressed a common feeling when he wrote "there is a freedom about motoring across the continent that is lacking in the train ride" as opposed to what he described as "the galling monotony of the stifling Pullmans."[21]

In the early days of motoring, particularly in the American West, driving offered not only freedom and intimacy, but also adventure, largely because of the poor quality of the roads. Tales of desert crossings and horrendous mountain tracks discouraged many potential transcontinental drivers. The interruption of train service during World War I and the "See America First" movement, however, encouraged traveling by car and the building of good roads. By 1921 one enthusiast assured motorists that "if you have hesitated because of supposed dangers, don't hesitate any longer." He noted further that "it is not necessary to carry a gun . . . the mountain roads are not difficult nor dangerous. Only a little care is required."[22]

The growing popularity and safety of automobile travel brought vast numbers of travelers into the West and into the national parks. Motoring made vacations possible for a much wider spectrum of the American population, although the family vacation would remain out of reach for the large majority of working-class people for another several decades. As early as 1916 one observer in Yosemite noted the ever-increasing stream of tourists traveling toward these mountains and commended "the far-sighted wisdom that is constructing automobile highways into the very heart of the amazing grandeur."[23]

This "ever-increasing stream," however, includ-ed new kinds of tourists who wanted to see the West and its national parks in new ways. Unlike the wealthy nineteenth-century tourists who trav-eled sedately across the continent in plush Pullman cars and demanded luxurious accommodations while observing the wonders of the American con-tinent, twentieth-century tourists often had lim-ited budgets and time. These travelers wanted to drive themselves and were content to "rough it" in the great American wilderness. In an article entitled "Autocamping—the Fastest Growing Sport," a wri-ter in *Outlook* noted that the automobile "has brought about a renaissance of the outdoors, and it has firmly planted a brand-new outdoor sport."[24] Americans, now happily ensconced in their automo-biles, wanted to savor the freedom of the road by camping out in the wilds through which they traveled.

Auto camping in Stoneman Meadow, Yosemite Valley, May 29, 1927. The clutter and congestion that would one day be brought to the valley by masses of auto campers is already evident in this early photograph. *Courtesy Yosemite National Park Research Library.*

Camping had several attractions for twentieth-century tourists. When the sport moved from the domain of aristocratic hunters, camping first became an upper-class activity attached to the expensive sport of motoring. Wealthy urbanites sought an escape from the pressures and luxuries of city life, hoping that direct contact with the wilderness would rejuvenate and ready them to participate in the hectic twentieth-century world. They feared that comfort and luxury had damaged the American spirit and that losing touch with the wilderness could spell doom for American ingenuity and toughness. From all facets of American culture came a call to renew contact with the wilderness, to "rough it" outdoors, in order to reclaim the vigor that many Americans believed was central to their national character.

Increasing numbers of people heeded this call and rushed into the wilderness hoping to experience its restorative effects. John Muir wrote in 1901 that "the tendency nowadays to wander in the wilderness is delightful to see." He noted happily that "thousands of tired, nerve-shaken, over-civilized people are beginning to find out that going to the mountains is going home." A promoter for the national parks promised that "in these work-filled American days . . . the deep forests of the Sierra call. The roar of Niagara can drown the buzz of the ticker. Old Faithful's gleaming column of spray shuts off the balance sheet."[25]

Not only did camping have the desired effect of encouraging Americans to throw off the shackles of modern civilization and to experience their primitive roots, but it also heightened the sense of freedom created by automobile travel. The car freed travelers from the limitations of railroad tracks and schedules and camping liberated them from the rules and regulations of hotels. Campers could avoid dressing for dinner and waiting for the bellhop. A car and a camping outfit gave the tourist the freedom to travel anywhere and anytime. Enthusiasts explained that camping allowed one "to throw off the impediments of civilization, the telephone, the silly conventions" and, as one woman wrote, "to put in their place the joy of being at least a healthy, if not an intelligent, animal."[26]

In addition to the spiritual renewal and the freedom offered by camping, it offered another attraction after World War I. As the price of automobiles came down, and as more Americans could afford to travel, camping became an inexpensive way to vacation. The car and the campground opened up the possibility of vacation travel to a much wider spectrum of middle-class Americans. The change in camping enthusiasts did not escape the notice of wealthier devotees who had pioneered the sport. They complained about the "ninety-thousand replicas of Maw" who now filled western roads and campgrounds. One rather peeved observer commented on this trend that "vacationing having ceased to be aristocratic and exclusive, it becomes more and more difficult to find an exclusive place in which to practice it." He added, "The trouble with our national parks is that there is no place in them for the man of means."[27]

In part, this snobbish observer was right. The automobile had democratized access to the national parks. No longer the domain of wealthy and leisured travelers, the national parks now captured the attention of a variety of American travelers who wanted to use the park in new ways. As more visitors began to travel to the parks and as they complained about the price and quality of the services that were available to them, it quickly became clear to the Department of the Interior that something would have to be done about the haphazard management of the parks. As early as 1911, the president of the American Civic Association, J. Horace McFarland, complained that "nowhere in official Washington can an inquirer find an office of national parks or a single desk devoted solely to their management."[28]

Several kinds of problems plagued park officials in the teens and 1920s, not the least being an inadequate and underfunded infrastructure for managing the parks in the face of the new volume of traffic brought by the automobile. In many of the parks, car traffic was treated with a certain amount of hostility, at least eventually, by the railroads that had once controlled access without much competition. Although some companies had initially welcomed the surge in tourism brought by the automobile, railroad management could hardly be expected to be enthusiastic for long about tourists who increasingly arrived in their own cars, who wanted to avoid railroad-built hotels, and who had little excess cash to spend. Even in Yosemite, where the railroads had little control over development, some local concessionaires regarded automobile traffic with some suspicion. Stage line operators and hotel owners saw no advantage in welcoming motorists who carried their own camping gear.

The combination of resistance from railroads and other park concessionaires and the commonly held view before World War I that cars were dangerous toys for eccentrics made officials ban automobile traffic in many of the parks. Even after automobiles were finally allowed in Yosemite, when motorists reached the valley floor they were at first required to chain their vehicles to logs and turn in their keys at a park office.[29]

More significant than automobiles, however, were the numbers of visitors they carried. New attitudes about the outdoors and the wilderness that had created the camping boom also increased interest in the national parks, and by 1910 unprecedented numbers of Americans were coming to visit. In addition, the outbreak of World War I in 1914 prevented Americans from traveling to Europe and encouraged people to see the wonders of their own country. The traveling public who wanted increased access to the parks, preservationists who wanted to call attention to the beauties of American scenery, railroads and other concessionaires who wanted to encourage use of their facilities, and government officials who wanted to please their constituents, all combined to demand new attention to the national parks. President William Howard Taft summed up these ideas in a message to Congress, stating that "every consideration of patriotism and the love of nature and of beauty and of art requires us to expend money enough to bring all of these natural wonders within easy reach of the people."[30] Most significantly, this movement resulted in the creation of the National Park Service in 1916.

The campaign after 1910 to create the Park Service, led by J. Horace McFarland, Secretary of the Interior Franklin K. Lane, and numerous others, brought the national parks enormous publicity and increased funding from the federal government. Finally the parks would have the money and management necessary to serve the needs of American travelers. Most important, with the appointment of Stephen Mather as director of the new Park Service, the parks had a tireless and innovative promoter. Mather, a Californian and a long-time enthusiast of Yosemite and the Sierra, would have particular impact on Yosemite.[31]

Mather's job as head of the newly formed Park Service involved several complex aspects. He had to build a bureau to manage thirteen parks and eighteen national monuments. Within the parks

themselves, Mather had to see that roads, hotels, and campgrounds were built to make these places accessible for all income levels. Mather knew that building public support for the park service idea was crucial to achieving these goals. He had to create public interest in the parks and to convince Congress that such interest warranted increased funding for the park system.[32]

Beginning in 1915, Mather began a public relations blitz that put the national parks on the pages of newspapers, national magazines, and promotional materials. Other park promoters, including the major railroads, *The Saturday Evening Post*, and *National Geographic* became important backers of Mather's publicity campaign. These efforts increased the number of visitors to the parks. Later, Mather noted proudly that in 1915, 344,799 people had come to the national parks and by 1919 the number had more than doubled to 756,027.[33]

Much of Mather's success in making national parks an important part of the American landscape rested on his recognition that automobiles represented the future of American tourism. He commented in 1919 that "it was inevitable that the automobile would revolutionize the park tour, just as it changed travel conditions everywhere and turned into memories cherished methods of seeing and doing things."[34] In 1915, when Mather took on the job of Assistant to the Secretary of the Interior in charge of the parks, he recognized the growing importance of the motoring public and the impact cars would soon have on the national parks. Decent roads would solve the problem of accessibility to the national parks. As more Americans could afford to buy cars and to take vacations, Mather reasoned, more of them would want to see the national parks. Increased numbers of visitors would give him the broad base of public support that he believed crucial to the park system's survival. He recognized the potential financial and political clout of the automobile industry, automobile clubs, and the motoring public, which already had nearly a million vehicles on the road in 1915. Demand for roads and facilities from from this rapidly expanding interest group would encourage congressional funding and would help to protect against exploitation of the parks' natural resources.[35]

Mather was one of the few people involved in the park system who foresaw the significance of the automobile so early and who welcomed motorists eagerly. His strongest opposition came from concessionaires, particularly railroads, who feared losing business to automobile traffic. Even in Yosemite, where railroads had less power, Mather met with resistance. In 1915 he tried to convince a Yosemite concessionaire to build a large hotel to attract the drivers of the one thousand cars he predicted would enter the valley that year. The concessionaire laughed at this grandiose prediction, but by 1916 more visitors entered Yosemite by automobile than by any other means, and by 1928, 136,689 cars poured into the park.[36]

Providing services for these new visitors challenged existing facilities in all the parks. In general, these had consisted of luxurious hotels built by railroads to attract their wealthy passengers. As Louis Hill of the Great Northern Railroad explained, "The railroads are greatly interested in the passenger traffic to the parks. Every passenger that goes to the national parks, wherever he may be, represents practically a net earning."[37]

In contrast to their later opposition, railroad companies and other concessionaires at first welcomed the novelty of automobile traffic, seeing these tourists as simply more bodies to put in their hotels and to carry over their stage lines. They welcomed the creation of the National Park Service and assisted Mather in his efforts to publicize the parks, believing that increased numbers of visitors, no matter how they arrived, could only mean profits for their companies. Unlike Mather, railroad officials did not immediately recognize the revolution signaled by motorists and their cars. During the 1915 international expositions in California, in fact, the Union Pacific and Santa Fe railroads spent more than half a million dollars on national park exhibits, hoping to convince travelers to California, many of whom had arrived in automobiles, to visit the parks.[38]

As it dawned on railroads by the 1920s, however, that automobiles competed directly with train travel and that automobiles carried a different breed of tourist, the enthusiasm of some companies began to wane. Railroad officials' dreams of wealthy travelers who boarded palace cars and lounged at expensive railroad hotels evaporated, as automobiles full of penny-pinching middle-class visitors arrived with camp kits tied to their running boards. The combination of new demands from tourists and the increasingly powerful role of the National Park Service aggravated tensions between the government and the railroads in parks where the companies had once dominated.[39]

This trend, however, did not occur in Yosemite. Its lack of major railroad facilities made the adjustment to automobiles and Park Service control easier. The conglomeration of concessionaires who offered facilities for visitors in Yosemite generally welcomed motorists. In addition, because no single concessionaire controlled services in the valley, Mather and the Park Service met with less organized resistance to change.

At first glance, Yosemite did not seem ideally suited for the automobile. The first car, a Stanley Steamer specially designed to withstand the rigors of mountain driving, arrived in the park in July of 1900. Claiming that automobiles frightened horses and disturbed tourists, park officials banned them from the park almost immediately after the Stanley Steamer's arrival. Such precautions were probably unnecessary, since few motorists had the machinery or daring to make the journey, and until 1915 the park had only twenty miles of unpaved government-built roads.[40] Despite bad driving conditions, park officials lifted the ban on automobile travel in 1913, as they did shortly thereafter in other parks, a change in policy that satisfied the demands of motorists and created a new source of income in the form of entrance fees. However, conditions for driving in Yosemite remained far from satisfactory for some time, and few drivers were willing to pay the $8 entrance fee or risk damaging their expensive machines.[41]

When Stephen Mather became the director of the national parks in 1915, however, accommodating automobiles and their drivers became a priority in Yosemite. Yosemite provided a perfect showcase for Mather's ideas about making the parks into attractive playgrounds for the American public. Central to Mather's plans was making the parks accessible to automobiles, and Yosemite seemed like a good place to start. What made Yosemite especially attractive to auto users was that it was the only major western park located within easy driving distance of two major urban centers—Los Angeles and San Francisco. In addition, in 1915 thousands of visitors were expected for the great world's expositions in San Francisco and San Diego. Many people would come by car, and many would want to see the famed Yosemite.

Mather immediately ordered the Tioga Road

Tent accommodations at Camp Curry in Yosemite Valley, ca. 1917. *Courtesy Huntington Library.*

improved to make it possible for a few cross-country motorists to enter the park on the rough road from the east, and he upgraded the quality of roads within the park. To help accommodate the increased number of tourists this would bring into the park, Mather awarded D.J. Desmond a permit to become the first big concessionaire in Yosemite. He also encouraged David A. Curry, one of the largest operators in the valley, to improve and expand his camp facilities. Camp Curry with its tents, camp-fires, and rudimentary plumbing, had opened in 1899. It represented the kind of service demanded by many automobile tourists—informal, inexpensive, and nominally out-of-doors—and in 1915, Camp Curry housed over a thousand guests. Mather's efforts were a success. By 1920 two-thirds of all visitors came to the park by car. Yosemite had entered the age of the automobile.[42]

These developments pleased most people. Better roads did make Yosemite more accessible and the number of tourists each year increased stead-

ily. In 1920, one visitor noted happily that "the Packard Twin Six took us down into the valley surely and splendidly." A park guidebook stated, "The long, hard trip over mountain roads . . . has given way to the comfortable automobile and train service and life in modern camps and hotels." The author concluded approvingly that "the policy of the National Park Service in making the Park 'liveable' is unquestionably the right one."[43]

Other observers had reservations about the changes that the automobile had brought. In 1913, Lord James Bryce had warned park officials who were planning to lift the early ban on automobile travel in the valley that "if Adam had known what harm the serpent was going to work, he would have tried to prevent him from finding lodgment in Eden; and if you were to realize what the result of the automobile will be in that incomparable valley, you will keep it out." Few people, however, had Bryce's foresight. For the most part, even staunch preservationists saw the car as a necessary evil that would bring increased public interest in Yosemite, protecting it from exploitation. A Sierra Club member commented that his first reaction to the sight of cars whizzing through Tuolumne Meadows was "to resent this intrusion into Nature's heart." On further reflection, however, he concluded that one can "but rejoice when increasing numbers of one's fellow-men find healthful pleasure in Nature's gifts."[44]

Some people felt that the natural beauty of Yosemite would not attract significant numbers of American tourists who wanted flashier entertainment. A participant in the first National Parks Conference complained that the park had "no attractions save an unkempt nature's wonderland." He recommended developing "golf, tennis, open-air concerts, skating, skiing, sleighing and similar attractions in the wonderful Yosemite," with the justification that "such civilized attractions would add much to the physical pleasure to thousands of the people of California alone, to say nothing of the people from other States, or even the world."[45]

Although Mather did not want to cover the valley floor with tennis courts and golf courses, he did believe that Yosemite must upgrade its tourist facilities to attract more visitors. When the new Park Service took over the operation of Yosemite in 1916, shoddy hotels, poor food, and high prices irked tourists, as they had decades earlier. The greatest difficulty facing Mather was the old one of the proliferation of small concessionaires, none of whom he thought provided high quality services at reasonable rates. He concluded that the solution would be to create a monopoly, making one concessionaire responsible for nearly all tourist services. He hoped such a system would make it easier for officials to regulate operations in the park, as well as improve the quality of service.[46]

Building such a monopoly, however, took some time. First, Mather had to find a concessionaire

Ahwahnee Hotel dining room (left) and main lounge (right), from a Yosemite Park and Curry Company advertising brochure, ca. 1930. American Indian designs are in keeping with the architectural theme of the hotel. *Courtesy Huntington Library.*

with enough capital to take over existing services and to create new ones. In 1920, Mather joined forces with the powerful editor of the *Los Angeles Times*, Harry Chandler, and raised a million dollars to create the Yosemite National Park Company. This operation faced continued competition from the Curry family, who ran the profitable and popular Camp Curry, the largest tourist facility in the park. In 1925, the two enterprises merged, creating the Yosemite Park and Curry Company, which was granted a monopoly on park services by the government. Finally, Yosemite had a concessionaire with the capital and experience to provide the services demanded by twentieth-century tourists.[47]

The merger occurred at an opportune moment. The state government had begun construction of an all-year road into Yosemite, designed to allow automobile travel into the park year-round. Park Service officials believed this paved road would greatly increase the numbers of visitors in the park,

particularly in the winter months.[48] Mather saw the opening of the road as an opportunity to push for one of his pet projects—a luxurious hotel designed to house wealthy tourists year round. Some other national parks had splendid hotels built by the railroads. Although Mather had argued for a first-class hotel in Yosemite for years, he was unable to convince any concessionaire that the necessary capital outlay would be profitable. With the all-year road and the new Yosemite Park and Curry Company, such a grand hotel was now possible.

On first glance, building an exclusive hotel in Yosemite seems a bit of an anomaly, given Mather's efforts to make national parks accessible to a wider range of visitors. He had worked hard to bring middle-class motorists to parks that had been the domain of rich and leisured travelers. By building roads, campgrounds, and inexpensive lodgings, he had opened the lands to the middle class. At the same time, Mather believed that Americans had

The title page of a Yosemite Park and Curry Company brochure advertising the Ahwahnee Hotel, ca. 1930. *Courtesy Huntington Library.*

the right to visit the parks "in as great luxury as each can afford" and that "it is the duty of the government to provide . . . the degree of comfort, even of luxury, that he requires."[49] Yosemite did not yet have the facilities to house wealthy visitors in the luxurious accommodations to be found at other parks, and Mather believed that this deficiency would hurt the park because such visitors had the political clout and spending power that national parks needed for protection.

With the impetus of the opening of the all-year highway, and with Mather's strong urging, the Yosemite Park and Curry Company began planning a glamorous hotel in 1925. They hired architect Gilbert Stanley Underwood, who had designed several station buildings for the Union Pacific Railroad. The hotel, named Ahwahnee, which means "deep grassy valley" in the local Miwok dialect, opened in July 1927, soon after the new highway brought cars into the valley on its paved, gently-graded surface.[50]

The great hotel demonstrated that Yosemite had indeed entered the modern age. Although the Ahwahnee resembled many of the other great rustic hotels built in the national parks in the first decades of the twentieth century, it was a modern, three-winged, six-story hotel for affluent tourists. Instead of the wood and stone used in the great hotels in Yellowstone, Glacier, and Grand Canyon, the Ahwahnee's steel-frame-and-concrete construction was stained to look like redwood and stone. With its combination of Indian, early Californian, English Tudor, Art Deco, and German Gothic motifs, the interior also reflected the modern cosmopolitan tastes of the post-war tourist. As one early brochure explained, the hotel "shuns the artificial unity of a definite period style, but the Ahwahnee attains consistency with . . . fundamental qualities of strength, simplicity, and directness."[51]

The aesthetics and luxuries offered by the new lodging appealed to wealthy tourists who wanted the freedom of automobile travel but not the discomforts of camping. The Ahwahnee, with its specially designed automobile entrance, garages, private bathrooms, ballroom, dining room, rock and wildflower gardens, and spectacular views, satisfied these requirements.

With the completion of the Ahwahnee in 1927, Yosemite National Park had achieved many of the goals that Stephen Mather had set for it. Because of Mather's efforts, his early recognition of the significance of the automobile, and the park's proximity to auto-crazed urban masses, Yosemite had been made accessible to more of the American people. Like the other great national parks, Yosemite offered accommodations and activities for a wide range of visitors. An easy drive up the new all-year highway or a more exciting trip over Tioga Pass carried tourists safely and quickly into the valley. Those who chose to could don dinner jackets or gowns for dinner at the Ahwahnee, while more economically-minded tourists could gather around the campfire at Camp Curry.

Most visitors found the new roads, hotels, and campgrounds in Yosemite to be far more appealing than the primitive roads, lurching stagecoaches, and crude tent hotels they had patronized earlier. Some tourists, however, recognized the price they paid for these improvements. The valley had lost the exclusiveness and remoteness that had characterized it in the nineteenth century. In 1933 an observer noted, "Nothing in all America is less wild than the floor of Yosemite Valley." He commented further that the "gleaming granite walls of the canyon and the tremendous water leaps" were all that he had imagined, but that "the floor of Yosemite is an amusement park, as crowded a city as New York's Central Park."[52]

A combination of physical beauty, convenient location near urban concentrations of middle- and upper-class people, and distinctive history made Yosemite a popular tourist attraction by 1930. Lacking extensive facilities developed earlier by railroads, the park was especially open to the efforts of the National Park Service and Yosemite Park and Curry Company to make it accessible to more Americans and their automobiles in the twentieth century. Building roads and facilities to handle cars and campers did encourage swarms of people to visit Yosemite and increase support for park appropriations. At the same time, however, dynamics had been set into motion that would after World War II culminate in crowding and automobile blight in the valley. As James Bryce had warned, a serpent had been admitted into the Garden of Eden.

Anne Hyde teaches history of the American West at Louisiana State University. Her book on far western tourism, An American Vision: Far Western Landscape and National Culture, 1820-1920, *was published by New York University Press in 1990.*

Professor Joseph Grinnell in his office at the Museum of Vertebrate Zoology at the University of California in Berkeley. Grinnell served as director of the museum from 1908 until his death in 1939. In addition to serving as the conscience of the national parks in matters of wildlife preservation and interpretation, Grinnell trained numerous graduate students who in their work for the national parks applied his belief that the parks should be preserved in a state of suspended animation as "samples of the earth as it was before the advent of the white man." *Courtesy Museum of Vertebrate Zoology, University of California, Berkeley.*

Joseph Grinnell and Yosemite

REDISCOVERING THE LEGACY OF A CALIFORNIA CONSERVATIONIST

by Alfred Runte

Understandably, every movement looks back to its founders for words of inspiration. The environmental movement is no different; mention Yosemite National Park, for example, and automatically most environmentalists will think of John Muir. And yet, by the time of Muir's death in 1914, the battle for Yosemite had only just begun. In truth, his hopes for the integrity of the national park were largely unrealized in his lifetime. It remained for a new generation of activists to carry on the struggle, to ensure, especially, that Yosemite won permanent status as a wilderness preserve. With further specificity to the fate of park wildlife, no one was more committed to Muir's unfinished agenda than Joseph Grinnell, director of the Museum of Vertebrate Zoology at the University of California at Berkeley. As a research scientist, Grinnell worked to infuse wildlife protection with scholarly accreditation and, in the process, forged one of the most important, yet least known, careers in American conservation.

Grinnell was born on February 27, 1877, at Fort Sill, Oklahoma, where his father, a physician, administered to Plains Indians living on the nearby reservation. A few years later the Grinnell family moved to California, settling east of Los Angeles in the suburb of Pasadena. It is hard to imagine now, but southern California in the 1880s still had large areas of open space, over which, for example, cir-

cled the great California condor. Here young Joseph was also free to pursue his boyhood interest in the study of birds. Nor was he content with observation alone. Rather, as an amateur ornithologist, he systematically collected and preserved a broad variety of field specimens. Just before his seventeenth birthday, a red shafted flicker became field number 72. Meanwhile, he completed high school in Pasadena, where, in 1897, he also received his A.B. degree from Throop Polytechnic Institute, later renamed the California Institute of Technology.[1]

Like many other young scientists, Grinnell mixed his years of formal training with personal fieldwork and adventure. In 1896, for example, he went to Alaska, collecting data and specimens in the area surrounding Sitka. His second trip to Alaska, from May 1898 to October 1899, combined attempts to find gold with zoological forays to Kotzebue Sound and the Bering Sea. As fate would have it, however, he was far more successful as a scientist than as a hopeful fortune hunter, a fact that was further underscored in 1901, when he received his M.A. degree from Stanford University.[2]

More seasons of fieldwork followed, three of which, the summers of 1905, 1906, and 1907, brought Grinnell back to southern California to conduct research in the San Bernardino Mountains. He further investigated the Salton Sea and the San Jacinto Mountains in 1908. He was forming, all the while, one of his lifelong beliefs, simply, that California had more than enough territory and biological diversity to occupy the career of even the most committed zoologist. Meanwhile, his own talent and discipline had not gone unnoticed. In 1908, at only thirty-one years of age—and with the completion of his Ph.D. at Stanford still five years in the future—he was appointed director of the University of California's new Museum of Vertebrate Zoology. For the rest of his life, Berkeley would be his intellectual base of operations.[3]

Predictably, his first few years at the Museum of Vertebrate Zoology were largely taken up with administrative duties and teaching. There remained, in addition, the task of finishing his Ph.D. With that milestone finally behind him, and with the Museum of Vertebrate Zoology more firmly established, he began to think seriously about several new projects, among them studying the natural history of Yosemite National Park. His choice was influenced by current events, as much as by the realization that Yosemite's flora and fauna had never been examined systematically. Along with a small cadre of other scientists, Grinnell was beginning to sense the value of national parks as wilderness laboratories. Consequently, on October 7, 1914, he asked Secretary of the Interior Franklin K. Lane for permission to begin a study "under the auspices of the University of California Museum of Vertebrate Zoology, along a line through Yosemite from Merced Falls to Mono Lake." As noted in the prospectus accompanying his request, the objectives of the survey included the identification of all mammals, birds, and reptiles in the area to be explored; the determination of their distribution, habits, and ecological relationships; "in other words," Grinnell reemphasized, "their natural history."[4]

From that goal logically followed another: concern for the future of the national park itself, especially for its viability as a wildlife preserve. The original Yosemite Grant of 1864, established by Congress and awarded to California, had taken in only Yosemite Valley and the Mariposa Grove of giant sequoias. Clearly, the intent in 1864 was to protect spectacular scenery and natural wonders. Then, in 1890, Yosemite National Park was established in the area surrounding the state park in the valley. At more than fifteen hundred square miles, compared to sixty in the valley grant, the national park had great potential as a wildlife preserve. Its territory, at least, was large enough to incorporate that ideal.

Unfortunately, the national park suffered a setback in 1905, when Congress reduced its area by fully one third, primarily in response to objections raised against the park by mining, logging, and grazing interests. California, meanwhile, agreed to return Yosemite Valley and the Mariposa Grove to the federal government, and Congress accepted the retrocession in June 1906. By then the city of San Francisco had pinned its hopes for fresh water on a dam and reservoir in the Hetch Hetchy Valley, this despite Hetch Hetchy's inclusion wholly within the confines of Yosemite National Park. The return of Yosemite Valley to the federal government aside, the loss of Hetch Hetchy to San Francisco's reservoir as a result of the passage of the Raker Act in 1913, coupled with the reduction of Yosemite National Park in 1905, was clear warning that Yosemite's status as a wildlife sanctuary had already been seriously jeopardized.[5]

Ultimately, Grinnell realized, whether in Yosemite or across the nation, further assaults on wildlife habitat would only be blocked by a concerned and knowledgeable public. Thus he repeatedly stressed to government officials, among them Secretary of the Interior Lane, the need for making natural history available to the public at large. "The Yosemite National Park is visited by thousands of people each year," Grinnell noted, for example, further justifying his proposed survey in terms of public education. Undoubtedly, curious Yosemite visitors "would find an account of its natural history of immediate service as a source of information concerning the animal life encountered." Likewise, a "natural history of so famous a region as that containing the Hetch Hetchy and Yosemite valleys would doubtless prove of wide acceptance among people not privileged to visit this National Park but who have a general interest in the out-of-doors."[6]

Here, it may be argued, lies the most important clue to Grinnell's thinking and effectiveness: he

Tourists viewing tule elk at the Elk Paddock, Yosemite Valley, ca. 1930. Until a change in Park Service policy promoted by Joseph Grinnell and others, Yosemite exploited its animals as tourist attractions. In contrast to Grinnell's ideal of the parks as living laboratories of wild nature, Yosemite differentiated between the scenic beauty and the animals that inhabited it. Paddocks or cages held the animals for the tourists' pleasure and one of the most popular entertainments was visiting the garbage dumps where the bears foraged for scraps. *Courtesy Yosemite National Park Research Library.*

did *not* believe that scholarship was only for other scholars. Rather, he insisted throughout his life that conservation would be advanced only if scientists worked with the general public. Scientific issues were too important to be discussed only by specialists. The key, then, he further realized, was a series of educational programs designed specifically for lay audiences. Indeed, literally from the moment of its founding, the Museum of Vertebrate Zoology sponsored public lectures on a wide variety of natural history subjects. Extension courses were also added, again with the hope that the Museum of Vertebrate Zoology might reach influential Californians about wildlife issues and conservation. One such course, entitled "Birds of California," drew twenty-seven students in September 1916. Its instructor, Harold C. Bryant, reported to Joseph Grinnell as follows: "Included in the class were three well-known physicians of San Francisco, and their wives; two well-known

business men, several teachers, and a number of other notables in San Francisco society." Grinnell could not have hoped for stronger proof of his program's acceptance and success. "I will be glad to incorporate the main facts into my report to the President for the current year," he replied to Bryant with thanks, then added a note of praise: "There is no one else in the University, or in the state, for that matter, to subserve the function you have chosen."[7]

Similar programs, it followed, could easily be adapted to the national parks. Thus Grinnell continued to build on his research in Yosemite, specifically, on his original reassurances to the Interior Department that both lay and professional readers would find his conclusions useful. The first of his major articles, "Animal Life as an Asset of National Parks," appeared on September 15, 1916, in *Science* magazine, coincidentally, only three weeks after the National Park Service was authorized. The gulf between science and bureaucracy was dramatically evident in Grinnell's article, which remains the best single expression of his lifelong commitment to wildlife conservation.[8]

With his associate Tracy I. Storer, Grinnell argued that the national parks were, in fact, universities of the wilderness. "As settlement of the country progresses," Grinnell and Storer remarked, "and the original aspect of nature is altered, the national parks will probably be the only areas remaining unspoiled for scientific study." It therefore seemed all the more imperative "that provision be made in every large national park for a trained resident naturalist who, as a member of the park staff, would look after the interests of the animal life of the region and aid in making it known to the public." But management, of course, took first priority; the naturalist's "main duty would be to familiarize himself through intensive study with the natural conditions . . . and to make practical recommendations for their maintenance." Once that task had been accomplished, however, the naturalist would devote the remainder of his time to public education, including "popularly styled illustrated leaflets and newspaper articles . . . and by lectures and demonstrations at central camps." The naturalist, in other words, would actively *promote* conservation, alerting "people to a livelier interest in wild life, and to a healthy and intelligent curiosity about things of nature."[9]

So often have these ideas been attributed to John Muir, Aldo Leopold, or some other "notable" of American conservation that Joseph Grinnell's contribution has been largely forgotten. It was simply not his style to insist on credit for his work. Wrote one of his later colleagues, E. Raymond Hall: "He liked to inspire the beginning of a movement, then sit back and watch it grow, fully content with, and even desirous of, anonymity for himself."[10] The point still remains that two significant movements, wildlife conservation and national park interpretation, owe as much to Grinnell as to anyone else. Until his and Storer's article appeared in *Science* magazine, the Department of the Interior had no established policy with regard to protecting wildlife in the national parks, let

alone to educating the public to the need for such a program. Even when Stephen T. Mather, the director-designate of the National Park Service, wrote Joseph Grinnell to acknowledge having read the article, he said only: "It contains much material which will be valuable to us in our plans for the parks." Mather said nothing substantive about any of Grinnell's proposals.[11]

Grinnell, not Mather, was to be the conscience of the National Park Service. Its first rangers were former cavalry troopers, mule skinners, guides, and adventurers; they were not trained biologists with any special fondness for wildlife. To the contrary, rangers in Yosemite, as well as in other parks, hunted and trapped fur-bearing animals for personal profit. Initially, Joseph Grinnell himself used that contradiction to special advantage, purchasing skeletons, skins, and carcasses for the Museum of Vertebrate Zoology. Yet he initiated those purchases in the interest of science. Beyond taking limited numbers of park animals for occasional research needs, he was alarmed that certain species of fur-bearing animals, especially Yosemite's predators, were apparently in decline. Trapping for its own sake, he concluded, was not only wrong but untenable. "I believe it would be in the interests of . . . the Yosemite National Park as a wild life refuge," he wrote the superintendent on July 8, 1920, "if all trapping of wild animals were henceforth absolutely prohibited."[12]

In effect, he had already argued as much four years previously in his article for *Science*: "It almost goes without saying that the administration should strictly prohibit the hunting and trapping of any wild animals within the park limits. A justifiable exception may be made when specimens are required for scientific purposes by authorized representatives of public institutions." Otherwise, "as a rule," even "predaceous animals should be left unmolested and allowed to retain their primitive relation to the rest of the fauna." The objectives of national parks should not be sanitized and civilized; rather, national parks should serve as refuges of biological diversity, "samples of the earth as it was before the advent of the white man." And that meant protecting predators as well as so-called desirable animals. "Another point worth emphasizing," Grinnell and

Jay C. Bruce, a predator hunter for the California State Fish and Game Commission, 1927. Until the practice was abolished in 1931, Yosemite National Park permitted, and sometimes even encouraged, the hunting of predators within park limits, despite Grinnell's warning that, in the interest of healthy wildlife balance, predators had to be "allowed to retain the primitive relation to the rest of the fauna." *Courtesy Yosemite National Park Research Library.*

sizing," Grinnell and Storer observed in their article, "is that many of the predatory animals, like the
marten, the fisher, the fox and the golden eagle,
are themselves exceedingly interesting members
of the fauna, and as their number is already kept
within proper limits by the available food supply,
nothing is to be gained by reducing it still further."[13]

The Park Service disagreed, and, in fact, pursued a vigorous program against predatory animals until 1931, fully fifteen years after Grinnell
and Storer's path-breaking article in *Science*.[14] The
Park Service had initially succumbed, in effect, to
nineteenth-century visions of the national parks as
scenery. Grinnell and Storer argued against this
philosophy. "The birds and mammals, large and
small, the butterflies and the numerous other
insects, even the reptiles and amphibians," they
noted, "are of no less consequence than the scenery, the solitude and the trails. To the natural
charm of the landscape they add the witchery of
movement."[15] Slowly the Park Service came around
to that opinion, but again, not before many predatory animals had been systematically eradicated
from the major western parks.

Thanks largely to Grinnell, an important breach
in that policy occurred in November 1925, when
Superintendent Washington B. Lewis finally banned all trapping in Yosemite National Park. "I have
just learned of your official action," Grinnell wrote
him enthusiastically. "This is mighty good news to
me, for I believe that you have acted in the best
interests of the Park, as regards its best use."
Granted, the rangers most affected would object
"for a time," but certainly their bitterness would
eventually "die out." Meanwhile, Grinnell hoped
the precedent would catch on in other national
parks, "to the end that no native animals in them
will be any longer considered as 'vermin' to be
continually harrassed." Nor could he resist the
temptation to close more philosophically. "The old
phrase, 'let nature take its course,' applies rightly
to National Parks, if to no other areas in our land."[16]

As always, the basis for his conviction was his
research in Yosemite. Again with Tracy Storer,
Grinnell completed his natural history of the park
in 1924.[17] To be sure, in preparing the book, Grinnell
evinced moments when he scrutinized his own

opinions. He occasionally relented, for example,
on the advisability of reducing the populations of
certain predatory animals, among them wolves,
mountain lions, coyotes, and rattlesnakes. But such
lapses in his conviction are best seen for what they
really were—not convincing evidence of self-doubt,
but rather, in the interest of protecting his credibility, attempts to strike a balance while criticizing
Park Service personnel. Whenever government per-
secution seemed to be getting out of hand, even
the largest native predators won his admiration
and defense. "I wish to repeat my belief," he thus
wrote the acting superintendent of Yosemite in
1927, "that it is wrong to kill mountain lions within
Yosemite, or within any other of our National Parks
of large area. They *belong* there, as part of the
perfectly normal, native fauna, to the presence of
which the population of other native animals such
as the deer is adjusted." Reasonable exceptions to
the rule should be perfectly obvious, such as individual animals that might pose a real danger to the
safety of park visitors.[18] Otherwise, Grinnell was
constantly troubled by what appeared to be pur-
poseful relaxations of national park philosophy,
generally to appease someone's personal preju-
dice or to satisfy bureaucratic expedience. "It would
seem to me," he confided to Superintendent Lewis,
"that national parks should comprise pieces of the
country in which natural conditions are to be left
altogether undisturbed by man. The greatest value
of parks from both a scientific and recreational
standpoint will thereby be conserved."[19]

Given the Park Service's reluctance to abide by
such directives, Grinnell's patience over the years
seems nothing less than amazing. But again, that
reflected his self-effacing personality. Observed
his colleague E. Raymond Hall: "He refused to
give public lectures; and even before his classes he
at times suffered from stage fright. A few persons
possessed of a certain dominating manner of speech
and greeting, he truly dreaded."[20] Obviously,
Grinnell was not the kind of person who gravitated
toward the limelight. He was at his best behind the
scenes, especially when dealing with government
officials. In those instances, he was perfectly suited
to accepting the bureaucratic truth that change
is incremental. However legitimate, none of his

reforms would be likely to win acceptance overnight. Dealing effectively with government officials required tolerance and patience, and patience especially was another of Grinnell's lasting virtues.

Grinnell further recognized the need to infiltrate bureaucracy, to effect change from within and not just from without. Interpretation, in that regard, was more than a means to educate the general public; it was also his method of seeding the Park Service with the incentives for its own reform. More knowledgeable visitors, it stood to reason, would insist on better park management. Similarly, some of the young people initially hired as naturalists should eventually rise within the organization, making changes, it also followed, where change really counted.

Indeed, contrary to the recollections of senior Park Service officials, the idea of interpretation was Joseph Grinnell's.[21] Beginning with his article in *Science*, and every year thereafter, he campaigned for such a program in every major park. On June 6, 1919, for example, he again wrote to Stephen Mather, suggesting that even though a small natu-

ral history museum had recently been opened in Yosemite Valley, the park's educational program was still incomplete. Specifically, he still had in mind "a natural history leader or guide" who would "be available for service at the several public camps of the Valley, particularly those with the largest registration, such as Camp Curry." The guide should have "the highest standing as a biologist," be of a "pleasing personality," and be "a facile and polished speaker." In short, "he should *not* be a casual pick-up, of unpolished language and manner." The leader or guide would "give twenty minute evening talks on local natural history —birds, mammals, reptiles, fishes, forests, flowers —perhaps two or even three such talks could be given at different centers in one evening." He suggested it be arranged for the guide "to take out 'bird classes' forenoons." "Simply to illustrate the type of man needed," Grinnell concluded, "I would name, as eminently qualified, Professor J.O. Synder, of Stanford University; Dr. Loye Holmes Miller, of the State Normal School, Los Angeles; Dr. Harold C. Bryant, of the University of Califor-

Naturalist/interpreters, many of them university students and instructors, were trained in the Yosemite Field School, shown here in session along the Merced River on July 3, 1940. At Grinnell's urging, the Park Service began hiring such naturalists as part of the staffs of Yosemite and other parks. By 1940, these scientist/rangers were educating thousands of visitors about park ecology during guided walks and evening campfire programs. *Courtesy Yosemite National Park Research Library.*

and Mr. Tracy I. Storer, of the University of California, and also of the Museum of Vertebrate Zoology."[22]

Rather than wait for the Park Service to make up its mind, Grinnell worked closely with his supporters to place one or more of those teachers at other locations. That summer, for example, Harold Bryant and Loye Holmes Miller gave lectures and led nature walks at Lake Tahoe, California, generally under arrangements with Fallen Leaf Lodge. Then, on July 19, Bryant wrote to Grinnell, informing his mentor that Mather had stopped by. "He stated the nature guide proposition had gone through," Bryant noted. "He wanted me to go to Yosemite immediately under civil service appointment." But of course Bryant was already committed and had to turn Mather down. "I certainly hope that the matter does not drop there," Grinnell replied, obviously disappointed, but fully sympathetic. "The main thing is to get a precedent set."[23]

Fortunately, Mather held his offer to both Bryant and Miller until the following year, when they and two other naturalists, Ansel F. Hall and Enid Michael, officially inaugurated park interpretation in Yosemite Valley.[24] "Am getting a fine start," Bryant reported to Professor Grinnell early in June 1920. "There is plenty of interest. Could keep several [more] guides busy. Have great difficulty in limiting the classes. Started with 20 this morning and ended with 27."[25] No words could have been sweeter music to Joseph Grinnell's ears.

Indeed, that Bryant would even submit such a report—revelling in the numbers of people his classes were attracting—again does much to reveal Grinnell's own personality. Although *he* may have suffered from stage fright, he was not by any means the insecure academic, insisting, for example, that the size of one's class is not evidence of good teaching, but, to the contrary, proof of pandering to a mass audience. In Grinnell's estimation, numbers *were* important. The more people his colleagues reached, the more secure the future of parks and conservation. So, too, clarity of expression was vitally important. "It was his habit," observed E. Raymond Hall, "to submit selected manuscripts of his own for criticism to his pupils, who often were impressed at his ready willingness to acknowledge imperfections. Then it was that he would make the point that any statement of which the meaning is not clear, even to one person, should be reworded, because there is a way of stating the thought so that everyone will understand it."[26]

The point of education, Grinnell thought, was to build bridges to the public, to make the university responsive to the community and its needs. "It is a splendid thing," he wrote in that vein to Harold C. Bryant, "that there is, in the State, a properly qualified person to make known to people at large a knowledge of our natural history. I particularly congratulate you upon your success in getting the nature-guide work in national parks upon an almost assured permanent basis."[27] True to form, Grinnell took no credit for himself. But even more significant, he reserved his highest praise for his students and colleagues who taught the general public. Education must have a purpose beyond the university campus. If conservation in particular were to have a stronger base, concerned scientists must do more than talk only among themselves.

A complete summary of Grinnell's philosophy of education would be impossible here. So, too, just listing his accomplishments would require an article in itself. Yet of all his contributions, none was more important than his ceaseless devotion to the national parks. Until his death in 1939, he was literally the biological conscience of the National Park Service. Every major reform in wildlife conservation owed something— if not everything—to his conviction and persistence. Among those reforms, the elimination of predator-control programs most certainly stands apart. Grinnell also figured prominently in efforts to rid the national parks of artificial displays of wildlife, such as cages, fenced enclosures, and various exotic species.[28] Meanwhile, the students and colleagues he inspired rose to the forefront of conservation, and, in many instances, were the first to conduct systematic surveys of the flora and fauna on the public lands.[29] As always, Grinnell was the catalyst, providing encouragement, assistance, and oftentimes research facilities for the advancement of both conservation and scientific knowledge of native wildlife.

In the national parks, the idea of "letting nature take its course" originates as much with Grinnell as anyone else. He figured prominently in efforts to eliminate artificial displays of wildlife, as depicted in this 1920s photograph of a deer in the "Yosemite zoo." *Courtesy Yosemite National Park Research Library*.

His own proving ground was Yosemite. The park, after all, met every criterion for his convictions as a scientist. It was large, biologically diverse, and obviously mismanaged. Any scholarly treatment of Yosemite was almost certain to make a difference, improving not only conditions in Yosemite but in comparable protected areas. Equally important, Yosemite had a large and enthusiastic following. It was the park of history, the first of its kind in California and the first in the United States.[30] Practically everyone in the nation had at least heard about Yosemite. If public education, like science, were to take hold in the national parks, Yosemite seemed the logical point of origin for both special programs.

Finally, there was the location of Berkeley itself. Like Los Angeles and San Francisco, the University of California was but a day's journey from Yosemite's gates. Grinnell could teach class one morning and be in Yosemite the very next. Nor did he fail to appreciate that the trip he could make so easily was also within reach of thousands of other people. Here again, it made sense to him to concentrate his attention on what mattered to society as a whole. Yosemite obviously mattered, and so Grinnell quite naturally thought first of Yosemite when he thought of national parks.

These and other advantages he used to perfection, securing, through the natural sciences, the legacy of John Muir and other famous activists. For his own part, Grinnell contributed more than 550 published works, dozens of which dealt specifically with the national parks.[31] Even today, his monumental *Animal Life in the Yosemite* is a significant research tool. More important, Grinnell wrote literally thousands of letters, notes, and memoranda to Park Service officials, stressing the need for education and wildlife reforms. If his ideas and accomplishments have long since been forgotten —or credited to others—that is what he wished. Time, in either case, would eventually set the record straight. What mattered most to him was results, especially instilling Park Service officialdom with greater sensitivity and attentiveness to the needs of the natural world.

In that regard, perhaps none of Grinnell's accomplishments as a scholar can ever equal his legacy as a teacher. He constantly motivated his best students to think of careers in conservation, especially as professionals in the National Park Service. Harold C. Bryant, who began his Park Service career in Yosemite, went on to become superintendent of Grand Canyon National Park.[32] Joseph S. Dixon, another of Grinnell's pupils, became field biologist in the new Wildlife Division of the National Park Service, established in 1933. And it was George M. Wright, perhaps Grinnell's most gifted and dedicated undergraduate, who sponsored, co-authored, and produced the first two volumes in the distinguished faunal series, *Fauna of the National Parks of the United States*, published in 1933 and 1935, respectively. With all of the conviction that imbued Grinnell's own letters and publications, Wright and his colleagues set forth, collectively and park by park, the steps needed for wildlife maintenance and long-range recovery.[33]

The faunal series itself bore the unmistakable imprint of Joseph Grinnell, emphasizing many of the ideas he and Tracy Storer had formally enunciated nearly two decades earlier in "Animal Life as an Asset of National Parks." In 1963 Grinnell's ideas were promulgated yet a third time, when the Wildlife Management Advisory Board, appointed by Secretary of the Interior Stewart L. Udall, and chaired by Professor A. Starker Leopold, released its own sweeping report, *Wildlife Management in the National Parks*. "As a primary goal," the committee suggested, "we would recommend that the biotic associations within each park be maintained, or where necessary recreated, as nearly as possible in the condition that prevailed when the area was first visited by the white man." In short, Leopold and his colleagues concluded, "A national park should represent a vignette of primitive America."[34]

The ideal was Joseph Grinnell's. "Herein lies the feature of supreme value in national parks," he and Tracy Storer had written in 1916: "they furnish samples of the earth as it was before the advent of the white man." George M. Wright, in 1933, changed the wording, but not the concept: "The American people intrusted the National Park Service with the preservation of characteristic portions of our country as it was seen by Boone and La

Salle, by Coronado, and by Lewis and Clark." And so the idea had come full circle in 1963. "A reasonable illusion of primitive America could be recreated using the utmost in skill, judgment, and ecologic sensitivity," Professor Leopold and his colleagues wrote.[35] Only those who had forgotten Joseph Grinnell could have failed to see the tie, for Leopold himself had received his Ph.D. in zoology from the University of California at Berkeley.[36]

Granted, from Grinnell to Leopold, it was naive to suppose that protection of the national parks might best be accomplished by holding each of them in a state of suspended animation, "samples of the earth as it was before the advent of the white man." If there is any constant in nature that constant is change. Although romanticism was much to be preferred over blind manipulation of nature, Grinnell personally could not stand by and allow ignorance of wildlife resources to prevail. "We must have the *facts*," he remarked as early as 1915, "in all their bearing, before generalization."[37] Until scientists had completed their research, he would not approve of the manipulation of either plant or wildlife resources. Throughout his life, that was his standard. That his students further embraced it, and carried it into the national parks, does much to explain the origins of modern principles of environmental conservation. As for his own part in the movement, he left the telling of that story to someone else. Now that historians have rediscovered Joseph Grinnell, they are finding his legacy most significant indeed.[38]

Alfred Runte is a public historian and author living in Seattle. A specialist on the national parks, he received his Ph.D. in history from the University of California, Santa Barbara. His highly-acclaimed National Parks: The American Experience *(University of Nebraska Press, 1979) has now appeared in a second, revised edition (1987), and he has also recently revised his popular* Trains of Discovery: Western Railroads and the National Parks *(Roberts Rinehart, 1990). Runte's latest work is* Yosemite: The Embattled Wilderness *(University of Nebraska Press, 1990).*

Stoneman Bridge over the Merced River near Camp Curry, Yosemite Valley, 1939. Designed to accommodate heavy automobile traffic and built in 1933 of reinforced concrete and faced with native granite, the Stoneman Bridge reflected the National Park Service's commitment to modernizing structures in the parks, while still keeping them in harmony with natural surroundings. *Courtesy Yosemite National Park Research Library.*

In Harmony with the Landscape

YOSEMITE'S BUILT ENVIRONMENT, 1913-1940

by Robert C. Pavlik

Yosemite National Park is best known for its spectacular scenery. Its discovery and subsequent establishment as a park has also been well documented.[1] Scant attention has been paid, however, to the park's roads and structures, or built environment. Beginning just before World War I and lasting roughly until 1940, a special effort was made to blend Yosemite's built environment with its renowned natural setting. There was a strong desire on the part of park officials to rebuild Yosemite's facilities in an organized and aesthetic manner, the better to serve its increasing influx of visitors. The successes and failures of that effort tell us much about Yosemite in particular and the evolution of national parks in general. Put simply, the question still remains: Is it possible to allow development inside the national parks and yet protect their distinctive natural features?

In 1913, three important events shaped the evolution of Yosemite's cultural and natural landscape: the shift from Army administration to civilian control; the admission of automobiles into Yosemite Valley; and the passage of the Raker Act, authorizing the city of San Francisco to dam the Hetch Hetchy Valley for a municipal water supply. Yosemite was on the verge of momentous changes, among them a dramatic surge in historical patterns of visitation. How government officials responded to these changes, especially in terms of the infrastructure and built environment, would forever determine the fate of the park's natural heritage.

Early Years of National Park Service Management: Contradictory Beginnings

The National Park Service's first director, Stephen T. Mather, and his hand-picked choice for superintendent, Washington B. Lewis, ushered in a new era of development for Yosemite. Their mission was to remake the park into a public pleasuring ground and resort that was readily accessible and accommodating to the public, while preserving the natural features. In a "Statement of Policy," written in 1918 and coauthored with Assistant Director Horace M. Albright, Mather stated that

In the construction of roads, trails, buildings, and other improvements, particular attention must be devoted always to the harmonizing of these improvements with the landscape. This is a most important item in our programs of development and requires the employment of trained engineers who either possess a knowledge of landscape architecture or have a proper appreciation of the esthetic value of park lands. All improvements will be carried out in accordance with a preconceived plan developed in special reference to the preservation of the landscape . . . [2]

Despite Mather's general concern for the landscape, there appeared to be little objection to using park resources for construction projects, or regard for the preservation of features considered less than scenic or aesthetic. An example was the Cas-

When the National Park Service was formed in 1916, its first director, Stephen T. Mather (right), chose Washington B. Lewis, (left) to run Yosemite National Park. Taken at the New Village, this photo dates from 1924. *Courtesy Yosemite National Park Research Library.*

cades power plant, the first significant development to take place under Mather's direction. A new electrical generating facility, it was designed to meet not only the current needs of the park, but to allow for expansion of government and concession facilities for years to come. The power plant consisted of a log crib dam, 17 feet high and 170 feet long, a penstock, and a powerhouse, a large concrete structure situated below the level of Highway 140 and next to the Merced River.[3] The diversion dam was located on the Merced River at the head of the rapids, above Cascades, yet below the floor of the valley, so it would not affect the falls or rapids on the valley floor above Pohono Bridge.[4] The large pool of water created by the dam was also thought to be a scenic attraction that park visitors would find pleasing. The power plant was first put into operation on May 28, 1918. A dedication was held on September 7, with Interior Secretary Franklin K. Lane and Park Service Director Mather in attendance. In his remarks, Mather illustrated the important role the plant would play in Yosemite's development, stating that "the installation of this plant . . . symbolizes the new and greater function for which the Yosemite National Park is preparing, and which it will assume in the very near future."[5] At the time, no mention was made of the questionable practice of erecting a

dam within a national park, especially so close on the heels of the Raker Act, which had legalized San Francisco's Hetch Hetchy project. The prevailing attitude at the time was that the park's development was necessary to provide for increased public use, even if some of the resources had to be sacrificed.

Building the New Village

The first major rehabilitation of Yosemite Valley to take place after the construction of the powerhouse was the relocation and construction of the New Village north of the Merced River. Rather than continue to develop and occupy the Old Village site on the south side of the river, an area park managers and visitors thought to be seedy and run down, a new location near Yosemite Falls was identified and plans were drawn up for its development. A maintenance yard—consisting of shops for carpentry, plumbing, electrical work, and blacksmithing, as well as a livestock barn—had already been established on the north side of the valley (on its present site) in 1916-1917.[6] Employee residences, administrative offices, and operations facilities were relocated adjacent to the maintenance shops over the next ten years. A new bridge near the Old Village replaced the dilapidated Sentinel Bridge in

1918-1919, and hastened the traffic flow between the two areas of development. Anticipating the need for more residences and their placement on the north side of the valley, a new schoolhouse was erected there in 1917-1918, the first unit of the new planned village area. With the school on its new site, the children and their parents were not far behind. In the 1918-1919 season, four cottages for government workers, the first of a series of employee residences in this area, were completed in the vicinity of the old Camp Lost Arrow.

The next improvement in the new village area was the erection of a Ranger's Clubhouse in 1920. Mather called upon landscape engineer Charles P. Punchard, Jr., working in conjunction with architect Charles Sumner, another Mather affiliate, to produce the initial design for a dormitory that would also serve as model for the construction in the new village of an administration building, museum, and post office.[7] Punchard and Sumner produced a striking building of steep-pitched roofs and rustic scrollwork more fitting for the Swiss Alps than a Sierran canyon. Their design reflected a preference for European scenic imagery carried over from the early years of national park development. For those American travelers who desired a foreign, exotic experience and could not afford the trip overseas, the national parks at first attempted to provide not only spectacular scenery but architecture that could compete with the European originals. Such an approach to scenery was also some compensation for a nation that was still unsure of its own heritage and history and that continued to rely on the cultural precedents set in the Old World.[8]

During this transition period between 1916 and 1925, the park headquarters remained in a makeshift structure in the Old Village. Ideal for summertime, this site's lack of sunshine during the winter combined with the building's poor construction to make the office uncomfortable most of the year. The building was not only inefficient; park managers feared that it left visitors with a negative impression of the park and that the wretched conditions contributed to employees' "indifference in their work."[9] In order to reduce discontent in the workplace, Congress in 1923 appropriated $35,000 for the construction of a new administration building. Architect Myron Hunt designed the structure, which was completed in October 1924. The park managers lost no time in

moving into their new quarters, and the former administration building in the Old Village was razed the following March.[10]

Another element of the new village construction was the museum. Park Naturalist Ansel Hall organized the Yosemite Museum Association in 1920 for the purpose of soliciting private donations to a permanent museum program in the park. His fundraising efforts caught the attention of the American Association of Museums, which secured a $75,500 donation from the Laura Spelman Rockefeller Memorial Foundation for the construction of a fireproof museum building in Yosemite.[11] The building was completed in May 1925, the first official museum in a national park.

The emergence of the administrative center was widely heralded in the 1920s as a giant step toward the elimination of the Old Village and the removal of the "unsightly, ramshackle" buildings across the river. Although the new buildings did not conform to the Ranger Club's Swiss chalet style of architecture, as had originally been planned, they were a powerful statement of the new "Rustic" architecture style. They also illustrated the rapidly changing attitudes of landscape architects and planners who were involved in the development of national parks in the early 1920s. As architects continued to exercise their creative skills in designing buildings that were harmonious with the landscape, an approach compatible with American architectural movements in general in the early twentieth century, they depended less on existing European styles and started to experiment with native building materials and designs that were integral with the intended building site.

What the National Park Service designers created came to be known as the "Rustic Style." Borrowing from the Arts and Crafts Movement, Native American Indian traditions, and the Shingle, Oriental, and Prairie styles, with a degree of San Francisco Bay Area architectural influence, park architects introduced buildings similar to those found on streets adjacent to California colleges. The distinguishing feature of park buildings was the design and placement of these same structures within the forests, near giant sequoia groves and high mountain lakes, and bordering the subalpine meadows and waterfalls of Yosemite National Park. Adherence to a comprehensive design plan, as well as a philosophy guiding the style and method of construction, also made these buildings important

A major step toward moving the center of Yosemite National Park activities away from the Old Village was taken when the Administration Building, shown here in 1927, was constructed. Taking their cue from the Arts and Crafts Movement, the park's designers used local materials and landscaping with native plants to blend the community as much as possible with natural surroundings. *Courtesy Yosemite National Park Research Library.*

and unique. Because each building was individually designed for its site and much of the construction material came from the surrounding area, the buildings truly became a part of the landscape.

Influence of Automobiles

In addition to the influence of changing architectural styles, the introduction of the automobile was crucial to the development of the modern Yosemite National Park built environment. The automobile's legal entry into the park in 1913 necessitated the improvement of the entire road system. Park planners decided that Yosemite Valley, the focus of visitor activity and overnight accommodations, would be favored first with a road improvement program that included widening, straightening, relocating, and paving the valley's haphazard thoroughfares. A stunning ninety percent increase in travel to the national park in 1915,

occasioned by the Panama-Pacific International Exposition in nearby San Francisco, provided the immediate impetus to improve roads built originally for horse-drawn wagons. The 1915 tourist season suggested that the automobile as a new method of conveyance for potential park enthusiasts could no longer be ignored.

For almost fifteen years, however, Yosemite motorists were forced to drive on unpaved, dusty, gravel roads, and the increasing numbers of motorists made driving in the valley a most unpleasant experience. Complaining that "of 138 miles of government owned roads in the park, only eight miles have been constructed under Congressional appropriations," Superintendent W.B. Lewis in 1923 called for the improvement of the entire road system, including construction of a road from Happy Isles, at the upper end of Yosemite Valley, to Tuolumne Meadows via the Merced Canyon, and a branch road from the top of Nevada Falls to Glacier

Point, following the approximate route of the Glacier Point-Panorama trail.[12] Although such an elaborate project was never built, it shows the vigor with which men like Lewis promoted schemes to make the park accessible to a desirous public.

Lewis's call for action was answered in part, however, by a congressional appropriation of $1.5 million for improvement of the Yosemite road system. The April 9, 1924, act made funds available for the paving of the valley floor and El Portal roads, approximately twenty-nine miles in all, and the modification of the remaining 110 miles of park roads.[13] This generous funding package was probably inspired in part by the imminent completion of the All-Year Highway from Merced to El Portal, constructed by the state of California and promising to bring even greater numbers of motorists to the park. In 1925 the federal Bureau of Public Roads and the National Park Service approved an interagency agreement providing for the engineering and construction of new roads within all national parks, a function that the Department of Transportation continues to this day.[14] In Yosemite, the resident park superintendent, engineer, and landscape architect had final say over the location of such roads, and they took great interest in the placement, design, and construction for minimal impact on the landscape.

Sanitation and Health

Garbage disposal and sanitation were pressing issues to be confronted with the increased tourism brought by the invasion of automobiles. Initially, the problem became acute in Yosemite Valley, where the greatest concentration of people occurred, but later it spread to other areas as their popularity grew. The problem first began to be addressed with the arrival of the Army Cavalry into Yosemite Valley in 1906. Park Supervisor Gabriel Sovulewski recalled that, "as [is] always the case with Army officers, sanitation took precedence over all other

Old Village, Yosemite Valley, in the 1920s. Until 1913, automobiles were banned from the park. The world's fairs at San Francisco and San Diego in 1915, however, brought thousands of tourists to the state, and Yosemite experienced its first mass invasion by motorists. By the 1920s, park roads, though narrow and unpaved, were regularly jammed with automobiles, particularly during the summer vacation season. *Courtesy Yosemite National Park Research Library.*

problems."[15] The conditions that greeted the Army officials were not conducive to good public health. Campers occupying the meadows below the Old Village had no sanitary facilities, and all campers and concessioners in the park were responsible for their own garbage disposal by whatever means they deemed appropriate.[16] As a result, sewage from the multiplying hotels, camps, and residences often flowed untreated into the Merced River, resulting in a badly polluted stream and serious health hazards for those living downstream from the valley.[17] The Army responded by restricting the campers to meadows above the Old Village and by instituting in 1912 a garbage collection and disposal service. Acting Superintendent George V. Bell succinctly described this operation: "The garbage is disposed of in a very up-to-date method, being gathered daily in garbage wagons, hauled to a pit, and buried."[18] Of course, this practice proved to be a boon to the bears, who flocked to the pits to scavenge and thereby developed a dependence on human offal that has continued to be a park management problem.

The first major improvement in sanitation came in 1920, when Congress appropriated funds for a sewage disposal system in Yosemite Valley. The tremendous surge in tourist visits to the valley after 1913 alarmed park managers, who feared that the inadequate sanitary facilities might turn the national parks into "breeding grounds for the dissemination of disease," damage the park's credibility, and lessen the possibility of continued appropriations for development.[19] Thus, they campaigned for and received authorization for the sewage treatment plant, which was located in a meadow south of the Three Brothers. At first the plant consisted of two Imhoff tanks, one sludge bed, and 6.3 acres of sand filter beds. Later, the system's capacity was expanded to dispose of sewage from 6,000 people.[20] Hotels and residences in the valley connected to this system, and a total of 31 restrooms were installed in the public campgrounds.[21]

The great amount of rubbish that larger crowds produced necessitated the building of an incinerator in the valley. Located behind the New Village in the maintenance area, the three units, capable of handling the garbage of 15,000 people daily, were installed by 1925. Wet refuse was burned, while cans were crushed and hauled away to be buried.[22] Refuse from the hotel kitchens continued to be hauled to the "bear pits," where nightly displays of ursine extravagance were witnessed by incredulous visitors and interpreted by misguided park naturalists. Garbage was not collected in other areas of the park until the late 1940s.

As visitation soared, the sewage plant quickly proved inadequate. Visitors and park personnel alike complained of the odor, conspicuous location, and inability to expand the facility.[23] Other towns and cities of the time shared similar problems. As one visitor reportedly remarked, "My, doesn't this valley smell refreshing—its just like San Francisco Bay."[24] Along with aggravating auto traffic, the sewage problem was a clear signal that Yosemite was already suffering some of the ill effects of urbanization.

Because the smell of San Francisco Bay was something park officials wanted to avoid, they once again coaxed Congress to fund a new treatment plant. After great debate, the park superintendent, public health officials, and landscape architects finally approved a site in the meadow north of Bridalveil Falls, where the plant would be sufficiently screened from visitors by the thick growth of oaks, pines, and cedars.[25] The project also required reducing odors and noise, preventing contamination from reaching the river, protecting fish from chlorine in the effluent, and screening from the approach roads to the valley and from the valley rim.[26] Constructed in 1930 and 1931, the disposal system met all of those requirements admirably. In May 1934 the California Sewage Works Association bestowed on the park its Award of Merit for the best operated and maintained sewage plant in the state.[27] With additions and improvements, the plant served well until a new facility was constructed in El Portal in the mid-1970s.

As improvements occurred in outlying areas of the park and more visitors took advantage of expanding roads and trails, more restrooms were also installed. Shortly after the Glacier Point Four-mile Trail was rebuilt in 1928-1930, the park replaced an unsightly pit privy at Union Point with an attractive Rustic Style restroom with a battered stone foundation, redwood siding, and shake roof.[28] Similar structures appeared on or near all trail heads, including three in 1934 alone (Vernal Falls Bridge, Glacier Point, and Hetch Hetchy).[29] In the era of park modernization, even the most basic of utilitarian structures commanded the careful attention of the Park Service's planners, landscape architects, and administrators, in order to preserve land-

Union Point Restrooms, Four Mile Trail, Yosemite National Park, 1932. As tourism increased in the automobile era, larger and more modern sanitation systems, as unobtrusive as possible, were called for. The Union Point rest area on the road to Glacier Point is a perennial attraction. *Courtesy Yosemite National Park Research Library.*

scape values while accommodating park visitors comfortably.

Relocating the Indian Village

Providing adequate medical facilities also concerned park officials. Superintendent Lewis pleaded this case with the Secretary of the Interior in 1923 when he noted that the existing hospital, a "temporary" structure built in 1912, was so overcrowded that patients had to be housed on the hospital porch or in tents in the public campgrounds. In some instances, the ill were refused medical care due to the lack of space.[30] The site chosen for the new Yosemite medical center was at the mouth of Indian Canyon, east of the New Village, on the road to the recently constructed Ahwahnee Hotel.

The placement of the hospital at the entrance to Indian Canyon in 1929 supplanted an historic-era Indian village that extended from the hospital west to the post office.[31] Although Superintendent C.G. Thomson characterized the village site as too "rocky, rattle-snaky, and hot," the Indian inhabitants regarded it as a desirable location, one their ancestors had occupied for generations because it was warm and sunny in cold winter months.[32] The Indians lived there in makeshift tent cabins and shacks built from discarded materials. It is plausible that park planners and Yosemite Park and Curry Company executives were eager to remove this eyesore for visitors passing between the new luxurious hotel and the expanding park administration area at the New Village. The large parcel of land the Indians occupied was also coveted by the government as the logical space for expansion and development for the New Village. In the debate over proper location for the new Indian village, however, the rationale centered on the need to segregate the Indians from other park residents and visitors alike, and to find a place where they would be less visible, ostensibly to provide the Indians with a "private" place to reside.[33] Sites considered included the entrance to Indian Caves, at the eastern end of the valley, and an area between Rocky Point and El Capitan, at the far western end.[34] Either location would have sufficiently separated Indians from whites and provided a degree of control over the Indian village inhabitants by the ranger force. The original plan for the new Indian residences called for a Great Plains "tepee type of house," reflecting the widespread ignorance of Miwok culture and indifference to the distinctions between groups of Native Americans.[35]

The displaced Indians were finally moved to a less visible, more isolated location, segregated from the rest of the park and concession employees, at the far western end of the developed area on the north side of the valley. The location was finally selected by April 1931, and construction began in late July.[36] Specifically, the village was built west of the winter campground now known as "Sunnyside" or Camp Four. To his credit, Assistant Landscape Architect John Wosky abandoned the original ersatz tepee design in favor of a more dignified structure similar to two cabins constructed at Glacier Point earlier that year. The tiny Indian dwellings measured 19.5 feet by 22 feet and contained two small bedrooms and a combination kitchen/dinette. The only plumbing was a sink, located in the kitchen. A wood stove served as the source of heat and for cooking.[37] All the cabins

The old Indian village of tent cabins and shacks, shown here about 1915, was considered an eyesore by some park administrators. Because it was a sunny, cheery site, however, generations of Miwoks had occupied the village before they were relocated during park modernization. The park hospital is located there now. *Courtesy Yosemite National Park Research Library.*

In the early 1930s, park officials displaced Indian residents of Yosemite Valley to a new village in a remote location. The new dwellings, though more modern than the old tents and shacks, were only 429 square feet in size, with three small rooms, regardless of the needs or sizes of families inhabiting the buildings. *Courtesy Yosemite National Park Research Library.*

were constructed uniformly, without regard for the various needs of the residents or the sizes of their families. Some cramped cabins housed upwards of six or eight people, including children and adults. The Indian village's removal from a prominent location on the road to the Ahwahnee Hotel and its subsequent placement at the remote end of the valley suggests a contradiction between the Park Service's desire to capitalize in its interpretation programs on the romantic image of the pre-contact Native Americans, while relegating their actual descendants to isolated and substandard living conditions.

The Great Depression and the Emergence of the Modern Yosemite, 1933-1940

If the period between 1913 and 1933 constituted the beginning of a rapid and thorough makeover of the built environment of Yosemite National Park, the ensuing years between 1933 and 1940 proved to

be a continuation, expansion, and consolidation of the development program already under way. The stimulus for development was not increased visitation, as had been true during the teens and 1920s, but the appearance of a number of public relief programs aimed at combating the Great Depression. It was in this period that the employee and visitor facilities at Yosemite took their present form.

Within hours of assuming office on March 4, 1933, President Franklin D. Roosevelt sketched out a preliminary administrative plan for a "civilian conservation corps," which he presented to his cabinet within days.[38] By the end of the month, the president signed a bill calling for the enrollment of men who would be employed on "public works projects and conservation tasks." Roosevelt instructed the Department of Labor to recruit enrollees, the Army to prepare the young men for camp life and transport them to their work stations, and the National Park Service (NPS) and U.S. Forest Service to establish camps and devise and oversee appropriate projects for the enrollees. The Army would later take over the administration of the camps, while the NPS continued to direct the work projects. The program was initially referred to as "Emergency Conservation Work," but the more popular "Civilian Conservation Corps" (CCC) was adopted as the official name for the organization in 1937.[39]

Another of Roosevelt's "alphabet" agencies that found ready acceptance in the national parks was the Civil Works Administration (CWA). Due to the slow start of another federal relief agency, the Public Works Administration (PWA), the CWA was created on November 9, 1933, to give unemployed men and women work on local projects at the federal government's expense.[40] After an explosive four and one-half months, during which the federal government spent $1 billion and engaged 4 million Americans in a "vast work-relief army," the program was dropped as quickly as it had been organized.[41] A different plan of distributing relief money to states and local governments was devised, and by mid-1934 the PWA was ready to take its place in the lineup of federal projects.

In contrast to the Emergency Conservation Work (ECW) and CWA programs, the Public Works Administration was created to distribute monies in the form of loans to responsible state, local, and municipal agencies for the construction of public works projects, or to private contractors secured by the federal government. The first year of PWA began with a $3.3 billion appropriation, most of which was allocated for federal projects, because "the machinery already existed to get under way with a minimum of delay and without opening unprotected avenues where funds might be misused."[42] A further stipulation of the PWA program was that the public works projects conform to some established program of comprehensive planning.[43] The national parks, especially Yosemite, were well suited to the nature of this requirement. Far-sighted planning had become a trademark of the national parks, and they were ready to apply for any source of funding at least partially dependent on comprehensive design plans. Crews from the PWA, CCC, and CWA programs facilitated many Yosemite National Park improvements after 1933.

A fourth source of construction revenue, and one unique to Yosemite, was provided by the Raker Act, which required the city of San Francisco to expend $1.5 million on road and trail improvements near the Hetch Hetchy reservoir. The city was slow to respond to the park service's demands for compliance with this portion of the act, and when the city finally removed the Hetch Hetchy railroad (used in construction of the dam) in 1925 and began to build trails in the area, park officials considered the city's work less than satisfactory. Rather than risk the construction of an inadequate, poorly built, and little used road and trail system, park officials reached an agreement with the city in the summer of 1932, absolving the city of responsibility for road and trail construction in the Hetch Hetchy area in exchange for $1.25 million of city money to build roads in other parts of the park.

Comprehensive road improvement was only one example of the modernization of Yosemite made possible by the surge of funds and workers after 1933. PWA funds were expended on all Yosemite road projects from 1933 to 1940, with CCC enrollees providing assistance. Realignment of the Tioga Road was the first project slated for improvement following the agreement with San Francisco. The reconstruction work took place in three stages. The first was the relocation and construction of the section of road that extends from a point two miles west of Tuolumne Meadows east to Tioga Pass.[44] A new ranger station was erected at the pass in 1931. The windswept location and rugged nature of the surrounding peaks necessitated a structure that would not attempt to compete with the landscape, but one that blended readily with its harsh and beautiful environment. The ranger station was the first stone building of the Rustic Style built by the National Park Service along Tioga Road, in anticipation of the increased numbers of visitors who would brave the mountain pass after the road improvements were completed in a few years.

In the vicinity of Tuolumne Meadows a road bridge was required to span the Tuolumne River. Sand and gravel used in the construction of the bridge came from a borrow pit located upstream from the bridge site, at the junction of the Dana and Lyell forks of the Tuolumne River. The contractor created a large pool, approximately 300 feet square and up to 20 feet deep, where a large sandbar had once been. The excavation took place next to the public camping ground, with the justification that it would be a "scenic attraction" to replace an "unsightly" area, however natural.[45] Although the utilization of natural materials found within the national park is prohibited today, it was seen at the time as a logical and economical alternative to securing building materials from great distances. Improved roads into Yosemite helped abolish this practice in favor of obtaining building and construction supplies from sources outside the park.

The second portion of Tioga Road to be reconstructed was the eleven-mile section from Crane Flat to McSwain Meadows, terminating two miles east of White Wolf. The unfinished section of Tioga Road, between White Wolf and Tuolumne Meadows, was surveyed by the Bureau of Public Roads in 1935, but not completed until the early 1960s.[46]

In 1935, work began on the new Big Oak Flat Road from the All-Year Highway to Crane Flat, linking Yosemite Valley with Tioga Road. A formal dedication ceremony took place at Crane Flat on June 23, 1940. An estimated 1800 people were in attendance to hear veteran Sierra Club leader William E. Colby deliver the keynote address, which recounted the history of Yosemite's road system and emphasized the importance of increased access and availability of the wonders of the High

Sierra to the motoring public.[47] An entertaining and unusual "ribbon cutting" took the form of a log-sawing contest between two teams of Civilian Conservation Corps enrollees, who wielded crosscut saws as two camps raced side by side to cut the large log symbolically blocking the roadway. Cheered on by camp mates, the "home" team stationed at Crane Flat beat out their challengers from the Cascades camp.[48] As the log was severed, so was one of the last obstacles to free and complete automobile access to the park.

As in the case of roads, other facilities were modernized and expanded during the period from 1933 to 1940. New ranger residences and automobile checking stations were built at South Entrance, Chinquapin, and Crane Flat. A general utility building covering one-half acre was built in the Yosemite Valley maintenance area, the center of all park maintenance activities. Fire lookouts were strategically located along the park's western boundary, where fire guards could survey the cutover lands of the Stanislaus and Sierra National Forests. One of the finest examples of the Rustic Style,

Skiers at the Ostrander Lake Ski Hut, March 1941. *Courtesy Yosemite National Park Research Library.*

C. G. Lewis, the second superintendent of Yosemite National Park, whose administration lasted from 1929 to 1937. *Courtesy Yosemite National Park Research Library.*

Ostrander Lake ski hut, was built in 1940. Coming at the end of the rugged architecture's era in national parks, it is an important element of Yosemite's built environment.

Conclusion

The twenty-seven-year period between 1913 and 1940 was an era of revolution in the human landscape of Yosemite National Park. Prior to 1913, the park was dotted with simple wood frame or log structures that were minimally functional and temporary in nature. The road system was virtually unchanged since 1874, when the first horse-drawn wagons rattled into Yosemite Valley. The park's transformation was largely attributable to the automobile. The greatly increasing number of motor vehicles in the country, and in California in particular, stimulated a building boom throughout the state that has continued to this day. Yosemite could not exist in this region and not be affected. Through faster and more independent transportation, people previously bound to the vicinities of their homes

by the cost and difficulty of travel could now travel longer distances. With the automobile's appearance, the luxury of travel was no longer restricted to the leisure class, who had always possessed both the means and the time for distant sojourns. An egalitarian carrier, the automobile allowed more people to travel farther in less time, providing for a relatively inexpensive form of vacation.

Upon its inception, the National Park Service, under the leadership of Stephen T. Mather and Horace M. Albright, immediately recognized the importance of this newly mobile middle class to the success of the national parks. The NPS capitalized on the American public's love of mobility by promoting and improving the parks for the automobile. Mather and Albright, along with Yosemite's first two superintendents, W.B. Lewis and C.G. Thomson, knew that the public would follow any road into the "wilderness," as long as it was paved and there were facilities enroute and at their destination.

The Park Service also succeeded in creating and sustaining a romantic type of architecture that reflected prevailing aesthetic tastes and embodied the values that the parks were created to protect. This Rustic Style was a combination of styles promulgated throughout the western United States during the first three decades of the twentieth century. That the style was perpetuated on such a widespread scale, and yet was suited to the individual parks and various settings within the parks, makes it a unique and important architectural movement in its own right. Its use of native materials, the subjugation of the structure to the surrounding natural environment, an adherence to a comprehensive plan, and the ultimate devotion to harmony with the landscape are all elements of the Rustic Style, and their application is readily apparent in the current built environment of Yosemite.

The program of road building and facilities improvement reached its zenith during the Great Depression. With a large pool of unemployed men and readily available funds for construction, the national parks were able to reap some benefit from the nationwide tragedy, offering employment to the logger, road builder, carpenter, and stone mason, as well as to thousands of the nation's unskilled youth. The park also served as a place of retreat to the disillusioned and disheartened, who sought a respite from the rigors of the Depression. The positive effect the parks had on the American public, however, would not be fully known until after World War II, when millions of vacationers would flock to Yosemite each year, straining the capacity of facilities that had been more than adequate only a decade earlier.

The improvements that enabled Yosemite to foster a constituency during its first twenty-five years under Park Service management set a precedent for even more development, although improvements increasingly clashed in style and function with earlier facilities. The Mission 66 era (1956-1966), a ten-year effort to accommodate the greatly increased numbers of visitors to the national parks at any cost, would expand facilities substantially without taking into consideration natural or aesthetic park values. Changes in society's work force, as well as the reduction of park funding and the increased costs of building materials, necessitated a more commonplace and utilitarian style of architecture and more crowding of facilities. Placed side by side with the earlier works of craftsmen and artisans, the new buildings paled by comparison. However, many of the handcrafted Rustic structures require greater repair and maintenance expenses. While the roads and structures of the park's earlier age blend with the landscape and reflect the philosophical precepts of the National Park Service, they are not always considered in harmony with the park's present fiscal, political, and social realities, and pressure has mounted to raze, renovate, or replace them.

Robert C. Pavlik is State Historian II for the San Simeon Region, California Department of Parks and Recreation. He has a Master of Arts degree in Public Historical Studies from the University of California, Santa Barbara. He has taught environmental education for the Yosemite Institute in Yosemite National Park and worked as a student-historian for the National Park Service in Yosemite. He has authored a series of articles on the built environment in Yosemite.

Tehipite Valley on the middle fork of the Kings River was coveted during the 1930s for a reservoir by both Los Angeles and the San Joaquin Valley. Following John Muir's lead, conservationists continued a fifty-year-old fight to protect it. *Courtesy National Park Service.*

Conservation Conflict and the Founding of Kings Canyon National Park

by Lary M. Dilsaver

In the summer of 1873, John Muir made his first visit to the high country of the Kings River. He later remembered:

> In the vast Sierra wilderness, far to the southward of the famous Yosemite Valley, there is yet a grander valley of the same kind. It is situated on the south fork of the Kings River, above the most extensive groves and forests of the giant sequoia, and beneath the shadows of the highest mountains in the range, where canyons are the deepest and the snow-laden peaks are crowded most closely together.[1]

Before he wrote those words, Muir encouraged California senator John Miller in 1881 to propose the area as the country's second national park. Miller's bill failed even to clear committee.

Muir and Miller were not the only persons to recommend the Kings River watershed for park status. In subsequent years every secretary of the Interior, three secretaries of Agriculture, most Forest Service chiefs, and many San Joaquin Valley citizens also supported a park for the area. Congressmen offered more than a dozen bills between 1890 and 1935, two of which led to creation of Sequoia National Park in 1890 and its expansion in 1926. Yet no bill to make the Kings watershed a national park came close to passage.

The reason for these dismal failures lay in the number and diversity of anti-park forces. As with most proposed national parks, Kings Canyon threatened many special interests. Both the city of Los Angeles and farmers from the San Joaquin Valley planned huge reclamation projects for the river, while Fresno businessmen envisioned massive tourism development. Cattlemen, hunters, timber companies, and summer cabin owners all opposed restrictive Park Service control. They much preferred the Forest Service, which had assumed control of the earlier forest reserves in 1905, and, in keeping with the Service's policy of "multiple use for the greatest good," encouraged all their diverse uses and plans.[2]

Yet, between 1935 and 1940, park advocates overcame this opposition to establish the state's first wilderness national park. The history of this intense five-year campaign to make Kings Canyon National Park a reality illustrates the growth of conservation under Franklin Roosevelt, exposes the complex opposition to wilderness preservation, and demonstrates some political methods used both to win and to block environmental legislation. It also provides a case study of the problems and conflicts, within the government and the conservation movement, precipitated by wilderness preservation issues.

In the early 1930s, the only positive aspect park supporters could find in their situation was the stalling effect their various foes had on each other's plans. Seeking to establish superior claims to dam sites, Los Angeles and San Joaquin Valley irrigators

The Cedar Grove area on the south fork of the Kings River, looking west. This development area became the focus of controversy and compromise. From the turn of the century until 1990, various factions have competed to control it for a reservoir, massive tourist development, or wilderness. Eventually this site hosted camping and a modest tourist complex. *Courtesy National Park Service.*

and hydroelectric power developers dueled to a standstill before the Federal Power Commission. Developers waited anxiously to see what areas would be inundated by proposed reservoirs before committing to recreation investment. Like reclamation and park proponents, they were especially interested in two Yosemite-like canyons, Tehipite Valley and Kings Canyon.

Then, in 1933, the Forest Service released a comprehensive plan for the Kings River watershed, focusing on Kings Canyon along the south fork of the river. The plan proposed a huge tourism complex including campsites for 6000, four or five major hotels, three access roads, and an airstrip. One road, from General Grant Park, was already under construction; another to Tehipite Valley was on the drawing board. Untroubled by reclamation proposals, Forest Service planners had contingency plans to make any reservoir an integral part of the recreation package. Their plan also proposed wilderness designation for much of the territory previously sought by park proponents. In typical

fashion, the Forest Service was doing what it could to satisfy everyone.[3]

As the Forest Service released its plan for Kings Canyon, another event with profound consequences for the future park occurred. Newly elected President Franklin Roosevelt appointed Chicago lawyer Harold Ickes as Secretary of the Interior. Ickes was one of the most strong-willed, widely despised, and powerful Interior appointees in history. He took particular interest in the National Park Service, actively participating—some say meddling—in decisions on its funding and management, and attempting to expand its control of federal lands. Notable among his achievements as Interior secretary were takeovers of the national battlefields from the War Department and of the national monuments from the Department of Agriculture. In 1934, Ickes attempted to add the entire Forest Service to Interior, even as the Secretary of Agriculture campaigned to take over the National Park Service.[4] Corporations despised Ickes for his anti-trust stance, segregationists for his civil rights actions, and many politicians for his stinging verbal and written assaults. He once referred to a southern governor as a "bubonic plague-carrying rat."[5] He could be dictatorial, suspicious, and vindictive to both his enemies and his own employees. Yet, he was also highly principled and fought tenaciously for what he believed.

Among Ickes's strong beliefs was conservation. He had been influenced by Gifford Pinchot, but later also adopted the ideas of Stephen Mather, including that of wilderness preservation. In May 1933 he declared, "If I had my way about national parks, I would create one without a road in it. I would have it impenetrable forever to automobiles, a place where man would not try to improve upon God."[6] In Kings Canyon, Ickes had a chance to put those words into action. In 1935, he persuaded California Senator Hiram Johnson to propose a bill to create a wilderness park that would be called John Muir-Kings Canyon National Park. In the Johnson bill, horse trails, footpaths, and simple camping facilities would be encouraged, while roads, hotels, and other developments would be banned. Unlike the Forest Service plan, Ickes's wilderness park included the canyon of the south fork of the Kings River.

If nothing else could unify all the developers, this bill and the presence of Harold Ickes in the conflict could. Bitter protests from power, irrigation, tourism, grazing, and timber interests buried Johnson's bill in committee, and thereafter, the various developers returned to maneuvering for

Kings Canyon is approached by a steep and winding state highway that runs from Grant Grove to Cedar Grove. From 1932 to 1939, convict labor built the road, visible toward the lower right, to facilitate Forest Service recreation development. *Courtesy National Park Service.*

control of the watershed. Despite the bill's crushing defeat, one piece of good news did reach park advocates during 1935: its hydroelectric needs temporarily sated by the new Boulder (Hoover) Dam, Los Angeles dropped its application for Kings River power development.[7]

Having gauged the opposition with the 1935 bill, Ickes, National Park Service (NPS) Regional Director Frank Kittredge, and members of the Sierra Club began to plot how to overcome them. In discussions around the state with both pro-park and anti-park people, they discovered that the Park Service had a very poor reputation. Many local citizens perceived the Park Service as an agency opposed to development, unconcerned about the fate of local farmers, restrictive in managing its lands, and controlled by wealthy, urban pleasure-seekers. They preferred the Forest Service, which supported freer use of lands and resources, seemed anxious to promote the economic welfare of valley farmers, and allowed much easier access to hunting, fishing, and travel in their territories.[8]

Ickes and Kittredge also discovered that distrust of the Park Service was fostered by Regional Forester Stuart B. Show and local Forest Service men. Over the years a deep antagonism had developed in California between the two agencies, arising both from fundamental differences in land management philosophy and from perceived empire-building by Park Service leaders. Forest Service personnel believed that their policy of "multiple-use" was fair, democratic, and promised the greatest freedom and the greatest good for the people. They regarded the Park Service's mission of strict preservation as appropriate only for select, small areas of unusual scenic curiosity. The Park Service, on the other hand, saw their administration as the only way legally and absolutely to protect wilderness areas like Kings Canyon. A Forest Service promise to manage an area as wilderness could be overturned by the next chief forester.

Details of land management also brought the two agencies into conflict. Regional Forester Show accused Ickes of trying to force the Forest Service into buying private lands and then donating them to national parks. Fire fighting posed a problem because Forest Service men and money were used to fight park fires. The Park Service also applied pressure to have livestock grazing stopped on forest lands in order to open range for herds of park deer, swollen by decades of protection from hunting.[9]

Ickes and the National Park Service men discovered, however, that all factions in the valley, despite their radically opposed and bitterly defended

A backcountry scene near Colby Pass in Kings Canyon National Park. Both the Forest Service and the Park Service proposed the high country for wilderness management in 1935. *Courtesy National Park Service.*

Harold Ickes was a Chicago lawyer with strong ideas about wilderness and conservation. Serving under Roosevelt from 1933 to 1945, he used diplomacy to bring about the establishment of Kings Canyon National Park. *Courtesy National Park Service.*

proposals, shared an abiding fear that Los Angeles would invade their waters. Both San Francisco and Los Angeles had attacked distant watersheds for power and water in disregard of local interests and consequences. Los Angeles, in particular, had appropriated the water supply of the Owens Valley, siphoned water from the Colorado River, and was now casting eyes on distant Sacramento Valley rivers. What chance did San Joaquin Valley farmers and communities have in blocking this imperialistic giant?

This threat of Los Angeles's potential control of water resources was the unifying element park backers had sought. Ickes, Kittredge, and Sierra Club members like Joel Hildebrand and William Colby decided to play on the fear of Los Angeles to lure the major local irrigation group, the Kings River Water Association (KRWA), into a compromise. At the same time, they campaigned widely for a more positive image both for the proposed park and the National Park Service. Although this cast the cantankerous Ickes in the unusual position of persuasive diplomat, he proved equal to the task. The campaign began during the early months of 1938. Ickes and Kittredge delivered radio addresses and speeches aimed at newspaper publishers, influential women's and businessmen's groups, state and local legislators, and various social clubs. Most talks were delivered in San Francisco or Los Angeles, but both men also appeared in Fresno and other valley towns.

Meanwhile, Assistant NPS Regional Director B.F. Manbey conducted the real compromise negotiations. Through the spring and summer of 1938, Manbey met with KRWA officials, civic authorities, businessmen's clubs, farmers, and even timber and grazing interests to foster support for Kings Canyon National Park and the Park Service. Manbey told farmers and irrigationists that the Park Service sympathized with their needs. He assured them that Harold Ickes intended to meet their legitimate water demands through the Bureau of Reclamation, which he also controlled. Manbey also promoted the health and spiritual benefits a wilderness park might bring, as well as the expanded business opportunities possible along the valley roads approaching it.

Slowly but surely, through this media and personal campaign, a compromise was achieved between Ickes and the KRWA, local businessmen, and most farmers. Three conditions were to be met

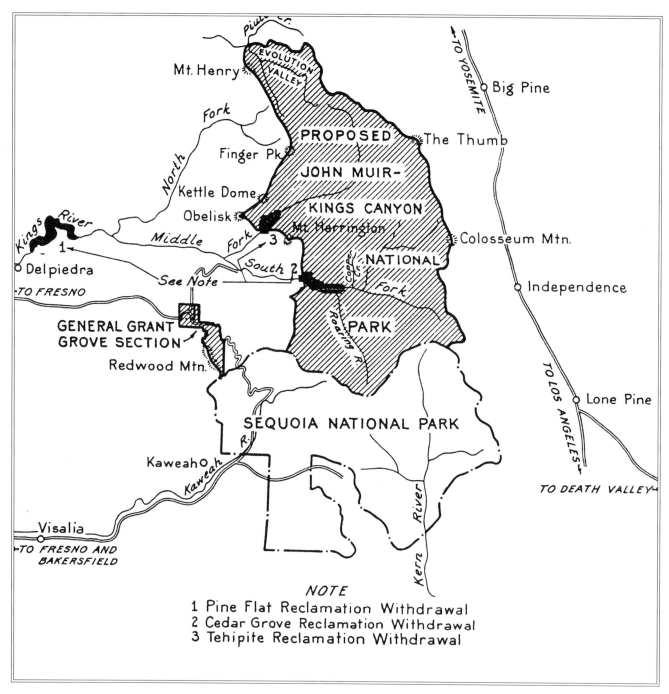

Map of John Muir-Kings Canyon National Park as proposed in the Gearhart bill of 1939. Also shown are the Pine Flat reclamation area (left), and the two valleys withheld for possible future reservoirs. *Courtesy National Park Service.*

by the Department of the Interior. First, the Bureau of Reclamation would build a large dam at Pine Flat. In addition, the department would support dams on the north fork of the river, outside the proposed park. Second, Tehipite Valley and Kings Canyon were to be excluded from the proposed wilderness park boundaries. Both sites had been important in all power and irrigation proposals. Although local farmers saw no immediate need for dams at these sites, they would not relinquish future opportunity there by allowing wilderness park status to be established. The exclusion of these canyons, the very heart of the proposed park, was a bitter pill for the Park Service to swallow, but one absolutely necessary in order to placate local water users. Finally, the Park Service would develop a major tourism complex in the canyon of the south fork of the Kings River. The preferred sites were adjacent to Copper Creek, near the entrance to the proposed wilderness park, and at Cedar Grove where the Forest Service had begun development.[10]

In March 1939, Representative Bertrand "Bud" Gearhart of the Ninth Congressional District (Fresno) introduced two bills. The first revived the John Muir-Kings Canyon National Park proposal, incorporating the small General Grant National Park, which had been established in 1890, as well as a magnificent adjacent stand of 7,000 giant sequoias known as Redwood Mountain. The second bill provided funds for construction of Pine Flat Dam. Unrelated in theory, the bills were interdependent in reality.[11]

As the House Committee on Public Lands took the Gearhart park bill under consideration, it still faced substantial opposition from some state irrigation associations, all grazing and hunting groups, several influential newspapers, the California legislature, the California Chamber of Commerce, a prolific letter-writing recreation group called California Mountaineers, Inc., and two conservation groups, the Wilderness Society and the National Parks Association (NPA).

Some of these opponents seemed so dissimilar that Roosevelt aide Irving Brant undertook an investigation of the last four groups. He found a startling connection. The conservation committee of the Chamber of Commerce was dominated by two retired Forest Service men, Ernest Dudley and Parker Friselle, along with Charles Dunwoody, a lobbyist for timber and power interests. Dudley and Friselle, in addition, comprised virtually the entire membership of California Mountaineers, Inc. The two conservation groups, meanwhile, were both

heavily influenced by William Wharton, a Massachusetts millionaire considered by other conservationists to be "an honest dumbbell," and whose closest friends and advisors were William Greeley, a lumberman, and Ovid Butler, a retired Forest Service man and director of an association of lumber companies. Wharton followed their advice to oppose any park proposal that excluded Tehipite Valley and Kings Canyon. The net effect was the alignment of the Wilderness Society and the NPA with anti-park forces. Frustrated park advocates dubbed Wharton's organizations "The Bewildered Society" and the "Anti-National Parks Association."[12]

The Forest Service was the connecting link between these odd allies, and to the NPS men that explained everything. Exposure of this Forest Service connection did not diminish anti-park forces, but the sense of their conspiracy helped the bill pass the House Committee on Public Lands over strenuous opposition by several western Congressmen.[13]

Through the spring of 1939, as the campaign for Kings Canyon intensified, so did the antagonism between the two federal agencies. Park Service officials accused the Forest Service of distortion and slander, while Show accused Park Service personnel of wire-tapping, bullying Forest Service personnel, and burglary of Ernest Dudley's home in Exeter in search of damaging papers. Thereafter, Show hid his records so they could not be summoned by Chief Forester Silcox, who was acting under orders from the president.[14]

With feelings running high, the final battle for Kings Canyon moved to the full House of Representatives. Republican Gearhart had introduced the bill and remained its principle champion. However, the park as proposed would also include acreage in the Tenth Congressional District, represented by Democrat Alfred Elliott of Visalia. Elliott bitterly opposed the bill for a variety of reasons. First, he favored the Forest Service, and its brand of management, over the NPS. Among his close friends were Forest Service allies Dunwoody and Dudley. Second, Elliott feared that creation of the wilderness park would damage the tourist business in adjacent Sequoia National Park, which also fell in his district. Finally, according to Irving Brant, Elliott was "sore at Gearhart" for some unspecified reason. Congress looked to these men for direction, and Elliott's opposition still made the bill's passage uncertain.[15]

Then, Elliott made a mistake, a mistake of such spectacular proportions that it eliminated the last serious obstacle to park creation.[16] On March 4,

1939, a park supporter, Mrs. Gertrude Achilles of Morgan Hill, California, had written to both congressmen Gearhart and Elliott urging passage of the park bill. She had also written a second note to Gearhart along with a $100 check for use in the campaign. Unfortunately, she had mistakenly enclosed this second note and the check in the envelope to Elliott.

When he received his letter and the check to Gearhart, Elliott saw a chance to defeat the bill by trapping his colleague in a bribery scandal. He notified the FBI and had the check photostated. Then Dunwoody typed a new envelope to Gearhart and mailed the check to him from San Jose, near Morgan Hill. When Gearhart received the check,

he returned it to Mrs. Achilles, suggesting she send the money to the Sierra Club.

The trap had not worked, yet Elliott began showing the photostatic copy of the check to prominent men in the San Joaquin Valley and to several other congressmen, ostensibly allowing them to draw their own inferences. Soon Gearhart received an anonymous phone call from a man who had been at one of the meetings and who warned, "He is out to frame you, Buddy, and I would not be a party to it. I had to tell you. Be on your guard."[17] Over the next few days three congressmen approached Gearhart with the same news.

Gearhart, a former district attorney, then began collecting the evidence to protect himself and show

A National Park Service planning team looks over the canyon of the Kings River in August 1951. This portion of the canyon, over 8,000 feet from mountaintop to riverside, is the deepest in the United States. From left to right are Dr. Harold C. Bradley of the Sierra Club, Park Superintendent Eivind Scoyen, lawyer Thomas Crow, NPS Director Conrad Wirth, and Regional Director Lawrence Merriam. *Photograph by Howard Stagner, park naturalist.*

Elliott's misconduct. He obtained an affidavit from Mrs. Achilles stating that she had not typed an envelope and that she had mailed her letter from Morgan Hill, not from San Jose. Step by step Gearhart pieced the entrapment story together. As Gearhart quietly continued his investigation, however, Elliott continued to suggest to San Joaquin created because he would personally profit from it.[18]

Finally, on May 2, Representative Gearhart rose before the House on a question of personal privilege. With controlled and deliberate emotion he systematically reported the entire plot, demonstrating at the same time his shock and sorrow that a colleague would use character assassination to defeat a bill. Word of his address quickly circulated through the halls, and by the time Gearhart reached his conclusion, the House and gallery were packed with rapt listeners:

I have searched the precedents of this body, searched them down through the last 150 years of the history of this body, and I fail to find one case referred to in those proceedings that even approaches that which I have been compelled to lay before you.

I ask no action. There was a time when I thought of expulsion. There was a time when I thought of disciplinary action. But all that is past now. The record is made. I am content.[19]

With the exception of Elliott, every person rose and gave Gearhart a standing ovation. They then turned to see how Elliott would answer these charges. During Gearhart's testimony, the representatives around Elliott had quietly moved away one by one, until he now sat separated from his nearest colleague by more than twenty feet. The Democrat's attempts to defend his actions were futile, consisting chiefly of an attack on the park bill and on Secretary Ickes. Frequently interrupted, peppered with questions on his actions, and laughed at, Elliott finally blurted in frustration, " . . . Some of you might think you are making a monkey out of me, but that cannot be done."[20] Roars of derisive laughter followed, and Elliott sat down, an embarrassed and lonely figure.

Horrified at the thought that this sort of character assassination could be levelled at each of them, representatives demanded Elliott's ouster. But Gearhart knew that when the passion died down a move to oust Elliott might become a partisan contest. As such, it would probably fail and in the process cloud the wilderness park issue. Instead, as the vote on the bill approached, Gearhart read

into the record a number of San Joaquin Valley newspaper accounts of the scandal to refresh the minds of his colleagues. When the vote came up, the remaining opponents tried one last sabotage by adding an amendment to allow dams in the new park. In the ensuing arguments the amendment was defeated, but with it went the John Muir portion of the park's name. Once this last-minute opposition had failed, the bill passed easily.[21]

The Senate received the bill too late to act in 1939, but, with the support of both California senators, sent it to Roosevelt in early 1940. The president signed the Kings Canyon National Park bill on March 4, 1940. Twenty-five years later, after completion of the dams at Pine Flat and on the north fork of the Kings River, Congress added Kings Canyon and Tehipite Valley, completing acquisition of all the territory of Ickes's 1935 proposal.[22] As he watched the arguments to add the two canyons, a bitter Show recalled how they had "fit [sic], bled and finally died." While admitting that Elliott's behavior had been "highly injudicious," the loyal Forest Service man still complained about the "morality of tactics" within the Park Service, and wondered "whether the end always justifies the means."[23]

The anti-climactic end to this struggle showed how successfully park advocates had divided, converted, conquered, or discredited their opponents. The creation of Kings Canyon National Park represented a stinging rejection of the Forest Service and its mandate. The philosophical division between the Park Service and the Forest Service would erupt again into internecine conflict in the 1960s during the debate over whether the Mineral King Valley should be added to Sequoia National Park or developed as a ski resort, as well as in other park campaigns around the nation. The five-year battle to establish Kings Canyon National Park consisted of a competition of manipulative conspiracies engineered by two government agencies and readily backed by special interests. In the end the Park Service won through skillfull diplomacy and an egregious error by overzealous opponents.

Lary M. Dilsaver is an associate professor of historical geography at the University of South Alabama, and a volunteer researcher for the National Park Service. With William Tweed he recently completed Challenge of the Big Trees, *a centennial history of Sequoia and Kings Canyon National Parks.*

Prescribed burn along the Merced River, Yosemite Valley, 1991. For centuries
before the first white people entered the Sierra Nevada, Indians regularly burned
the grass and underbrush in Yosemite Valley to preserve open meadows and
maximize growth of large seed-bearing trees. Along with natural lightning-
caused fires, Indian burning established fire as an indispensable force shap-
ing Yosemite's ecology. When early park managers, in keeping with the limited
scientific knowledge of the day, suppressed Indian-set and natural fires, the
valley quickly became choked with underbrush, meadows receded, views of the
waterfalls became constricted, and the danger of truly devastating forest fires
mounted. Relying on the oral tradition of Indians and modern scientific understanding of the importance of fire in maintaining the long-range health of wild
lands, the National Park Service in the past few decades has stopped fighting
some natural fires and has instituted controlled burning of meadows and forest
lands in Yosemite, as well as other parks. Since fire can endanger human property and interrupt short-term recreational and economic activities, the new policy
has provoked some controversy. *Photograph by Phillip Scholz Ritterman. Courtesy
Yosemite Photographic Survey.*

Planning Yosemite's Future

A HISTORICAL RETROSPECTIVE

by Alfred Runte

In its original format, this collection of essays ended here, with the National Park Service triumphant in the establishment of Kings Canyon, Sequoia National Park lacking all but the gem of Mineral King, and Yosemite—despite growing pressures from visitation and development—still as magnificent as ever. It was fitting, perhaps, that a book largely commemorative of the national park idea should conclude on an optimistic note. The point, however, is that the modern history of California national parks has not been nearly as uplifting. To be sure, new parks have been added in the state, while former ones have been enlarged. But there is an "edge" to most recent park histories that visibly contrasts with earlier congratulatory anecdotes and narratives. The historian Susan Schrepfer, for example, has written of the 1960s *fight* for Redwood National Park. Similarly, the title of my own recent book defines Yosemite as an *embattled* wilderness. Still focusing on the West, if outside California, Richard Bartlett has further described Yellowstone as a wilderness *besieged*, much as Carsten Lien, writing for the Sierra Club, considers Olympic National Park in Washington state to be another Pacific Coast *battleground*.[1]

As such combative metaphors imply, the national parks today are immersed in a struggle between preservation and use. Granted, that has always been the case to some degree; it just seems that now the stakes have so measurably increased. Even twenty-five years ago, it was still possible to

believe that California and the nation would ultimately protect the national park system regardless of any alleged sacrifices to the economy. Now, it would appear, even the most isolated national parks cannot escape the consequences of civilization.

As early as 1910, John Muir bitterly summarized the problem as follows: "Nothing dollarable is safe, however guarded."[2] There followed, three years later, the worst reversal ever in the history of any national park: federal approval of a request by San Francisco to flood Yosemite's Hetch Hetchy Valley for a municipal water supply. Nonetheless, it could still be argued that America in 1913 did not know any better, or that the decision to turn the gorge over to San Francisco reflected the consensus of the time. Indeed, the national park system as a whole has been expanding ever since. Perhaps Hetch Hetchy was an anomaly. That interpretation, at least, still seemed valid well past the midpoint of the century.[3]

It was tenable, that is, until the 1960s, when plans to dam the Grand Canyon itself were brazenly unveiled, including one that would actually flood into the existing national park. Arguing its case for the construction of two major reservoirs, the U.S. Bureau of Reclamation pointed to the Southwest's burgeoning population, thirsting for abundant water and cheap hydroelectric power. Besides, the Bureau maintained, no one but environmental "elitists" got to see the bottom of the canyon in the first place. In contrast, once the reservoirs had filled, even the frailest senior citizen could make the pilgrimage by motorboat. "SHOULD WE ALSO FLOOD THE SISTINE CHAPEL SO TOURISTS CAN GET NEARER THE CEILING?" asked an outraged Sierra Club. Indeed, exclaimed David Brower, the club's outspoken executive director, "If we can't save the Grand Canyon, what the hell can we save?"[4]

Merely establishing the parks, it was finally obvious, had done nothing to protect them permanently. Beyond the lofty rhetoric of each park's enabling legislation lay a widening gulf between promise and reality. On the one hand, the United States had pledged that every park would be held inviolate. On the other—shades of John Muir's bitter observation that Americans valued the dollar more—such commitments to perpetuity seemed hopelessly naive in the face of continuing pressure on park resources by both public and private economic interest groups.

It was enough that historical threats to the national parks—especially calls for more dams—were clearly on the rise in the mid-twentieth century. So too, visitation had increased dramatically since the close of World War II. Suddenly, Muir's definition of what was "dollarable" had taken on a new twist. Might not millions of park visitors be a gold mine in their own right? Why log, dam, or excavate lands that so many people would actually *pay* to see? Sensing that opportunity, turn-of-the-century preservationists had courted the western railroads, risking the problem of overvisitation for the promise of park security. Obviously, the preferred scenario was parks crawling with too many tourists, rather than no parks at all. Fortunately, visitation was still kept in check by distance, time, and income. Only the well-to-do could afford the investment in transcontinental pleasure travel. By the end of World War II, however, such barriers were coming down. Rising wages, cheaper cars, and faster highways were finally putting the national parks within reach of the middle-class visitor.[5]

Increasingly, the eyes of the preservation community were fixed on California, whose three Sierra parks—and most notably Yosemite—had already begun to experience that fundamental shift in American travel patterns. As early as 1916, automobile vacationists to Yosemite had surpassed those arriving by rail, 14,527 as opposed to 14,251. The following season the ratio was nearly three to one, and by 1918 almost seven to one, 26,669 in contrast to 4,000. Although ridership on the Yosemite Valley Railroad quickly recovered following the close of World War I, the spurt to an average of more than 20,000 riders annually lasted but a few years, and was still dramatically outpaced by the number of visitors arriving by car. Then came the final blow to the fortunes of the Yosemite Valley Railroad—the completion in 1926 of the so-called All Year Highway between Merced and El Portal. By the close of the next fiscal year, September 30, 1927, a whopping 490,430 visitors had entered Yosemite National Park, only 13,565 of whom had taken the train.[6]

Even in the depths of the Great Depression, an average of 300,000 auto-tourists annually found their way into Yosemite Valley. On the eve of World War II, yearly visitation fell just short of 600,000.[7] Clearly, Yosemite was already an important test case in the art of accommodating such numbers while still upholding the integrity of the national parks as natural environments.

Or was the hope of accommodation merely wishful thinking? "When there was a vast reservoir of wilderness, when areas such as Yosemite were difficult of access," observed Ansel Adams, writing to David Brower in 1957, "there was a different kind of visitor; he came primarily for the *experience of the place*, and he was willing to sacrifice certain comforts and undergo considerable difficulties to gain this experience. As the areas became accessible, as the comforts increased, as the 'services' became more general, the character of the visitor-in-the-aggregate changed." Likewise, visitor services had mushroomed from the provision of basic necessities, namely food and shelter, to a long list of

Photographs document the effects of human intrusion, and its cessation, in Yosemite. *Opposite, above:* Yosemite Falls and Old Village store, 1953, photographer unknown. *Opposite, below:* the same scene as photographed in 1991 by Willie Osterman. By then, the Old Village had been relocated by the Park Service as part of its Mission 66 program. These and most of the other illustrations in this essay are from the ongoing Yosemite Photographic Survey. Under Project Director Brian Grogan and sponsored jointly by the Yosemite Association and the Ansel Adams Gallery, along with other benefactors, the survey has organized the talents of historians and some of the finest contemporary photographers to gather a representative set of historic photographs of Yosemite, and then to rephotograph the same views in order to produce a comprehensive photographic record of the park. The Yosemite Photographic Survey is creating a unique visual resource, of great value to historians and park managers alike, that will reveal changes in the landscape introduced by human actions and provide insights into evolving attitudes toward the national parks and wilderness. *Courtesy Yosemite Photographic Survey.*

comforts and luxuries more appropriate to a purely recreational setting. For example, Adams noted, Yosemite's park concession, "(which should have always been kept at a modest 'service' level) has become a 'resort' enterprise to which people are attracted for other reasons than the simple experience of the Natural Scene."[8]

As government statistics already implied, few assessments of the changing face of park tourism were more on target. As of 1954, total annual visitation to Yosemite had surpassed one million people. Even so, the Park Service was still determined to accommodate rather than discourage the flow of visitors. In 1955, for example, the agency won congressional approval for Mission 66, a ten-year, billion-dollar program intended to upgrade roads, parking lots, campgrounds, utility systems, and visitor centers in national parks coast to coast. This was in anticipation of the Park Service's golden anniversary in 1966, when fifty million visitors were expected to crowd the flagship western parks alone. In Yosemite, for example, the Park Service moved aggressively to complete the modernization of the historic Tioga Road, running east-west across the High Sierra via Tenaya Lake and Tuolumne Meadows. Here again, Ansel Adams and David Brower, among other leaders of the Sierra Club, bitterly protested the project, noting the deep scarring caused during preparation of the new right of way. In its defense, the Park Service reminded the Sierra Club that the flood of Yosemite visitors still continued to exceed expectations. Indeed, by 1967 annual visitation stood at two million, and by 1987 the National Park Service estimated that more than three million people a year were passing through Yosemite's entrance stations.[9]

Visitation itself, such figures confirmed, had evolved into a dominant threat to the sanctity of the national parks. Accommodating more and more people, no less than allowing public works, made uncompromising demands on wilderness, scenic landscapes, and the dwindling wildlife habitat. "One situation begets another," Ansel Adams complained, continuing his analysis in 1957. "Developments in the National Parks are more sharply tuned to the requirements of the average tourist— as a tourist—than to the nature and necessities of the areas themselves." Writing in agreement, the distinguished naturalist and social critic Joseph Wood Krutch also saw a linkage between the aimlessness of modern tourism and the problem of overcrowding. "Ours is so much an age of technology and the machine that machines come to be

loved for their own sake rather than used for other ends," he maintained. "Instead, for instance, of valuing the automobile because it may take one to a national park, the park comes to be valued because it is a place the automobile may be used to reach."[10]

The only viable solution, preservationists argued, was to do everything possible to discourage so-called frivolous visitation. "I am in complete agreement," Ansel Adams further confided in his memorandum to David Brower, "with the idea of removing from Yosemite ALL unnecessary operations, buildings, and activities." Granted, at this point in the park's evolution, it would be "a hard decision to make." Yet postponing it bore an even greater risk—the eventual destruction of the valley. "People, things, buildings, events, and evidence of occupation and use simply will have to go out of Yosemite if it is to function as a great inspirational shrine for all our people. That means me, you, hotels, stores, bars, shops—everything but the barest service necessities." While a bit less outspoken, Joseph Wood Krutch was equally convinced that the prevention of overcrowding hinged on restricting access and development to minimum service standards. "It would hardly be practicable to examine every visitor...to make him prove that he has come for a legitimate purpose," Krutch admitted, for example. Yet it seemed "perfectly possible to make the test automatically by having the road ask the question: 'Are you willing to take a little trouble to get there?'"[11]

And so, inevitably, Yosemite took center stage in the latest debate over access to the national parks, providing, as prophets since John Muir had long predicted, a classic example of too many people in too little space. In other western parks, such as Yellowstone and Glacier, visitation tended to disperse among widely scattered points of interest. In Yosemite, unfortunately, such was not the case. With the exception of the Mariposa Grove of giant sequoias, the most popular attraction was Yosemite Valley proper, barely seven miles long and only one mile wide. On any given day, the majority of visitors tended to funnel into the valley, choking roads, overflowing parking lots, and tramping across meadows. To make matters worse, visitation further concentrated in the eastern third of the valley, where the park's hotels, shops, stables, campgrounds, and restaurants had historically been located.

Yet, as Ansel Adams had observed as early as 1957, even original visitor services had been radically transformed. Turn-of-the-century summer camps and rustic hotels had evolved into a sophisticated infrastructure whose very air of permanence discouraged any call for its removal. Nonetheless, still voicing the concerns of a growing number of preservationists, Adams rejected the notion of "welcoming many millions to Yosemite per season, simply because there can be 'room' made for them. There has to be some kind of logical selectivity imposed." A perfect example, he suggested, was the National Gallery of Art. The gallery was naturally "pleased that its attendance has been so good—but the important fact is that the attendance is based solely on Art and the basic attraction of ART, and not on dances, bars, movies, nightly firefalls and vaudeville, swift roads, super-comfortable beds and adequate food, cocoa-cola stands, 'dude' rides and atrocious curios. No, the National Gallery of Art belongs to the people and serves *those who wish to attend* for the purpose of getting experience in art." His frustration now painfully obvious, Adams asked "why cannot the National Parks be planned and operated along the same logical lines?"[12]

Ironically, the more Yosemite Valley drifted from a natural area into a resort, the more that Adams himself was to prove the power of economic self-interest over principle *or* consistency. As John Muir had earlier implied, the fundamental flaw in park legislation was the privatization—for profit—of the sale of food, lodging, supplies, and transportation to incoming visitors. Obviously, anyone holding a concession had constant incentive to promote rather than discourage that flow of new business. Adams may have thought himself immune, but such was not the case. Through his father-in-law, Harry Best, he had already inherited Best's Studio in Yosemite Village. In 1972, Adams and his wife Virginia renamed the historic concession the Ansel Adams Gallery.[13] Fifteen years earlier, Adams had vehemently complained to David Brower that *everything* ought to be removed from Yosemite Valley. Now, however, the renowned photographer was not so sure. Granted, he may simply have changed his mind. Or was it that his business, like his reputation, had suddenly begun to soar?

Whatever his motives, his reversal was complete. "Any attempt to reduce Yosemite Valley to a wilderness area would be futile—socially and politically—and would be a real disservice to the people at large," he wrote just prior to renaming his gallery. "The maximum appropriate number of people

should see Yosemite and should experience its incredible quality. To shut it off from the world would be somewhat similar to closing St. Paul's Cathedral for the sake of the architecture!" Perhaps anticipating the reaction of astonished critics, he qualified his view: "This statement does not imply any relaxation of the wilderness qualities of all other areas of the park!" There was an exception, he immediately interjected: "The present High Sierra Camps do not, in my opinion, violate wilderness qualities as they now exist. I personally feel that a High Sierra Camp near the north rim of Yosemite Valley would be a logical link in the chain. Likewise, establishment of more public camp grounds along the existing Tioga Road and the Glacier Point Road, and at Wawona, would not violate wilderness."[14]

In short, whether he admitted it or not, Adams the preservationist had turned into Adams the concessionaire. In his emerging role as a businessman, wilderness preservation (defined as an absolute commitment to the protection of natural values) was suddenly more or less objectionable in direct proportion to the distance of that wilderness from any of the park's centers of *commercial* activity. Yet the inescapable truth remained. Yosemite Valley, not the distant high country, was still the heart of the park, the very reason for its founding and later enlargement in the first place. Which scenario, then, would prevail—one leading to the eventual restoration of the valley floor as the soul of Yosemite National Park, or, as underscored by Adams's own dramatic about face, one tending to allow even greater commercial appropriation?

The recent history of Yosemite may be summarized as a series of disquieting answers—disquieting, that is, if by the term *national park* is meant a commitment to the protection of natural values free of commercial distraction. As so often occurred in the past, every reaffirmation of that commitment in the last few decades was again to be discredited or diluted. The most recent period of controversy erupted in 1973, when the Music Corporation of America (commonly known simply as MCA) purchased the Yosemite Park and Curry Company, thereby releasing to MCA the remaining twenty years of the thirty-year concessions contract that was to run from 1963 to 1993. The new owner immediately embarked on a program to increase profits from its subsidiary. Barely months after its purchase, MCA began promoting a host of new projects, including expanded commercial facilities throughout the national park. Yet it was the company's proposals for Yosemite Valley that quickly alarmed preservationists. "Why is a primary goal to eliminate or substantially reduce automobiles from Yosemite Valley?" asked Edward C. Hardy, the newly appointed chief operating officer of the Yosemite Park and Curry Company. "The costs of such a plan far exceed any marginal benefits." All across Yosemite the actual problem was not the number of automobiles or tourists, but rather the *lack* of parking lots. "Planning," he therefore maintained, "should focus on alternate travel options, such as the Aerial Tramway to Glacier Point and increased parking within the valley."[15]

As part of a multi-year effort to prepare a master plan for Yosemite, the Park Service had already studied—and shelved—the cable car proposal. Similarly, Hardy's call for more parking lots violated a fragile—but nonetheless sincere—consensus that all private automobiles should eventually be barred from Yosemite Valley proper. As a significant first step, the former owners of the Yosemite Park and Curry Company had already agreed in 1970 to cooperate with the Park Service by closing the eastern third of the valley to all private vehicles, and to inaugurate in their stead a public shuttle system of propane-fueled motor buses. Hardy's now apparent opposition to extending the shuttle system at the expense of auto-access, as well as high-level support within MCA for the cable car proposal, suggested that the company was then still trying to determine the final outcome of the entire planning process.

In fact, no definitive proposals for the future of Yosemite had apparently been reached. Even in published form, each version of the master plan was still labeled as a draft. Yet, whatever the case, preservationists objected, insisting that the entire process had been tainted from the outset. Most notably, MCA alone had been given access to government planning teams and senior park officials. Finally, in December 1974, the Park Service agreed to start anew. Led by the Sierra Club and other national environmental groups, preservationists won further concessions, including public participation through a series of citizens' workshops. All told, more than sixty thousand people contributed their views on the future of Yosemite, most by choosing from among a range of development options on a standardized planning kit. In 1978 the results of those surveys allegedly found their way into a revised master plan; following two more years of public comment and additional open

forums, a so-called general management plan was finally released on October 30, 1980.[16]

Essentially, the plan called for maintaining the status quo. Other than modest reductions (roughly ten to fifteen percent) in obviously non-essential buildings, facilities, and visitor services, nothing radical had emerged over five years of public input. Even so, full implementation of the plan was never a serious option. It *did* call for some reductions, however modest, all of which were challenged by MCA officials. Proposals to limit visitation in Yosemite were also contrary to the views of the new federal administration, led by President Ronald Reagan and his secretary of the interior, James Watt. Management plan or not, its particulars could be thwarted simply by starving it for funds.[17]

This itself, accordingly, became another excuse to manipulate the plan, or, when convenient, to ignore it entirely. Pressure from the concessionaire to improve park facilities and profits continued. To be sure, there would be no cable car built to Glacier Point. In 1983, however, a once spacious lounge at Yosemite Lodge was gutted, subdivided, and wholly replaced by a $282,000 bar, conference meeting rooms, and lodge store annex, all in violation of the general management plan.[18] Predictably, Park Service and MCA officials objected to that interpretation, arguing that the bar, although greatly expanded, was really not a new *facility*. Rather, it was the former lodge bar, just in a different location. Park Superintendent Robert Binnewies further applauded its brightness and spaciousness, noting that for once problem drinkers would be "forced into the light." The old location, he explained, was very cramped and too dark, making it difficult for park rangers to monitor anyone's behavior. "We tried to create an atmosphere where you can come in, relax, and enjoy the beautiful surroundings while enjoying your favorite beverage," further explained Debbie Price, general manager of the lodge. It was, indeed, "a guest improvement we can be proud of."[19]

That the sale of alcoholic beverages might invite exactly the opposite interpretation—namely, how far Yosemite had drifted from the principles of preservation—escaped all but those who openly admitted that the park had been consistently undermined by commercial pursuits. If nothing else, alcohol was another symbol of how easily a commonplace product might invade an uncommon resource. As of March 1989, there were thirty-five outlets for beer, wine, or liquor in Yosemite

The Yosemite National Park hamlet of Foresta after the great fire of 1991. The ever-present danger of forest fire, aggravated by human activities—such as fire suppression—haunts Yosemite and other national parks, exposing contradictions between recreation and preservation and causing reevaluation of management policies. *Photograph by Steve Dzerigian. Courtesy Yosemite Photographic Survey.*

National Park, twenty-three of them located on the valley floor alone.[20] Even so, as late as 1991, yet another superintendent, Michael V. Finley, refused to acknowledge (at least publicly) that there might be a direct correlation between Yosemite's rising crime rate and the promotion of alcohol. As proof of that correlation, the Yosemite Valley jail had recently been expanded from sixteen to twenty-two beds. A nearby courthouse, completed in 1987, now heard one thousand cases annually, several hundred involving assault, drunk and disorderly conduct, and driving while intoxicated. Yet other visitors, Finley noted, objected just as

strongly to the sale of candy and pizza (although no one jailed in Yosemite Valley had apparently ever been arrested for driving under the influence of sugar or tomato paste).[21] Obviously, anyone, not just Ansel Adams, could forget the distinction (or purposely ignore it) between making a valid comparison and retreating into subterfuge.

Throughout the 1980s, the increasing frequency of such statements rationalizing the further development of Yosemite foretold that the park might be approaching another moment of truth. As one barometer that change was in the offing, the existing concessions contract would expire in 1993. For another, 1989 would mark the 125th anniversary of the original Yosemite Grant, and 1990 the centennial of Yosemite National Park. Finally, there were those three million visitors pushing at Yosemite's gates, a figure that had further climbed to an estimated 3.75 million by 1992.[22]

As predicted, the approach of each milestone or anniversary rekindled public interest in Yosemite National Park, not only in the history of its evolution but even more so in its future. And what that future should be, it was also apparent, was still as controversial as ever. Taking up where they had left off during the late 1970s, preservationists continued to press, at the very least, for implementing the broader proposals of the general management plan of 1980, especially limitations on day use, motor vehicles, and overnight accommodations. Just as vehemently, however, MCA officials still argued that those goals were much too restrictive. In particular, the suggestion that visitation was too high was seen by MCA as purely an arbitrary judgment, and at that, one that reflected only a few days out of the entire year. Yosemite could take the load, MCA insisted, if just a bit more attention were paid to expanding parking lots in strategic locations. Although caught in the middle, the Park Service itself still seemed to side with its traditional mandate to promote access. In the future, as in the past, denying anyone the privilege of seeing Yosemite would be condemned as selfish and elitist.[23]

In 1990, however, both the Park Service's and MCA's alleged concerns for the average visitor were again seriously undermined by yet another revelation indicating that profit was still the driving force behind the park concession. Specifically, journalists revealed in widely disseminated sensational accounts, the franchise fee the company paid for conducting business in Yosemite amounted to a mere three-quarters of one percent of the Curry Company's gross receipts.[24] The concessionaire was, in effect, being allowed to conduct business in Yosemite with virtually no return to the public, while the company continued to exert influence to thwart implementation of the 1980 plan. A second major bombshell was not far behind. In late December 1990, the Matsushita Corporation, a major Japanese electronics firm, bought out MCA, thereby gaining full control over all of its subsidiaries, including the Yosemite Park and Curry Company. Ever since acquiring the Yosemite franchise in 1973, MCA had always maintained that the proportion of its profits from Curry alone had been relatively small. Nevertheless, leading the opposition to foreign ownership of a national-park franchise, Secretary of the Interior Manuel Lujan demanded that Matsushita sell the Yosemite Park and Curry Company back to American investors.[25]

If reluctantly, Matsushita acceded to Lujan's demands. As agreed, the company would retain certain rights to the concession for the remaining life of the contract, only two and a half years. In effect, however, Matsushita would entrust the period of transition—including a portion of the profits and terms of the final sale—to the National Park Foundation, chartered by Congress in 1967 to oversee private gifts to the national parks. There matters stood on the eve of the next concessions contract, slated to take effect on September 30, 1993, and, as promised by Secretary Lujan, to reflect higher franchise fees for the privilege of doing business inside the national parks.[26]

Despite Secretary Lujan's general promise, the question of Yosemite's future is still no closer to being resolved as the twentieth century draws to a close. And thus there remains that "edge" to modern park histories. For Yosemite, especially, the story trails off without a clear and unmistakable finish. The secretary of the interior pledged change, but what in fact will *really* change? Has the system been truly reformed or has the government once again merely switched the players, perhaps modifying, but not *eliminating,* the fundamental sources of Yosemite's long history of conflict and controversy? Are the sources of the controversy mechanical, or in truth philosophical? In other words, is the solution as easy as tinkering with an outmoded concessions contract, or will Yosemite's problems in fact defy resolution until Americans decide, once and for all, what the *primary* purpose of the national parks ought to be?

If history is any guide, whoever wins the right to manage the renewed concessions contract will just as quickly embrace the argument that the popular mood of American tourism should govern every means of park access and that facilities, especially in the valley, should be maintained, if not expanded. Consequently, the stake of development will remain poised at the heart of Yosemite National Park, still in recognition of the fact that the vast majority of visitors come not to see wilderness but rather the fabled grandeur of Yosemite Valley itself. "The first point to be kept in mind then," warned Frederick Law Olmsted as early as 1865, "is the preservation and maintenance as exactly as is possible of the natural scenery, the

Ranger and visitor cabins, Yosemite Valley. One of the most controversial provisions of the management plan for Yosemite National Park adopted by the Park Service in 1980 is the relocation of employee housing and many visitor services from the valley to the new "towns" to be built around the periphery of the park. Shortage of funds, in addition to conflicts of values and interests between environmental preservation and expanding visitor services, even within the Park Service itself, have so far stalled implementation of most of the 1980 plan. The de-urbanization of Yosemite Valley remains a vital issue into the foreseeable future. *Photograph by Robert Dawson. Courtesy Yosemite Photographic Survey.*

restriction, that is to say, within the narrowest limits consistent with the necessary accommodation of visitors, of all artificial constructions and the prevention of all constructions markedly inharmonious with the scenery or which would unnecessarily obscure, distort, or detract from the dignity of the scenery."[27]

Fundamentally, the problems of Yosemite and all national parks derive from the nation's reluctance to embrace Olmsted's first principle—absolute concern for the *dignity* of the scenery. The common rebuttal, predictably, is that dignity is only relative. It is possible, for example, to mix scenery with alcohol, provided that enjoyment of the one does not conflict with the other. The problem, Olmsted forewarned, was that any such con-

cession was only bound to escalate. "Before many years," he carefully explained, Yosemite's current "hundreds" of visitors would "become thousands and in a century the whole number of visitors will be counted by the millions." Accordingly, any "injury to the scenery so slight that it may be unheeded by any visitor now, will be one of deplorable magnitude when its effect upon each visitor's enjoyment is multiplied by these millions."[28] To be sure, Olmsted was no elitist. As the co-designer and first superintendent of New York City's already fabled Central Park, he more than anyone stood firmly behind the principle of full public access. But access was only that—the *privilege* of entry and nothing more. The question to be asked of Yosemite's current "hundreds" as

Already a noted landscape architect and creator of New York City's famous Central Park, Frederick Law Olmsted came to California in 1863 as superintendent of John C. Frémont's estate in Mariposa, near the newly discovered Yosemite Valley. Although there was little direct evidence for his participation, historians agree that he was probably influential in the national campaign that resulted in the 1864 creation by Congress of Yosemite Valley as the nation's first wilderness park. Olmsted became a leader of the state of California's Yosemite Valley commission appointed to govern the park. Later in the 1860s, he participated in the landscape planning for the new University of California in Berkeley, as well as for Stanford University in Palo Alto in the 1880s. *Courtesy Bancroft Library.*

well as its future "millions" was simple and straightforward: Is the privilege of your being here access enough? Are you here for the experience of the *place,* for what this park, as a natural environment, has to offer you in and of itself?

If there is any regrettable chapter in Yosemite's long and intriguing history, it is that Olmsted's visionary pronouncements were purposefully ignored. Even as he resigned his nominal appointment as head of the first state Board of Yosemite Park Commissioners, two standards of access were replacing his one. His, unavoidably, was also left more vulnerable to protestations regarding "fairness." Yosemite, it was increasingly argued, could safely be compartmentalized into developed and undeveloped zones, thereby accommodating everyone's perception of dignified scenery. Inevitably, in future decades Yosemite was only further pressured, as managers, concessionaires, and visitors alike—again forgetting Olmsted—chose expedience over stewardship, arguing that Yosemite might be no better—but it could be no worse—if dignity bent just a little more to the latest national obsession, addiction, or public whim. As enumerated by Ansel Adams, it might be the automobile one day, and alcohol the next. Yet Adams himself proved incapable of resisting individual temptation for the sake of a common good. Ultimately, Olmsted's challenge was too difficult, and Adams's personal struggle for consistency was representative of the nation's very own.

On this point, at least, history is clear—all across the national park system Olmsted's predicted "millions" have finally come true. Yosemite's unarguable uniqueness may not survive unless, heeding Olmsted, the nation ultimately agrees to allow only his vision of proper access. Will Americans, then, have the courage to restore Yosemite to a semblance of its former grandeur? Will they insist that mild inconvenience, rusticity, or public transportation should act as social filters, while remembering that fundamental question: Are you in fact here for the experience of the place, for what Yosemite, free of distraction, has to offer in and of itself? Not without precedent, in the perception of the national parks as an inviolable public trust—rather than in any standard less demanding—still seems to lie the only legitimate set of choices for guiding the visions of both 1864 and 1890 into the twenty-first century.

Alfred Runte is a public historian and author living in Seattle. A specialist on the national parks, he received his Ph.D. in history from the University of California, Santa Barbara. His highly acclaimed National Parks: The American Experience *(University of Nebraska Press, 1979) has now appeared in a second, revised edition (1987), and he has also recently revised his popular* Trains of Discovery: Western Railroads and the National Parks *(Roberts Rinehart, 1990). Runte's latest work is* Yosemite: The Embattled Wilderness *(University of Nebraska Press, 1990).*

Notes

RUNTE, "Introduction," pp. 1–5.

1. *Congressional Globe*, 38th Cong., 1st sess., May 17, 1864, 2301.
2. U.S., *Statutes at Large*, 13 (1864): 325.
3. Ibid. For more on the precedent-setting importance of the Yosemite Park Act of 1864, see Alfred Runte, *Yosemite: The Embattled Wilderness* (Lincoln and London: University of Nebraska Press, 1990), chapter 2.
4. State of California, Geological Survey, J.D. Whitney, State Geologist, *The Yosemite Book: A Description of the Yosemite Valley and the Adjacent Region of the Sierra Nevada, and of the Big Trees of California* (New York: Julius Bien, 1868), 22.
5. *Hutchings v. Low*, 82 U.S. (1872), 94.
6. The ongoing management controversy in Yosemite Valley was referenced in both the House and Senate debates leading to the establishment of Yellowstone. See *Congressional Globe*, 42d Cong., 2d sess., January 30, 1872, 697, and ibid., February 27, 1872, 1243.
7. U.S., *Statutes at Large*, 26 (1890): 478, 650-52. U.S., Department of the Interior, *Report of the Secretary for the Fiscal Year Ended June 30, 1891* (Washington, D.C.: Government Printing Office, 1891), 123-26.
8. A valuable reference to the changing status of all national-park lands is U.S., Department of the Interior, National Park Service, *The National Parks: Index 1985* (Washington, D.C.: Government Printing Office, 1985).

DILSAVER & STRONG, "Sequoia & Kings Canyon," pp. 13–31.

1. This article is based primarily on Douglas H. Strong's unpublished dissertation, "A History of Sequoia National Park" (Syracuse University, 1964); Strong, *Trees—or Timber? The Story of Sequoia and Kings Canyon National Parks*, rev. ed. (Three Rivers, California: Sequoia Natural History Association, 1986); and Lary M. Dilsaver and William C. Tweed, *Challenge of the Big Trees: A Resource History of Sequoia and Kings Canyon National Parks* (Three Rivers, California: Sequoia Natural History Association, 1990). The authors are grateful to Deborah Osterberg for aid in obtaining illustrations, Beret Strong for editorial assistance, and William Tweed for suggested revisions.
2. See Douglas H. Strong, "Sequoia National Park: Discovery and Exploration," *The Western Explorer* 4 (September 1966): 1-27.
3. See A.B. Elsasser, *Indians of the Sequoia and Kings Canyon National Parks*, rev. ed. (Three Rivers, California: Sequoia Natural History Association, 1988).
4. Strong, "Discovery and Exploration," 22-27.
5. Clarence King, *Mountaineering in the Sierra Nevada* (New York: W.W. Norton, 1935), 295.
6. John Muir, "God's First Temples," *Sacramento Daily-Record Union*, February 5, 1876. See also William Tweed, "John Muir in the Southern Sierra," *Valley Trails* (Stockton: Stockton Corral of Westerners, 1976), 7-12.
7. See Samuel T. Porter, "The Silver Rush at Mineral King, California, 1873-1882" (M.A. thesis, Fresno State College, 1961).
8. Strong, "A History of Sequoia National Park," 61, 65.
9. U.S., Senate, *Congressional Record*, 47th Cong., 1st sess., 1881, 13, pt. 1:78. For a brief history, see William Tweed, *Kaweah Remembered* (Three Rivers, California: Sequoia Natural History Association, 1986).
11. The account that follows is based on Douglas H. Strong, "The History of Sequoia National Park, 1876-1926, Part I: The Movement to Establish a Park," *Southern California Quarterly* 48 (June 1966): 137-167. See also "The History of the Sierra Forest Reserve," June 13, 1902, and "The Sequoia National Park," *Bakersfield Morning Echo*, June 18, 1902.
12. U.S., Congress, House, *Congressional Record*, 51st Cong., 1st sess., 1890, 21, pt. 8:7834.
13. U.S., *Statutes at Large*, 26:478.
14. Ibid., 26:651.
15. Richard J. Orsi, "'Wilderness Saint' and 'Robber Baron': The Anomalous Partnership of John Muir and the Southern Pacific Company for the Preservation of Yosemite National Park," *Pacific Historian* 29 (Summer/Fall 1985): 148. See also George Stewart to Colonel White, June 8, 1929, Sequoia National Park Archives (cited hereafter as SNPA), and "General Grant National Park," *Bakersfield Morning Echo*, June 21, 1902.
16. Tweed, *Kaweah Remembered*. Also see Strong, "The History of Sequoia National Park," Part I, 161.
17. U.S., *Statutes at Large*, 26: 1095. The account that follows is based on Douglas H. Strong, "The Sierra Forest Reserve: The Movement to Preserve the San Joaquin Valley Watershed," *California Historical Society Quarterly* 46 (March 1967): 3-17.
18. The petition is located in the National Archives, General Land Office Records, Record Group 49, Sierra National Forest File, Box 143, Part 7. SNPA also has a copy.
19. U.S., *Statutes at Large*, 27:1059.
20. The account that follows is based on Strong, "A History of Sequoia National Park," 193-292. For a briefer treatment, see Strong. "The History of Sequoia National Park, 1876-1926, Part III: The Struggle to Enlarge the Park," *Southern California Quarterly* 48 (December 1966):

369-399.

21. U.S., *Statutes at Large*, 44:818.

22. The movement to establish Kings Canyon is discussed in Dilsaver and Tweed, *Challenge of the Big Trees*, chapter 7, and in Lary Dilsaver, "Conservation Conflict and the Founding of Kings Canyon National Park," also in this issue of *California History*. See also Francis P. Farquhar, "Legislative History of Sequoia and Kings Canyon National Parks," *Sierra Club Bulletin* 26 (February 1941): 42-58.

23. U.S., *Statutes at Large*, 54:41.

24. The account that follows is based on Strong, *Trees—or Timber*, 48-49.

25. U.S., *Statutes at Large*, 79:446.

26. For an insider's view, see John L. Harper, *Mineral King: Public Concern with Government Policy* (Arcata, Ca: Pacifica Publishing Co., 1982).

27. Susan R. Schrepfer, "Perspectives on Conservation: Sierra Club Strategies in Mineral King," *Journal of Forest History* 20 (October 1976): 176-190.

28. U.S., *Statutes at Large*, 92:3479.

29. The account that follows is based on Douglas H. Strong, "The History of Sequoia National Park, 1876-1926, Part II: The Problems of the Early Years," *Southern California Quarterly* 48 (September 1966): 265-288.

30. *Report of the Acting Superintendent of the Sequoia and General Grant National Parks* (Washington: Government Printing Office, 1899), 10. Cited hereinafter as *Superintendent Report*.

31. Ibid., 1910, 13.

32. U.S., *Statutes at Large*, 39:535. For an insider's view, see Horace M. Albright, *The Birth of the National Park Service: The Founding Years, 1913-1933* (Salt Lake City: Howe Brothers, 1985).

33. *Superintendent Report*, 1890-1914, particularly 1903.

34. Strong, "A History of Sequoia National Park," 178-192.

35. See Dilsaver and Tweed, *Challenge of the Big Trees*, especially chapter 5. See also Rick Hydrick, "The Genesis of National Park Management: John Roberts White and Sequoia National Park, 1920-1947," *Journal of Forest History* 28 (April 1984): 68-81.

36. Jim Corson, "A Brief History of the Generals Highway," June 4, 1963, an unpublished chronology; John White to H.E. Patterson, July 16, 1921; Arno Cammerer to W.B. Greeley, July 20, 1922; and SNP,

"Press Bulletin on Completion of Generals Highway," June 19, 1935; all in "Roads and Trails" in SNPA. See also *Superintendent Report*, 1920-1926.

37. William Tweed, "Sequoia National Park Concessions, 1898-1926," *Pacific Historian* 16 (1972): 36-60. See also *Superintendent Report*, 1926-1930.

38. The *Sierra Club Bulletin* contains frequent references to the need for more and better trails. See also correspondence between White and William Colby and Francis Farquhar in "Sierra Club," SNPA.

39. U.S. Forest Service, "John Muir Trail: A History," 1933, SNPA; and William Tweed, *The High Sierra Trail* (Three Rivers, California: Sequoia Natural History Association, 1982).

40. William Tweed, "The Early Natural History Association" (1978), SNP library.

41. Marcella M. Sherfly, "The National Park Service and the First World War," *Journal of Forest History*, 22 (October 1978): 203-5. See also White to Horace Albright, August 2 and 6, 1931; Albright to John White, November 10, 1931; SNP, *Wildlife Management Plan* (March 1987), 11-15; and Walter Fry, "A Twenty-Five Year Survey of the Animals of Sequoia National Park" (1928); all in "Wildlife" and "Resource Management," SNPA.

42. *Superintendent Report*, 1931.

43. John White, "Atmosphere in the National Parks," an address at the Special Superintendent's Meeting, Washington, D.C., February 10, 1936, transcript in SNPA. The role of landscape architects is revealed in *Superintendent Report*, 1920-1934.

44. See John C. Paige, *The Civilian Conservation Corps and the National Park Service, 1933-1942: An Administrative History* (Washington, D.C.: National Park Service, 1985), 51-65, 183, and SNP, "Statement of Conditions in Sequoia National Park Before CCC (1933) and Now (1941)," a report to the superintendent filed under "Civilian Conservation Corps," SNPA.

45. Paige, *The Civilian Conservation Corps*, 51-65.

46. See Dilsaver and Tweed, *Challenge of the Big Trees*, chapters 5-9. For correspondence on this issue, see "Giant Forest Planning," especially White to Newton Drury, September 16, 1944, SNPA. *Superintendent Report*, 1930-1947, also contains a part of the story.

47. White to Newton Drury, November 23, 1944, summarizes the history of the re-

moval question, in "Giant Forest Planning," SNPA.

48. Dilsaver and Tweed, *Challenge of the Big Trees*, chapter 6.

49. White to Drury, November 23, 1944, SNPA.

50. Newton Drury, "The National Parks in Wartime," *American Forests* 49 (August 1943): 375-78. See also *Superintendent Report*, 1942-1946.

51. Dilsaver and Tweed, *Challenge of the Big Trees*, chapters 6 and 8. See also White to Drury, November 23, 1944 and September 16, 1944, SNPA.

52. See Conrad Wirth, *Parks, Politics and the People* (Norman: University of Oklahoma Press, 1980), especially 59-62 and 237-263; *Superintendent Report*, 1947, 1953; SNP, "Mission 66 Accomplishments, July 1, 1956-June 30, 1966," in "Developments," SNPA.

53. For one of the earliest contributions, see Charles C. Adams, *An Ecological Survey in Northern Michigan: A Report from the University Museum, University of Michigan* (Michigan Board of Geological Survey Report, 1905).

54. For a summary of early resource management, see Lowell Sumner, "Biological Research and Management in the National Park Service: A History," *The George Wright Forum* 3 (August 1983): 3-27.

55. Emilio Meinecke, "Memorandum on the Effects of Tourist Traffic on Plant Life, Particularly Big Trees, Sequoia National Park, California," May 1926, unpublished report, in "Vegetation," SNPA.

56. Sumner, "Biological Research and Management," 5-16.

57. See sections on wildlife and vegetation management in *Superintendent Report*, 1930-1941.

58. Emilio Meinecke, "Relocation of Public and Operator Developments in Sequoia National Park," a confidential report to the National Park Service, November 1944, in "Giant Forest," SNPA.

59. Yosemite National Park, *Report on the Effects of Human Impact Upon the Giant Sequoias of the Mariposa and Tuolumne Groves—Yosemite National Park*, report to Superintendent Preston, 1954, SNPA.

60. Carl W. Sharsmith, *A Report on the Status, Changes and Ecology of Backcountry Meadows in Sequoia and Kings Canyon National Parks* (1959), copy in SNP Library.

61. Richard Hartesveldt, "The Effects of Human Impact Upon Sequoia Gigantea and Its Environment in the Mariposa

Grove" (1959), a preliminary report to the National Park Service, copy in Resources Management Office, SNP.

62. Stanley Cain and others, "A Vignette of Primitive America," *Sierra Club Bulletin* 48 (March 1963): 2-11.

63. U.S., *Statutes at Large*, 88:577.

64. See David J. Simon and Joseph L. Sax, *Our Common Lands* (Washington, D.C.: National Parks and Conservation Association, 1988), especially chapter 4.

65. SNP, *Sierra District Backcountry Report, 1962-1972*, in Sierra District Ranger's Office, Ash Mountain Headquarters, SNP.

66. SNP and U.S. Forest Service, *A Use Limit Plan for Portions of the John Muir Wilderness and Kings Canyon National Park* (March 16, 1973).

67. Dilsaver and Tweed, *Challenge of the Big Trees*, chapters 7 and 8.

68. See John L. Harper, *Mineral King*.

69. SNP, *Mineral King Comprehensive Management Plan* (November 1980).

70. SNP, *Wildlife Management Plan* (March 1987), 11-15.

71. SNP, *Fire Management Plan* (April 1984 revision), 21-31.

72. SNP, "Recommendations of the Giant Forest Development Meeting," (June 1960), in "Giant Forest Development," SNPA.

73. SNP, *Giant Forest Development Concept Plan* (April 1980). For an earlier plan, see Sasaki, Walker and Associates, *Development Concept Plan, Giant Forest and Lodgepole, Sequoia and Kings Canyon National Parks, California* (1974). For a review of the evolution of the final plan, see Dilsaver and Tweed, *Challenge of the Big Trees*, chapter 9.

74. Interview of Harold Werner, SNP fisheries biologist, by Lary Dilsaver, October 16, 1985.

75. Interview of Tom Nichols, SNP fire management specialist, by Lary Dilsaver, June 23, 1989.

BLODGETT, "Yosemite," pp. 33–47.

1. Francis P. Farquhar, "A Scene of Wonder and Curiosity," in *Yosemite: Saga of a Century 1864-1964* (Oakhurst, CA: Sierra Star Press, 1964), 11-12; Linda Wedel Greene, *Yosemite: The Park and Its Resources: Historic Resource Study; A History of the Discovery, Management and Physical Development of Yosemite National Park, California.* (Washington, D.C.: United States Department of Interior, National Park Service, 1987), I, 32-34; David Robertson, *West of Eden: A History of the Art and Literature of Yosemite* (Yosemite National Park: Yosemite Natural History Association and Wilderness Press, 1984), 4-5; Carl P. Russell, *One Hundred Years in Yosemite: The Story of A Great National Park and Its Friends* (Yosemite National Park: Yosemite Natural History Association, 1959), 48-50; and Margaret Sanborn, *Yosemite: Its Discovery, Its Wonders and Its People* (New York: Random House, 1981), 79-81.

2. Greene, *Yosemite Resource Study*, I, 34-35; Bill and Mary Hood, "Yosemite's First Photographers," in *Yosemite Saga*, 49-52; Hans Huth, *Nature and the American: Three Centuries of Changing Attitudes* (Berkeley and Los Angeles: University of California Press, 1957), 144-146; and Huth, "Yosemite: The History of an Idea," *Sierra Club Bulletin* 33 (March 1948): 64-65.

3. The quotation from the early tourist is drawn from an article in *The Mariposa Democrat*, August 5, 1856, as edited by Ansel F. Hall and reprinted under the title, "The Early Days in Yosemite," in *The California Historical Society Quarterly* I (January 1923): 274. The letter from Raymond to Conness is quoted in Huth, "Yosemite," 67. The final quotation in the paragraph is taken from Kevin Starr, *Americans and the California Dream 1850-1915* (Santa Barbara and Salt Lake City: Peregrine Smith, 1981, paperback reprint), 173. Also see Greene, *Yosemite Resource Study*, I, 51-53, Huth, "Yosemite," 68, Sanborn, *Yosemite*, 99, and Starr, *California Dream*, 175-82.

4. The Yosemite legislation is reproduced in Greene, *Yosemite Resource Study*, III, Appendix D. The quotation is from Greene, *Yosemite Resource Study*, I, 61. Also consult Huth, "Yosemite," 68, and Alfred Runte, *National Parks: The American Experience* (Lincoln: University of Nebraska Press, 1987), 28-30.

5. Detailed information about the earliest services available for travelers in the Yosemite region may be found in Greene, *Yosemite Resource Study*, I, 40-45, Russell, *One Hundred Years*, 92-94, Sanborn, *Yosemite*, 81-87, and Shirley Sargent, *Yosemite and Its Innkeepers: The Story of a Great Park and Its Chief Concessionaires* (Yosemite: Flying Spur Press, 1975), 11-12.

6. The quotation is from a letter written by William E. Boardman to Benjamin Davis Wilson, July 21, 1861 (WN 1186), located in the B. D. Wilson Collection, Henry E. Huntington Library, San Marino, California. Also consult Francis P. Farquhar, editor, *The Ralston-Fry Wedding and The Wedding Journey to Yosemite, May 20, 1858* (Berkeley: The Friends of the Bancroft Library, 1961), and the 1870 account by Olive Logan entitled "Does It Pay to Visit Yo Semite?" reprinted in *Yosemite Saga*, 13-15.

7. Greene, *Yosemite Resource Study*, I, 78, 89-91; Russell, *One Hundred Years*, 61-63; and Sanborn, *Yosemite*, 198-199.

8. The guidebook quoted is *Bancroft's Tourist Guide: Yosemite, San Francisco and Around the Bay (South)* (San Francisco: A. L. Bancroft and Co., 1871), 9-10. Similar advice was proffered by Charles Nordhoff, *California, For Health, Pleasure, and Residence: A Book for Travelers and Settlers* (New York: Harper and Brothers, 1872). Also consult Greene, *Yosemite Resource Study* I, 80-97, Russell, *One Hundred Years*, 93-97, and Margaret Schlichtmann, "Memories of the Big Oak Flat Road," in *Yosemite Saga*, 29-31.

9. Greene, *Yosemite Resource Study* I, 115-117; Russell, *One Hundred Years*, 93-94; Sanborn, *Yosemite*, 94-98; and Sargent, *Innkeepers*, 12-13.

10. The quotation is from an undated brochure advertising the saloon in the "Yosemite National Park" file, Ephemera Collection, Rare Books Department, Huntington Library. Also refer Greene, *Yosemite Resource Study*, I, 122-132, 126-127, 133, 135-138, Russell, *One Hundred Years*, 101-106, and Sanborn, *Yosemite*, 83-91.

11. Greene, *Yosemite Resource Study*, I, 69-77 and 89-98, Russell, *One Hundred Years*, 150-151, and Sanborn, *Yosemite*, 99-100.

12. The figures are assembled from Walter E. Dennison, compiler, *Information for the Use of Yosemite Visitors* (Sacramento: James J. Ayres, Supt. State Printing, 1886), 9-13. The 1884 party to Yosemite Valley is described in H. M. Barton, *A Trip to the Yosemite Valley and the Mariposa Grove of Big Trees, California* (Dublin: Ponsonby and Weldrick, 1885), 7. Similar parties are described in W. F. Butler, *Far Out; Rovings Retold* (London: Wm. Isbister, Ltd., 1880), and Constance F. Gordon Cumming, *Granite Crags* (London and Edinburgh: W. Blackwood and Sons, 1884), among other accounts.

13. Greene, *Yosemite Resource Study* I, 126-132 & 156-157; Russell, *One Hundred Years*, 101-103 & 111, and Sargent, *Innkeepers*, 14.

14. For a description of the renovated Hutchings' House under J. K. Barnard's management, consult *Barnard's Hotel and Cottages, Yosemite Valley, California* (n.p., 189?). The broader story of private operators in the valley can be traced through Greene, *Yosemite Resource Study*, I, 126-133, and Russell, *One Hundred Years*, 99-101.

15. The quotation is from Charles Nordhoff, *California* (n.p.: Ten Speed Press, 1973, paperback reprint), 71. Also see Greene, *Yosemite Resource Study*, I, 145-146, and Russell, *One Hundred Years*, 106-07.

16. The quotation about accommodations in Yosemite is from C. F. G. Cumming, *Granite Crags*, 127. The quotations about the Yosemite journey are from C. F. G. Cumming, 68-69, and Barton, *Trip to the Yosemite*, 8-9. Other accounts that contain similar details about travel to the valley include the manuscript diary of Janet Jacks, May 1885, in Family Papers, Box 1, David Jacks Collection, Huntington Library; Brantz Meyer to Cornelia (Poor) Meyer, June 28, 1872 (HM 21313), Huntington Library; and Lilias Napier Rose Robinson, *Our Trip to the Yosemite Valley and Sierra Nevada Range* (London: J. Martine and Sons, 1883).

17. The quotations are from Barton, *Trip to the Yosemite*, 25, the Jacks diary (Jacks Collection), 17, and Butler, *Far Out; Rovings Retold*, 137. Other accounts that contain similar expressions of wonder are "On the Fourth Raymond Excursion to Colorado, New Mexico and California," a manuscript diary kept by Amy T. Bridges in 1882 (HM 48977), Huntington Library; Reverend J. M. Buckley, *Two Weeks in the Yosemite and Vicinity* (New York: Nelson and Phillips, 1873); C. F. G. Cumming, *Granite Crags*; and Brantz Meyer to Cornelia (Poor) Meyer, June 28, 1872 (HM 21313), Huntington Library.

18. These controversies are summarized in Greene, *Yosemite Resource Study*, I, 69-77, 100-102, 258-259, and 289-96; Holway Jones, *John Muir and the Sierra Club: The Battle for Yosemite* (San Francisco: Sierra Club, 1965), 33-36; Russell, *One Hundred Years*, 150-152; and Shirley Sargent, *Galen Clark, Yosemite Guardian* (San Francisco: Sierra Club, 1964), 73-75 and 129-131.

19. Greene, *Yosemite Resource Study*, I, 289-296; Jones, *Muir and Sierra Club*, 36-43; and Sargent, *Clark*, 136-137.

20. The quotation is taken from the editorial entitled "Amateur Management of the Yosemite Scenery," in *The Century Magazine* 40 (September 1890): 797-798. Criticism of the same variety is raised in "The Case of the Yosemite Valley," *The Century Magazine* 39 (January 1890): 494-495, and the open letters published under the heading of "Destructive Tendencies in the Yosemite Valley" in the same issue. The background of the alliance between Muir and Johnson is described in Stephen Fox, *John Muir and His Legacy: The American Conservation Movement* (Boston: Little, Brown, 1981), 86-88 and 97-99; Jones, *Muir and Sierra Club*, 43-44; and Sanborn, *Yosemite*, 227-228.

21. The two articles by Muir are "The Treasures of the Yosemite" and "Features of the Proposed Yosemite National Park" which appeared in *The Century Magazine* 40 (August 1890): 483-500, and 40 (September 1890): 656-667, respectively. The campaign is outlined in Fox, *Muir and His Legacy*, 104-107, Greene, *Yosemite Resource Study*, I, 304-309, Jones, *Muir and Sierra Club*, 44-47, and Richard J. Orsi, "'Wilderness Saint' and 'Robber Baron': The Anomalous Partnership of John Muir and the Southern Pacific Company for the Preservation of Yosemite National Park," *The Pacific Historian* 29 (Summer/Fall 1985): 136-156.

22. Michael P. Cohen, *The History of the Sierra Club, 1892-1970*. (San Francisco: Sierra Club, 1988), 8-22; Greene, *Yosemite Resource Study*I, 402-412; Jones, *Muir and Sierra Club*, 55-80; Sanborn, *Yosemite*, 229-36; and Orsi, "The Anomalous Partnernship."

23. Greene, *Yosemite Resource Study*, I, 318-341 and 370-374, and H. Duane Hampton, *How the U.S. Cavalry Saved Our National Parks* (Bloomington: Indiana University Press, 1971), 130-63.

24. The quotations are from Earl Pomeroy, *In Search of the Golden West: The Tourist in Western America* (New York: Alfred A. Knopf, 1957), 112-13. For further discussion of the general phenomenon, consult Pomeroy, 112-124.

25. The history of the Yosemite Valley Railroad is ably encapsulated in an essay by Alfred Runte entitled "Yosemite Valley Railroad: Highway of History, Pathway of Promise," printed in Runte's informative study, *Trains of Discovery: Western Railroads and the National Parks* (Flagstaff, AZ: Northland Press, 1984), 60-75. It is also reviewed in Greene, *Yosemite Resource Study*, I, 388-390 and 513-516. Several contemporary brochures that advertise the progressive new means of transport furnished by the railroads include Sierra Railway Company and Hetch Hetchy and Yosemite Valley Railway, *In Old Tuolumne* (n.p., n.d.); Yosemite Valley Railroad, *Yosemite The New Way Open All Year* (San Francisco: Bolte & Braden Co., c.1907); and Oliver W. Lehmer, *Yosemite National Park* (Chicago: Poole Bros., 1912).

26. Greene, *Yosemite Resource Study*, I, 433-439. The developing importance of automobile-borne tourist travel in the West is examined in Pomeroy, *Golden West*, 125-131 and 146-151.

27. The details of Raymond and Whitcomb's enterprise are drawn from Pomeroy, *Golden West*, 13-16, while the quotations are taken from the Bridges diary (HM 48977) and the manuscript recollections of Stephen Merrit, "From Ocean to Ocean! Or Across and Around the Country: Being an Account of the Raymond and Whitcomb Pacific, Northwest and Alaska Excursion of 1892," II, 2 (HM 53278), respectively, both in the Huntington Library.

28. The quotations are from Lehmer, *Yosemite National Park*, and Yosemite Valley Railroad Company, *Yosemite The New Way*, respectively. Similar arguments are advanced in many examples of period advertising literature, such as *Miami Lodge on the Road to Yosemite* (San Francisco: J. C. Marshall, 1915) and Andrew Jackson Wells, *The Yosemite Valley and the Mariposa Grove of Big Trees of California* (San Francisco: Southern Pacific Railroad Passenger Department, 1907).

29. The quotations are from Sargent, *Innkeepers*, 19 and 22. Sargent, 17-24, and Greene, *Yosemite Resource Study* I, 351-352, review Camp Curry's founding and early development.

30. The attendance figures are compiled from Sargent, *Innkeepers*, 27, 38, and 53. Camp Curry's history up to the establishment of the National Park Service in 1916 is discussed in Sargent, 35-62, and Greene, *Yosemite Resource Study*, I, 470-472.

31. Greene, *Yosemite Resource Study* I, 446-449 and 516-517, and Sargent, *Innkeepers*, 26-28. D. J. Foley, editor of *The Yosemite Tourist*, provides a contemporary description of the valley's tourist industry in *Foley's Yosemite Souvenir and Guide* (Yosemite, CA: D. J. Foley, 1908, eighth edition), 66-71.

32. The quotation is from William Lee Popham, *Yosemite Valley Romance* (Louisville,

Kentucky: The World Supply Co., 1911), 3. Descriptions of various concessionaires can be found in Greene, *Yosemite Resource Study* I, 349-354, 462-466, and 472-480.

OGDEN, "Sublime Vistas," pp. 49–67.

I am especially grateful to Peter E. Palmquist and Alfred C. Harrison, Jr., for their assistance in recent months.

1. I am indebted to Barbara Novak, my advisor at Columbia University, for many of the ideas expressed here. See Novak, *Nature and Culture: American Landscape and Painting, 1825-1875* (New York: Oxford University Press, 1980). See also Herbert Hovencamp, *Science and Religion in America, 1800-1860* (Philadelphia: University of Pennsylvania Press, 1978).

2. See Kevin Starr, *Americans and the California Dream, 1850-1915* (New York: Oxford University Press, 1973), 183.

3. Sources on the geologists of Yosemite include William H. Goetzmann, *Exploration & Empire: The Explorer and the Scientist in the Winning of the American West* (New York: W.W. Norton & Co., 1978; originally 1966), 355-89; and Michael L. Smith, *Pacific Visions: California Scientists and the Environment, 1850-1915* (New Haven: Yale University Press, 1987).

4. Sources on art and tourism include John F. Sears, "Doing Niagara Falls in the Nineteenth Century," *Niagara: Two Centuries of Changing Attitudes* (Washington, D.C.: The Corcoran Gallery of Art, 1985), 103-115; and Kenneth Myers, *The Catskills: Painters, Writers, and Tourists in the Mountains, 1820-1895* (Yonkers, NY: The Hudson River Museum of Westchester, 1987). See also Alfred Runte, *National Parks: The American Experience* (Lincoln: University of Nebraska Press, 1979).

5. James Mason Hutchings, "The Yo-Ham-i-te Valley," *Hutchings' California Magazine* 1 (July 1856): 1-8.

6. Joseph Hutchinson to his father, June 7, 1859, typescript, No. 979.447 Y-1-28, Yosemite Research Library: 14.

7. Franz Stenzel, *James Madison Alden, Yankee Artist of the Pacific Coast, 1854-1860* (Fort Worth, Texas: Amon Carter Museum, 1975), 110-14.

8. See David Robertson, *West of Eden: A History of the Art and Literature of Yosemite* (Yosemite: Yosemite Natural History Association and the Wilderness Press, 1984), 9-11; and Marjorie Dakin

Arkelian, "Artists in Yosemite," *The American West: The Magazine of Western History* 15 (July/August 1978): 39.

9. On the early artists of Yosemite, see also Jeanne Van Nostrand, *The First Hundred Years of Painting in California, 1775-1875* (San Francisco: John Howell Books, 1980); and Edan Milton Hughes, *Artists in California, 1786-1940* (San Francisco: Hughes Publishing Company, 1986).

10. George Tirrell's *Vernal Falls*, September 3, 1858, and *Cap of Liberty and Nevada Falls*, September 1858, are now owned by the Yosemite Museum (Nos. 1945, 1946). See also James Mason Hutchings, "The Great Yo-Semite Valley," *Hutchings' California Magazine* 4 (March 1860): 386.

11. James (Joseph) Lamson, "Nine Years' Adventures in California, From September 1852 to September 1861, with Excursions into Oregon, Washington, and Nevada," entries for June 29 and 30, 1859, California Historical Society. See also Hutchings, "The Great Yo-Semite Valley," 394. Lamson's watercolor *Mount Broderick and the Nevada Fall*, 1859, is in the California Historical Society Collection.

12. James H. Lawrence, "Discovery of the Nevada Fall," *Overland Monthly* 4 (October 1884): 370.

13. For historical information of this type I have used Carl P. Russell, *One Hundred Years in Yosemite: The Story of a Great Park and Its Friends* (Yosemite Natural History Association, 1968; originally 1931).

14. Jeanne Van Nostrand, "Thomas A. Ayres: Artist-Argonaut of California," *California Historical Society Quarterly* 20 (September 1941): 277.

15. Peter E. Palmquist, "Yosemite's First Stereo Photographer, Charles Leander Weed (1824-1903)," *Stereo World* 6 (September-October 1979): 8, 10-11.

16. "Art Items," New York *Evening Post* (December 11, 1862), 2.

17. Benjamin P. Avery, "Art Beginnings on the Pacific, Part I," *Overland Monthly* 1 (July 1868): 34.

18. Benjamin P. Avery, "Art Beginnings on the Pacific, Part II," *Overland Monthly* 1 (August 1868): 114.

19. See Gordon Hendricks, *Albert Bierstadt: Painter of the American West* (New York: Harry N. Abrams, in association with the Amon Carter Museum of Western Art, 1974), 154-5; and Nancy Anderson, *Albert Bierstadt: Cho-looke, The Yosemite Fall* (San

Diego: Timken Art Gallery, exhibition catalogue, May 3-June 15, 1986), n.p.

20. See Hans Huth, "Yosemite: The Story of an Idea," *Sierra Club Bulletin* 33 (March 1948): 66-7.

21. "Local Art Items," San Francisco *Bullein* (May 25, 1869), 3. Reference courtesy Alfred C. Harrison, Jr.

22. *Kennedy Quarterly* 5 (New York: Kennedy Galleries, May 1965): 162. Thomas Hill's *Yosemite Valley*, 1864, was carried by North Point Gallery, San Francisco, in 1989.

23. Alfred C. Harrison, Jr., *William Keith: The Saint Mary's College Collection* (Moraga, California: Hearst Art Gallery, Saint Mary's College, 1988), 5, 48 (notes 55 and 56).

24. See Weston Naef, *Era of Exploration: The Rise of Landscape Photography in the American West, 1860-1885* (Boston: New York Graphic Society, 1975), 34-41.

25. See for example Harriet Errington to Lottie, August 10, 1865, in "Letters and Journal from California, 1864-65," typescript, Yosemite Research Library, 60; and Josiah D. Whitney, *The Yosemite Book* (New York: Julius Bien, 1868), 12.

26. Whitney, *The Yosemite Book*, 12-13 and plates 25-28.

27. Laura Wood Roper, "The Yosemite Valley and the Mariposa Big Trees: A Preliminary Report (1865) by Frederick Law Olmsted," *Landscape Architecture* 43 (October 1952): 12. See also Laura Wood Roper, *FLO: A Biography of Frederick Law Olmsted* (Baltimore: Johns Hopkins University Press, 1973), 287.

28. Olmsted's letter of August 9, 1865, is reprinted in Huth, "Yosemite," 70.

29. Information on Haseltine courtesy Andrea Henderson.

30. Constance F. Gordon-Cumming, *Granite Crags* (Edinburgh and London: William Blackwood & Sons, 1884), 282-3. Two of Washington F. Friend's Yosemite watercolors are now at the Bancroft Library at the University of California, Berkeley; another is in a private collection in California.

31. See Peter Palmquist, "California in Stereo 1850-1950," *Return to El Dorado: A Century of California Stereographs* (Riverside: California Museum of Photography, *Bulletin* 5, 1986), 6.

32. Fritiof M. Fryxell, "The Thomas Moran Art Collection of the National Parks," *Yosemite Nature Notes* 15 (August 1936): 60.

33. James D. Smillie, "Diaries," entry for June 30, 1870, Roll 2849, Frame 1003, Archives of American Art, Smithsonian

Institution. Smillie saw Samuel Colman's California sketches on June 30.

34. See "Art Notes," *Overland Monthly* 15 (August 1875): 201; and Gordon-Cumming, *Granite Crags*, 282.

35. *Memoir, Gilbert Munger, Landscape Artist, 1836-1903* (New York: DeVinne Press, 1904), 11; and Hildegard Cummings, "Gilbert Munger on the Trail," *The William Benton Museum of Art Bulletin* no. 10 (Storrs: University of Connecticut, 1982), 7-11.

36. Smillie, "Diaries," entries for July 1-August 21, 1870, Roll 2849, Frames 1215-1240.

37. "Art Notes," *Overland Monthly* 12 (June 1874): 575. Reference courtesy Alfred C. Harrison, Jr.

38. Marjorie Dakin Arkelian, *Thomas Hill: The Grand View* (Oakland: The Oakland Museum Art Department, 1980), 23-26.

39. C.D. Robinson, "Painting a Yosemite Panorama," *Overland Monthly* 22, second series (September 1893): 243-256.

40. Dwight Miller, *California Landscape Painting, 1860-1885: Artists Around Keith and Hill* (Exhibition Catalogue, Stanford University Art Gallery, December 9, 1975-February 29, 1976), 12.

41. Brother Cornelius, *Keith, Old Master of California* (New York: G.P. Putnam's Sons, 1942), 217.

42. See Robert Cahn and Robert Glenn Ketchum, *American Photographers and The National Parks* (New York: Viking Press, 1981), 37 and catalog.

43. Yelland's painting is at the San Diego Museum of Art; the others are privately owned.

44. "Art in California," *Alta California* (October 30, 1859), 1.

45. See Ted Orland, *Man & Yosemite: A Photographer's View of the Early Years* (Santa Cruz, California: The Image Continuum Press, 1985).

46. Jewett's *Yosemite Falls* is at the Newark Art Museum, New Jersey; *Bridalveil Falls* is privately owned.

47. Marjorie Dakin Arkelian, *William Hahn, Genre Painter, 1829-1887* (Oakland: The Oakland Museum, 1976), 27.

48. See for example Charles Nordhoff, *California: For Health, Pleasure, and Residence. A Book for Travellers and Settlers* (New York: Harper & Bros., 1872), 69.

49. See Paul Hickman and Peter Palmquist, "J.J. Reilly, Photographer and Manufacturer of All Kinds of Stereoscopic Views, Part II," *Stereo World* 11 (January/February 1985): 10, 12. Therese Yelverton was then

notorious because of the long series of courtroom battles in which she tried to establish the legality of her Irish marriage ceremony.

50. Benjamin F. Taylor, *Between the Gates* (Chicago: S.C. Griggs & Co., 1878), 216.

51. Palmquist, "California in Stereo," 6.

52. Peter B. Hales, *William Henry Jackson and the Transformation of the American Landscape* (Philadelphia: Temple University Press, 1988), xii, 268-9.

53. Photographs RG57-PS(28-43), RG200-S-JH (10-38), and RG273-JH(78-82), National Archives, Washington, D.C. Hillers's Yosemite photographs are mentioned in the 1893 *Annual Report* of the U.S. Geological Survey. Information courtesy Don D. Fowler.

54. See Peter E. Palmquist, *Lawrence & Houseworth/Thomas Houseworth & Co., A Unique View of the West, 1860-1886* (Columbus, Ohio: National Stereoscopic Association, 1980), 36-7.

55. Peter E. Palmquist, *Carleton E. Watkins, Photographer of the American West* (Albuquerque: University of New Mexico Press and the Amon Carter Museum, 1983), 51-2.

56. Sarah A.J. Locke, "Diary of Events for a Trip to Yo Semite, June 5-21, 1879," typescript, 9, Yosemite Research Library.

57. James Mason Hutchings, *In the Heart of the Sierras* (Oakland: Pacific Press Publishing Co., 1886), 351.

58. Adam Clark Vroman, "Southern California and Yosemite Valley, 1900-1901," album of original prints, Center for Creative Photography, Tucson.

59. Carleton Watkins, 1864 Notebook, Miscellaneous Watkins Papers, Bancroft Library. See also Whitney, *The Yosemite Book*, and Whitney, et al., *Geology of California. I. Report of Progress and Synopsis of the Field-Work, from 1860 to 1864* (Philadelphia: Caxton Press of Sherman & Co., 1865).

60. Gordon Hendricks, *Eadweard Muybridge: The Father of the Motion Picture* (New York: Grossman Publishers, 1975), 17-18; and Mary V. Jessup Hood and Robert Bartlett Haas, "Eadweard Muybridge's Yosemite Valley Photographs, 1867-1872," *California Historical Society Quarterly* 42 (March 1963): 17.

61. Smillie, "Diaries," August 26, 1871, Roll 2849, Frames 1228, 1243-47.

62. Hickman and Palmquist, "J.J. Reilly," 10.

63. Arkelian, *Thomas Hill*, 37.

64. Hutchings, *In the Heart of the Sierras*, 350.

65. Thomas Hill, "Notebook with Entries Dated 1884-1887," Hill Memorabilia Collection, the Crocker Art Museum, Sacramento.

66. Charles D. Robinson, "The Artists of California," list enclosed in a letter to Mr. Newbegin, San Rafael, August 8, 1927, n.p., Bancroft Library (copy at Oakland Museum Library).

67. J. Gray Sweeney, *American Painting at The Tweed Museum of Art and Glensheen* (Duluth: The University of Minnesota, 1982), 52.

68. "Art Notes," San Francisco *Morning Call* (January 18, 1880).

·69. Clark's *Yosemite Valley* was copyrighted by Charles H. Crosby in Massachusetts in 1872 and 1873, and by D.S. Norris in 1873 (copyright no. 4425, Library of Congress). Chromos by Key and Wilkie can be seen at the Boston Public Library Print Collection.

70. Paul Hickman and Terence Pitts, *George Fiske, Yosemite Photographer* (Flagstaff, Arizona: Northland Press in cooperation with the Center for Creative Photography, 1980), 15.

71. See Katherine Mather Littell, *Chris Jorgensen, California Pioneer Artist* (Sonora, California: Fine Arts Research Publishing Co., 1988).

72. Virginia Best Adams, "Best's Studio," in Jack Gyer, ed., *Yosemite: Saga of a Century, 1864-1964* (Oakhurst, California: The Sierra Star Press, 1964), 46-7.

73. Robertson, *West of Eden*, 94-5, 134-6.

HYDE, "Stagecoach to Packard," pp. 69–83.

1. Technically, Yellowstone was the first *national* park. Created in 1872, it was the first chunk of land set off under control of the United States government to be a "pleasuring ground" for the people. Yosemite Valley, however, granted by the federal government to the state of California in 1864, originated the idea of setting aside scenic wilderness to be protected from exploitation. For details, see Alfred Runte, *National Parks: The American Experience* (Lincoln, Nebr., 1979).

2. Anne F. Hyde, "An American Vision: Far Western Landscape and the Formation of National Culture, 1820-1920" (Ph.D dissertation, University of California, Berkeley, 1988), 401-77.

3. Quoted in Stephen Fox, *John Muir and His Legacy: The American Conservation Movement*

(Boston, 1981), 14.

4. Olive Logan, "Does It Pay to Visit Yosemite?" *Galaxy* 10 (October 1870): 498; Miriam Leslie, *California: A Pleasure Trip From Gotham to the Golden Gate* (New York, 1877), 213.

5. George A. Crofutt, *Crofutt's Transcontinental Tourist's Guide* (New York, 1871), 192; N.C. Carnall, *California Guide for Tourists and Settlers* (San Francisco, 1889), 27; Leslie, *California*, 234.

6. Carl R. Russell, *One Hundred Years in Yosemite: The Story of A Great National Park* (Yosemite Natural History Association, 1957), 61.

7. Susan Coolidge, "A Few Hints on the California Journey," *Scribners* 6 (May 1873): 26; Caroline M. Churchill, *Over the Purple Hills, Or, Sketches of Travel in California* (Denver, 1884), 117.

8. Churchill, *Purple Hills*, 118-19; Rose Pender, *A Lady's Experiences in the Wild West in 1883* (Lincoln, Nebr., 1978), 101.

9. Russell, *One Hundred Years*, 93-109; Robert Shankland, *Steve Mather of the National Parks* (New York, 1951), 131.

10. *To San Francisco and Back* (n.p., 1868), 94; Churchill, *Purple Hills*, 144.

11. Russell, *One Hundred Years*, 111; John Ise, *Our National Park Policy* (Baltimore, 1961), 72.

12. Hyde, "An American Vision, 418-470.

13. Muir, quoted in Fox, *John Muir*, 84; Charles Nordhoff, *California for Health, Pleasure, and Residence* (New York, 1872), 69; Logan, "Does It Pay," 505.

14. Coolidge, "A Few Hints," 30; Susie C. Clark, *The Round Trip From the Hub to the Golden Gate* (Boston, 1890), 125; Logan, "Does It Pay," 501.

15. John H. Beadle, *The Undeveloped West: or, Five Years in the Territories* (Philadelphia, 1873), 251; Pender, *A Lady's Experiences*, 32, quoted in Clark, *The Round Trip*, 143.

16. Quoted in Ise, *Park Policy*, 73-74.

17. Russell, *One Hundred Years*, 61; Ise, *Park Policy*, 208-11; Churchill, *Purple Hills*, 120.

18. John B. Rae, *The Road and Car in American Life* (Cambridge, Mass., 1971), 48-50; John A. Jakle, *The Tourist: Travel in Twentieth Century North America* (Omaha, 1985), 101-2.

19. Richard A. Bartlett, *Yellowstone: A Wilderness Besieged* (Tucson, 1985), 82-86; Tom Dillon, *Over the Trails of Glacier National Park* (St. Paul, 1912), 6; Shankland, *Steve Mather*, 63-66.

20. Rae, *Road and Car*, 50; James J. Flink, *The Automobile Age* (Cambridge, Mass., 1988), 129-131.

21. Warren James Belasco, *Americans on the Road: From Autocamp to Motel, 1910-1945* (Cambridge, Mass., 1979), 18-22; James Montgomery Flagg, *Boulevards All the Way—Maybe!* (New York, 1925), 138.

22. Vernon McGill, *Diary of a Motor Journey from Chicago to Los Angeles* (Los Angeles, 1922), xvi.

23. Herbert A. Jump, *The Yosemite: A Spiritual Interpretation* (Boston, 1916), 1.

24. Frank E. Brumner, *Outlook* 137 (July 16, 1924): 437.

25. Muir, *Our National Parks*, 1; J. Horace McFarland, "Are National Parks Worthwhile?" *Sierra Club Bulletin* 8 (January 1912): 236.

26. Mary Roberts Rinehart, *Through Glacier Park: Seeing America First with Howard Eaton* (Boston, 1916), 24-25; Grace Gallatin Seton-Thompson, *A Woman Tenderfoot* (London, 1901), 4.

27. Belasco, *Americans on the Road*, 106-113; Earl Pomeroy, *In Search of the Golden West: The Tourist in Western America* (New York, 1957), 198-205; Emerson Hough, *Yellowstone National Park* (n.p., 1922), 5; R.L. Duffus, "America Works Hard at Play," *New York Times Magazine*, September 1, 1929, 21.

28. Quoted in Shankland, *Steve Mather*, 6-7.

29. Flink, *Automobile Age*, 178-180; Shankland, *Steve Mather*, 65.

30. Runte, *National Parks*, 90-95; Quoted in Jenks Cameron, *The National Park Service: Its History, Activities, and Organization* (New York, 1922), 12.

31. Shankland, *Steve Mather*, 16-23.

32. Shankland, *Steve Mather*, 56-57; Ise, *Park Policy*, 194-195.

33. Ronald A. Foresta, *America's National Parks and Their Keepers* (Washington, D.C., 1984), 25; William C. Everhart, *The National Park Service* (Boulder, Col., 1983), 16; Stephen Mather, "Progress in the National Parks," *Sierra Club Bulletin* 11 (January 1920): 5.

34. Quoted in Peter J. Schmitt, *Back To Nature: The Arcadian Myth in Urban America* (New York, 1969), 161.

35. Flink, *Automobile Age*, 171-173; Shankland, *Steve Mather*, 146.

36. Flink, *Automobile Age*, 173; Shankland, *Steve Mather*, 147.

37. Quoted in Shankland, *Steve Mather*, 145.

38. Ise, *Park Policy*, 196.

39. Hyde, "An American Vision," 498-504.

40. Flink, *Automobile Age*, 174; Russell, *One Hundred Years*, 69.

41. Ise, *Park Policy*, 203; Ansel F. Hall, *Handbook of Yosemite National Park* (New York, 1921), 45.

42. Foresta, *National Parks*, 27; Shankland, *Steve Mather*, 131-32; Hall, *Handbook*, 45.

43. James E. Rother, "Three Weeks in the San Joaquin—Kings," typescript in the Bancroft Library, 1919, 27; Hall, *Handbook*, 45.

44. James Bryce, "National Parks—The Need of the Future," *Sierra Club Bulletin* 9 (January 1913): 29; Charles A. Noble, "The Sierra Club Outing of 1919," *Sierra Club Bulletin* 11 (September 1920): 15.

45. R.B. Mitchell in *Proceedings of the National Park Conference* (Washington, D.C., 1912), 109.

46. Ise, *Park Policy*, 182; Shirley Sargent, *Yosemite and its Innkeepers: The Story of A Great Park and Its Chief Concessionaires* (Yosemite, 1975), 70-71.

47. Shankland, *Steve Mather*, 133-135; Sargent, *Yosemite*, 84-85.

48. Hall, *Handbook*, 307.

49. Stephen Mather, "Sieur De Monts and Yosemite: The Problem of Our National Parks," *Outlook* 15 (April 5, 1917): 750.

50. Jeffrey Limerick, Nancy Ferguson, and Richard Oliver, *America's Grand Resort Hotels* (New York, 1979), 221-223.

51. Limerick, Ferguson, and Oliver, *Resort Hotels*, 221-223; Hyde, "An American Vision," 478-481; Curry Company, *The Ahwahnee, Situated in Yosemite National Park* (n.p., 1928).

52. Lewis Gannett, *Sweet Land* (Garden City, N.Y., 1934), 161.

RUNTE, "Grinnell," pp. 85–95.

I am indebted to Resources for the Future, Washington, D.C., and the Eastern National Park and Monument Association, Cooperstown, New York, and Philadelphia, Pennsylvania, for financial assistance in making this article possible.

1. E. Raymond Hall, "Joseph Grinnell (1877 to 1939)," *Journal of Mammalogy* 20 (November 14, 1939): 409, 411.

2. Ibid.

3. Ibid.

4. Grinnell to Lane, October 7, 1914, and attached Prospectus, "Natural History Survey of Yosemite National Park," File 12-13, pt. 1, Yosemite National Park, Privileges, Joseph Grinnell, Central Files, 1907-39,

Records of the National Park Service, Record Group 79, National Archives, Washington, D.C. (hereinafter cited as R.G. 79).

5. The history of Yosemite's changing boundaries is well-treated in Holway R. Jones, *John Muir and the Sierra Club: The Battle for Yosemite* (San Francisco: Sierra Club, 1965).

6. Grinnell to Lane, October 7, 1914, and attached Prospectus, File 12-13, pt. 1, R.G. 79.

7. Bryant to Grinnell, June 18, 1917, and Grinnell to Bryant, June 19, 1917, both in the Bryant File, Records of the Museum of Vertebrate Zoology, University of California, Berkeley (hereinafter cited as MVZ).

8. Joseph Grinnell and Tracy I. Storer, "Animal Life as an Asset of National Parks," *Science* 44 (September 15, 1916): 375-380.

9. Ibid., 379.

10. Hall, "Joseph Grinnell," 413.

11. Mather to Grinnell, October 3, 1916, Mather File, MVZ.

12. Grinnell to W.B. Lewis, July 8, 1920, Lewis File, MVZ.

13. Grinnell and Storer, "Animal Life as an Asset of National Parks," 377-78.

14. Thomas R. Dunlap, *Saving America's Wildlife* (Princeton: Princeton University Press, 1988), 79-80; Horace M. Albright, "The National Park Service's Policy on Predatory Mammals," *Journal of Mammalogy* 12 (May 1931): 185-86. Some predator controls continued throughout the 1930s. For a further summary, see John Ise, *Our National Park Policy: A Critical History* (Baltimore: Johns Hopkins University Press, 1961), 592-97.

15. Grinnell and Storer, "Animal Life as an Asset of National Parks," 377.

16. Grinnell to Lewis, November 25, 1925, Lewis File, MVZ.

17. Joseph Grinnell and Tracy I. Storer, *Animal Life in the Yosemite: An Account of the Mammals, Birds, Reptiles, and Amphibians in a Cross Section of the Sierra Nevada* (Berkeley: University of California Press, 1924).

18. Grinnell to E.P. Leavitt, October 4, 1927, File 710, pt. 1, Yosemite Fauna, General, Central Classified Files, 1907-49, R.G. 79. Grinnell further published his "Open Letter" as "Recommendations Concerning the Treatment of Large Mammals in Yosemite National Park," *Journal of Mammalogy* 9 (February 1928): 76.

19. Grinnell to Lewis, September 14, 1920, Lewis File, MVZ.

20. Hall, "Joseph Grinnell," 417.

21. See, for example, Horace M. Albright as told to Robert Cahn, *The Birth of the National Park Service: The Founding Years, 1913-33* (Salt Lake City and Chicago: Howe Brothers, 1985), 121-22. Joseph Grinnell's contribution to park interpretation is not even mentioned.

22. Grinnell to Mather, June 6, 1919, Mather File, MVZ.

23. Bryant to Grinnell, July 19, 1919, and Grinnell to Bryant, July 29, 1919, both Bryant File, MVZ.

24. Carl P. Russell, *One Hundred Years in Yosemite: The Story of a Great Park and Its Friends* (Yosemite: Yosemite Natural History Association, 1968), 189. Russell, who began his career in Yosemite as a park naturalist and later served as superintendent (1947-52), was also among the few people who carefully acknowledged the contributions of Enid Michael, the first woman interpreter in the natural history program. See especially 134-35.

25. Bryant to Grinnell, June 9, 1920, Bryant File, MVZ.

26. Hall, "Joseph Grinnell," 416.

27. Grinnell to Bryant, June 9, 1922, Bryant File, MVZ.

28. In Yosemite, for example, these displays included a herd of exotic Tule elk, which, at Grinnell's insistence, were finally removed to the Owens Valley in 1933. See the C.G. Thomson File, MVZ. A contemporary account of the issue is A.E. Borell, "Yosemite Elk Herd Moved to Owens Valley," *Yosemite Nature Notes* 12 (December 1933): 107-109.

29. An important inventory of early studies affecting the national parks is U.S., Department of the Interior, National Park Service, *Research and Education in the National Parks*, by Harold C. Bryant and Wallace W. Atwood, Jr. (Washington, D.C.: Government Printing Office, 1932).

30. On the issue of the origins of the national park idea, see Alfred Runte, *National Parks: The American Experience* (2d ed., rev.; Lincoln: University of Nebraska Press, 1987), 28-32; and Hans Huth, "Yosemite: The Story of an Idea," *Sierra Club Bulletin* 33 (March 1948): 47-78.

31. Hall, "Joseph Grinnell," 411.

32. A revealing summary of Bryant's career is Ann and Myron Sutton, "The Man from Yosemite," *National Parks Magazine* 28 (July-September 1954): 102-105, 131-32.

33. U.S., Department of the Interior, National Park Service, *Fauna of the National Parks of*

the United States: A Preliminary Survey, by George M. Wright, Joseph S. Dixon, and Ben H. Thompson (Washington, D.C.: Government Printing Office, 1933); and U.S., Department of the Interior, National Park Service, *Fauna of the National Parks of the United States: Wildlife Management*, by George M. Wright and Ben H. Thompson (Washington, D.C.: Government Printing Office, 1935).

34. U.S., Department of the Interior, Advisory Board on Wildlife Management, *Wildlife Management in the National Parks*, by A.S. Leopold, et al., Report to the Secretary, March 4, 1963, 4.

35. Grinnell and Storer, "Animal Life as an Asset of National Parks," 377; Wright, et al., *Fauna of the National Parks (1933)*, 1; Leopold Committee, *Report*, 5.

36. Although in 1944, five years after Grinnell's death.

37. Grinnell to Robert Sterling Yard, July 17, 1915, Yard File, MVZ. Yard, an Interior Department official, had asked Grinnell to advocate controlling gray squirrels in the national parks. Grinnell refused, citing the lack of evidence that gray squirrels destroyed birds' eggs, as Yard and others charged.

38. For more on Grinnell, see especially Dunlap, *Saving America's Wildlife*, and Alfred Runte, *Yosemite: The Embattled Wilderness* (Lincoln: University of Nebraska Press, 1990). An important collection of Grinnell's essays is *Joseph Grinnell's Philosophy of Nature: Selected Writings of a Western Naturalist* (Berkeley and Los Angeles: University of California Press, 1943).

PAVLIK, "In Harmony," pp. 97–109.

1. Among the best known titles regarding the park's discovery are Layfayette H. Bunnell, *Discovery of the Yosemite in 1851* (Golden, Colorado: Outbooks, 1980); Francis P. Farquhar, *History of the Sierra Nevada* (Berkeley: University of California, 1965); Bil Gilbert, *Westering Man: The Life of Joseph Walker, Master of the Frontier* (New York: Atheneum, 1983); Carl Parcher Russell, *100 Years in Yosemite* (Yosemite: Yosemite Natural History Association, 1968). Its establishment and administration are addressed in William C. Everhart, *The National Park Service* (Boulder, Colorado: Westview Press, 1983); John Ise, *Our*

National Park Policy: A Critical History (Baltimore: Johns Hopkins University Press, 1961); Holway R. Jones, *John Muir and the Sierra Club: The Battle for Yosemite* (San Francisco: Sierra Club, 1965); Alfred Runte, *National Parks: The American Experience* (Lincoln and London: University of Nebraska Press, 1979).

2. As quoted in William C. Tweed, *Parkitecture: A History of Rustic Building Design in the National Park System: 1916-1942* (Typewritten MS, 1978), 26, on file, Yosemite National Park Research Library.

3. Stephen T. Mather, *Annual Report of the Superintendent of National Parks to the Secretary of the Interior for the Fiscal Year ended June 30, 1917* (Washington: Government Printing Office, 1917), 60; Mather, *Annual Report of the Director of the National Park Service . . . for the Fiscal Year ended June 30, 1918*, 45; James Delgado, "National Register of Historic Places Inventory-Nomination Form: Yosemite Hydroelectric Power Plant," typewritten MS, September 1981, on file, Yosemite National Park Research Library. I relied on Delgado's nomination form as a concise, complete, and accurate secondary source of information regarding the construction of the power plant and its components.

4. Mather, *Annual Report of the Director of the National Park Service . . . for the Fiscal Year ended June 30, 1918*, 45; *Annual Report of the Superintendent of National Parks . . . for the Fiscal Year ended June 30, 1916*, 14-15.

5. James Delgado, "National Register . . . Nomination Form: Yosemite Hydroelectric Power Plant"; Mather, *Annual Report of the Director of the National Park Service . . . for the Fiscal Year ended June 30, 1918*, 45.

6. Mather, *Report of the Director of the National Park Service . . . for the Fiscal Year ended June 30, 1917*, Gabriel Sovulewski, "Monthly Supervisor's Reports," November 1916, December 1916, and various reports, 1917, on file, Yosemite National Park Research Library.

7. Tweed, *Parkitecture*, 30-31; Mather, *Report of the Director of the National Park Service . . . for the Fiscal Year ended June 30, 1920*, 113.

8. The works of Hans Huth, Roderick Nash, and Alfred Runte amply address the issue of a national identity "crisis" and the role of nature, parks, and wilderness in defining our heritage. Harold Kirker has accounted for the colonial nature of architecture in early California in the absence of an existing regional or local style. Hans Huth, *Nature and the American* (Berkeley: University of California, 1957); Roderick Nash, *Wilderness and the American Mind* (New Haven: Yale University Press, 3rd ed. 1982); Runte, *National Parks: The American Experience*; Harold Kirker, *California's Architectural Frontier* (San Marino: The Huntington Library, 1960).

9. Mather did his best to make the old administration building seem atrocious. In 1919 he wrote, "The present building . . . is the result of joining together two old abandoned buildings inherited from the state administration and to which was added later a second story . . . It is a ramshackle affair, the foundations of which have unevenly settled and rotted away, leaving the floors warped and uneven, infested with vermin impossible to eliminate, inadequately ventilated and lighted, and above all wholly lacking in space for the necessary office work for effective administration." See Mather, *Report of the Director of the National Park Service . . . for the Fiscal Year ended June 30, 1919*, 197.

10. W.B. Lewis, "Superintendent's Monthly Report, March, 1925," 13.

11. Lewis, "Superintendent's Annual Report, 1924," 14.

12. Lewis, "Superintendent's Annual Report, 1923," 7 and 28.

13. Lewis, "Superintendent's Annual Report, 1925," 3.

14. Lewis, "Superintendent's Monthly Report, October, 1925," 8.

15. Gabriel Sovulewski, "The Story of Campgrounds in Yosemite Valley," *Yosemite Nature Notes* 16 (November 1937): 81-4.

16. Ibid.; Donald Bertram Tresidder, "The National Parks: A Public Health Problem" (Ph.D. dissertation, School of Medicine, Stanford University, 1927), 119.

17. "Descriptions of Sewer Systems in Yosemite National Park," November 1931, typewritten MS, box 11, Yosemite National Park Research Library-Records Center (hereinafter referred to as "YNPRL-RC").

18. George V. Bell, *Report of the Acting Superintendent of the Yosemite National Park to the Secretary of the Interior for the Fiscal Year ended June 30, 1915* (Washington: Government Printing Office, 1915), 6.

19. Tresidder, "The National Parks," 71.

20. "Descriptions of Sewer Systems in Yosemite National Park."

21. Ibid.

22. Tresidder, "The National Parks," 131.

23. E.M. Hilton, "Yosemite Valley Sewage Treatment Plant," n.d., typewritten MS, Box 11, YNPRL-RC.

24. Ibid.

25. Ibid.; C.G. Thomson, "Superintendent's Monthly Report, June 1930," 2.

26. H.B. Hommon, "Treatment and Disposal of Sewage in the National Parks," *American Journal of Public Health* 25 (February 1935): 128-46.

27. Thomson, "Superintendent's Monthly Report, May 1934," 5.

28. Gabriel Sovulewski, "Monthly Supervisor's Report, May 1930," 2; Thomson, "Superintendent's Monthly Report, August, 1932," 5.

29. Thomson, "Superintendent's Monthly Report, April 1934," 6-7; "Glacier Point Comfort Station" file, box 59, YNPRL-RC.

30. Lewis, "Superintendent's Annual Report, 1923," 6.

31. The highly desirable nature of this area for development was recognized early by National Park Service officials, although it was not until the Mission 66 era (1956-1966) that residences, offices, a store, and a delicatessen were erected on the site.

32. "Minutes of the Meeting at Indian Village, 1929," typewritten MS, YNPRL-RC, Box 8.

33. "Memorandum of Tentative Conclusions in Regard to Certain Problems presented at Meetings of July 27, 28, 29, 30, 31, August 1 and 2," in Minutes of Yosemite National Park Committee of Expert Advisors, August 2, 1929, 3, box 10, YNPRL-RC.

34. Thomas C. Vint to Superintendent, March 9, 1928, "Landscaping" box, YNPRL-RC.

35. Ibid.

36. Thomson, "Superintendent's Monthly Report, April, 1931," n.p.; "Completion Report: Six Cabins, Indian Village," March 1932, Maintenance Office, Yosemite NP.

37. "Completion Report: Six Cabins, Indian Village"; Memorandum for the Regional Director, Region 4, from Frank A. Kittredge, Superintendent, October 6, 1947, box 8, YNPRL-RC.

38. John C. Paige, *The Civilian Conservation Corps and the National Park Service 1933-1942: An Administrative History* (Washington, D.C.: National Park Service, 1985), 7-10. There are few secondary works on the CCC, and all are of a general nature.

39. Ibid.

40. "The Crisis in Civil Works," *The Literary Digest* 117 (February 3, 1934): 10; Florence Peterson, "CWA: A Candid Appraisal,"

Atlantic Monthly 153 (May 1934): 587-90.

41. Wayne W. Parrish, "CWA Ends After Brightening Up Nation," *The Literary Digest* 117 (April 21, 1934): 9, 50.

42. Justus S. Wardell, "The Federal Public Works Program," *California Arts and Architecture*, October 1933.

43. Ibid.

44. J.A. Killalee, "Final Construction Report: Grading of the Tuolumne Meadows-Tioga Pass Section of the Tioga Road," January 22, 1936, box 51, YNPRL-RC.

45. Ibid.

46. During the 1950s, a dramatic battle ensued between and among Park Service officials and Sierra Club members over the completion of the Tioga road. One can only speculate that, had the road been completed prior to World War II, its impact on the landscape would have been minimized. For more information, see Alfred Runte, *National Parks: The American Experience* (Lincoln and London: University of Nebraska Press, 1979), 173; Michael P. Cohen, *The History of the Sierra Club 1892-1970* (San Francisco: Sierra Club Books, 1988), 134-142; and Ansel Adams, *Ansel Adams: An Autobiography* (Boston: Little, Brown and Company/New York Graphic Society, 1985), 154-156.

47. Lawrence C. Merriam, "Superintendent's Monthly Report, June, 1940."

48. Ibid.

DILSAVER, "Conservation Conflict," pp. 111–119.

1. John Muir, "A Rival of the Yosemite—The Canyon of the South Fork of the Kings River," *Century* 21 (April 1891): 77-82.

2. Lary Dilsaver and William Tweed, *Challenge of the Big Trees* (Three Rivers, CA: Sequoia Natural History Association, 1990), ch. 7; Douglas Strong, "A History of Sequoia National Park" (Ph.D. dissertation, Syracuse University, 1964), 63-292.

3. George Gibbs, *Preliminary Plan for Development of Kings River Canyon for Recreation* (San Francisco: United States Forest Service, California Region, November, 1933), found in Sequoia National Park (SNP) at the Ash Mountain Headquarters library.

4. Barry Mackintosh, "Harold Ickes and

the National Park Service," *Journal of Forest History* 29 (April 1985): 78-84; William Colby, transcript of an interview by Corrinne Gibb, 51-56, Bancroft Library, University of California, Berkeley.

5. Max Hayden, "Kings Canyon Becomes a National Park," an address to the Fresno Academy delivered during November 1968. A twenty-nine page transcript of the address is kept at Sequoia National Park in the museum archives vault at Ash Mountain Headquarters.

6. Quoted in Mackintosh, "Harold Ickes and the National Park Service," 82.

7. Dilsaver and Tweed, *Challenge of the Big Trees*, ch. 7.

8. Frank Kittredge, "Kings Canyon National Park," (Unpublished memoir, Sequoia National Park archives, Box 39691, filed in chronological order, April 26, 1950).

9. A good comparison of land management philosophy is available in Dyan Zaslowsky and the Wilderness Society, *These American Lands* (New York: Henry Holt and Company, 1986), especially 9-112; a discussion of the relations between the agencies in California and how they affected the Kings Canyon issue is found in Irving Brant, *Adventures in Conservation with Franklin D. Roosevelt* (Flagstaff, AZ: Northland Publishing Company, 1988), 147-218.

10. For a step by step reconstruction of the negotiations, see the sixteen reports from B. F. Manbey to Frank Kittredge, Sequoia National Park archives, Box 425629, File 602-02 in chronological order: February 11, 28, March 8, 21, April 4, 13, 26, May 4, 7, 25, June 3, 13, July 5, 25, August 20, 30, 1938.

11. Brant, *Adventures in Conservation*, 165-168.

12. Brant, *Adventures in Conservation*, 162-172, 185-199.

13. Ibid.

14. Stuart B. Show, transcript of an interview by Amelia Fry, 176-211, Bancroft Library.

15. Brant, *Adventures in Conservation*, 198.

16. There are several excellent accounts of the following bizarre story, each of which adds details that the others do not: Brant, *Adventures in Conservation*, 203-205: Hayden, "Kings Canyon Becomes a National Park"; and *Congressional Record, House*, Vol. 84, Part 5, 76th Congress 1st Session (May 2,

1939), 5033-5045.

17. Hayden, "Kings Canyon Becomes a National Park," 8.

18. Ibid., 8-15.

19. *Congressional Record, House*, 5040.

20. *Congressional Record, House*, 5044.

21. Brant, *Adventures in Conservation*, 205-213.

22. See Dilsaver and Tweed, *Challenge of the Big Trees*, ch. 8.

23. Show, interview by Amelia Fry, 207-208.

RUNTE, "Planning," pp. 121-130.

1. Susan R. Schrepfer, *The Fight to Save the Redwoods: A History of Environmental Reform, 1917-1978* (Madison: University of Wisconsin Press, 1983); Alfred Runte, *Yosemite: The Embattled Wilderness* (Lincoln: University of Nebraska Press, 1990); Richard A. Bartlett, *Yellowstone: A Wilderness Besieged* (Tucson: University of Arizona Press, 1985); and Carsten Lien, *Olympic Battleground: The Power Politics of Timber Preservation* (San Francisco: Sierra Club Books, 1991). For representative examples of an earlier perspective, see Harlean James, *Romance of the National Parks* (New York: Macmillan Company, 1939), and Freeman Tilden, *The National Parks*, 2d ed. (New York: Alfred A. Knopf, 1970).

2. John Muir, "The Hetch Hetchy Valley: A National Question," *American Forestry* 16 (May 1910): 263.

3. A comprehensive account of the Hetch Hetchy controversy is Holway R. Jones, *John Muir and the Sierra Club: The Battle for Yosemite* (San Francisco: Sierra Club, 1965). See also Elmo R. Richardson, *The Politics of Conservation: Crusades and Controversies, 1897-1913* (Berkeley and Los Angeles: University of California Press, 1962).

4. Roderick Nash, *Wilderness and the American Mind*, 3d ed. (New Haven: Yale University Press, 1982), 230-31.

5. Alfred Runte, *Trains of Discovery: Western Railroads and the National Parks* (Niwot, Colo.: Roberts Rinehart Publishers, 1990).

6. "Yosemite Visitors, October 1, 1916 to September 30, 1917," Yosemite National Park, Travel, pt. 1, Box 727, Central Files, 1907-39, Records of the National Park Service, Record Group 79, Na-

tional Archives, Washington, D.C.; U.S., Department of the Interior, National Park Service, Yosemite National Park, "Superintendent's Monthly Report(s)," September 1926 through September 1927.

7. Yosemite, "Superintendent's Monthly Report(s)," 1933, 1940, and 1941, inclusive.

8. Adams to Brower, January 6, 1957, H. C. Bradley Files, Records of the Sierra Club, Bancroft Library, University of California, Berkeley.

9. Yosemite, "Superintendent's Monthly Report," December 1954; Runte, *Yosemite: The Embattled Wilderness*, 193-96; U.S., Department of the Interior, National Park Service, Yosemite National Park, "3 Million People Visited Yosemite National Park Last Year," News Release, January 7, 1988, Yosemite National Park Research Library.

10. Adams to Brower, January 6, 1957, Sierra Club Papers; Joseph Wood Krutch, "Which Men? What Needs?" *American Forests* 63 (April 1957): 23.

11. Adams to Brower, January 6, 1957, Sierra Club Papers; Krutch, "Which Men? What Needs?" 23.

12. Adams to Brower, January 6, 1957, Sierra Club Papers.

13. Ansel Adams with Mary Street Alinder, *Ansel Adams: An Autobiography* (Boston: Little, Brown and Co. and New York Graphic Society Books, 1985), 106.

14. Adams to Richard Leonard, June 19, 1971, Carton 163, Sierra Club Papers.

15. Hardy to Arnberger, with attachment, "Yosemite Master Plan—Specific Comments," June 12, 1974, File D18, Yosemite National Park Research Library.

16. Runte, *Yosemite: The Embattled Wilderness*, 205.

17. Ibid., 206.

18. Anonymous, "The Mountain Room Bar: A Guest Improvement We Can Be Proud Of," *Yosemite Sentinel* 2 (November 1983): 1.

19. Robert Binnewies, interview with author, November 16, 1984; Anonymous, "The Mountain Room Bar."

20. Typed Inventory, "Alcoholic Outlets in Yosemite Valley—Outside Yosemite Valley," March 2, 1989, Yosemite National Park Research Library.

21. Runte, *Yosemite: The Embattled Wilderness*, 225; video-taped interview, American Broadcasting System, "Nightline," July 5, 1991.

22. Telephone interview with Yosemite Office of Public Affairs, October 15, 1992.

23. U.S., Department of the Interior, National Park Service, Denver Service Center, *Final Concession Services Plan and Environmental Impact Statement, Yosemite National Park, California* (August 1992) 92; Printed Circular, Yosemite Park and Curry Company, "Important Changes to Yosemite Are Being Considered ... You Can Help Influence Them," Fall 1989.

24. Kevin Roderick, "Park Service Reveals Yosemite Firm's Big Take," *San Francisco Chronicle*, January 20, 1990, sec. A.

25. Robert Reinhold, "MCA Agrees to Sell Interest in Yosemite to End Dispute," *New York Times*, January 9, 1991, sec. A.

26. Ibid.

27. Frederick Law Olmsted, "The Yosemite Valley and the Mariposa Big Trees: A Preliminary Report," ed. by Laura Wood Roper, *Landscape Architecture* 43 (October 1952): 22.

28. Ibid.

Index